PRAISE FOR *THE DARK SIDE OF SCHOOL REFORM*

"Skillfully captured in teachers' real voices, this account of a school reform effort draws the reader in so deeply that you'll feel as though you're an invisible presence in busy classrooms and hot and crowded meeting rooms. The writing is superb and the message is enlightening."—Lisa D. Delpit, author of *Other People's Children* and editor of *The Skin We Speak*

"Jeff Brooks' perceptive account plunges us headfirst into the everyday messiness of school reform at ground level, where teachers struggle mightily to hold on to their ideals amid the whirlwind that whips around them. In an educational universe where the wisdom of classroom practitioners is too often disregarded, Brooks' greatest contribution may be his willingness to listen carefully to teachers and to take seriously what they have to say."—Gregory Michie, author of *See You When We Get There: Teaching for Change in Urban Schools*

"Teaching is intellectual and ethical work, transcendent work that at its best encourages students to reach the full measure of their humanity. Teaching is also gritty work—grinding, draining, back-breaking, mind-wrecking, and as common as mud. How do teachers experience these conflicting pulls? How do we understand the contradictions at the heart of what we do? How do we negotiate the turbulence? Jeffrey Brooks dives directly into the whirlwind, and invites us to sail along with him. It is not an easy ride, but it is well worth it. In this book he provides a nuanced and complex look at that special place between heaven and earth where every teacher must somehow make a life."—William Ayers, Distinguished Professor of Education, The University of Illinois at Chicago, author of *Teaching toward Freedom: Moral Commitment and Ethical Action in the Classroom*

"While Jeffrey Brooks portrays the ___ ___ of being a teacher, he does it in a shining, even brilliant multi____ ___. The effect, not depressing, is exciting ___ itself. Through multiple lenses, he foc___ ___acher's struggle, a group of teachers and ___ies, experiences, contradictions, and problems. ___ in the book with the teachers, feeling and interacting. For as one teacher, Jim, asked, 'Why can't you use common language to describe something so common?' The author's response: 'Okay, Jim, maybe I will. Thanks.' But nothing's common about this marvelous book."—Bruce S. Cooper, professor and chair, Division of Educational Leadership, Administration, and Policy, Fordham University, coauthor of *The Promises and Perils Facing Today's School Superintendent*

"*The Dark Side of School Reform* is an eye-opening look at the difference between appearance and reality in schools today. There will be laughter, tears, and gasps as you read the journey one school has taken. This book will serve as an inspiring and practical tool for school leaders."—Julie Gawarecki, assistant principal, South Valley Junior High, Liberty, Missouri

"Education reform efforts generally start off with good intentions, but often lose their effectiveness as they unfold within the daily life of schools. *The Dark Side of School Reform* is a skillfully-written book that speaks to a wide variety of audiences about this deterioration, but does not alienate any of them. Indeed, policy-makers, researchers, teachers, administrators, and vested constituents alike are bound to find this book approachable, insightful, and useful."—Gerardo R. Lopez, assistant professor, Department of Educational Leadership and Policy Studies, Indiana University, coeditor of *Interrogating Racism in Qualitative Research Methodology*

"With a filmmaker's eye for detail and resonance, Jeff Brooks immerses readers in the voices of teachers who care deeply about what they do—in spite of the daily suffocations of bureaucracies and the constant stream of "reform movements."—Roy F. Fox, author of *UpDrafts: Case Studies in Teacher Renewal* and *Harvesting Minds*

"Evocative, provocative, and very well written. Brooks delves into the shifting complexities of multiple and contradictory school reforms, shedding light on how the layering of these competing demands shapes the lived worlds of teachers. It is "a must-read" for policy entrepreneurs, political leaders, school board members, educational leaders, teachers, researchers, and anyone who cares about public education."—Catherine A. Lugg, associate professor, Department of Educational Theory, Policy and Administration, Rutgers University

THE DARK SIDE OF SCHOOL REFORM

Teaching in the Space between Reality and Utopia

Jeffrey S. Brooks

Rowman & Littlefield Education
Lanham, Maryland • Toronto • Oxford
2006

Published in the United States of America
by Rowman & Littlefield Education
A Division of Rowman & Littlefield Publishers, Inc.
A wholly owned subsidiary of The Rowman & Littlefield Publishing Group,
Inc.
4501 Forbes Boulevard, Suite 200, Lanham, Maryland 20706
www.rowmaneducation.com

PO Box 317
Oxford
OX2 9RU, UK

British Library Cataloguing in Publication Information Available

Library of Congress Cataloging-in-Publication Data

Brooks, Jeffrey S., 1970-
  The dark side of school reform : teaching in the space between reality and
utopia / Jeffrey S. Brooks.
       p. cm.
  Includes bibliographical references and index.
  ISBN 1-57886-281-7 (hardcover : alk. paper) — ISBN 1-57886-305-8
(pbk. : alk. paper)
  1. Teaching. 2. Educational change. I. Title.

LB1025.3.B756 2006
371.102—dc22   2005023063

∞™ The paper used in this publication meets the minimum requirements of
American National Standard for Information Sciences—Permanence of
Paper for Printed Library Materials, ANSI/NISO Z39.48-1992.
Manufactured in the United States of America.

CONTENTS

FOREWORD

Harry F. Wolcott

With this book, Jeff Brooks adds to our growing collection of cases of discontent among high school teachers. But this one is so well written, so engaging, that readers will be propelled along to see how it all "ends." It doesn't, of course—we are left with teachers and the school in perpetual discontent as his study comes to a close, caught in the space he describes as existing between reality and utopia. Still, the case is convincing, and we feel that we have been brought to the brink of understanding how this school, and many schools like it, carry on, year after year.

Jeff is an extraordinary observer. He captures his interviews so well that it is impossible not to feel they have been reported just as he heard them. When he himself interrupts what his interviewee is telling us, he includes the interruption, so it is as though we are one with the interview, and we, too, would want to get our two cents in. Seldom did I find a value judgment or disparaging comment; I can even forgive the observation that a teacher was "shuffling papers" during the brief period when her instructional partner took responsibility for the class, although I doubt that any high school teacher ever needs to create the *impression* of being busy.

But a case study should have a purpose other than being purely descriptive, and this one is devoted to understanding and explaining why those who work in public schools report acute dissatisfaction with various aspects of teaching. Because Jeff is willing to share with the reader early in his study his feeling that the "bad guy" in all this is contained within the concept of alienation, we have a chance from the outset to judge his key concept and to weigh its utility for the case. I think the teachers concurred with his preordained conclusion; he did not hide his tentative explanation and he did not hide from them his commiseration in their plight. One gets the impression that they also realize from the start that it is OK to "spill their guts" and say why they feel trapped. And his interviewees are so eloquent that their every observation comes across as both brilliant and plausible.

There has been the rare researcher who has approached schools with the idea that everything is beautiful, and who has made a good case for that happy circumstance. Approaching schools with a problem focus is more common. In my case, with an ethnographic study conducted now thirty years ago, I slipped in with the problem itself to be sure there would be one; I was guaranteed that things were wrong from the beginning, and sure enough, that is what I found (see *Teachers versus Technocrats*, reissued in 2003 by AltaMira Press). I took a more anthropological approach, in contrast to Jeff's sociological one, and came up with a different explanation. Like Jeff, I also hint at the problem with my title.

In these same thirty years, there have been many studies of schools and of their faculties. In each case the researcher poses an answer to what is wrong, and why teachers are unhappy (or again, in a small minority of cases, why they are happy). We have had studies that target isolation, autonomy, motivation, burnout, accountability, technology, communication, resistance to change, commitment—the list goes on and on. None of them seems to have it quite right, and I doubt that Jeff's study has it quite right, either. What is refreshing here is that he lets us look at the concept he is using and allows us to watch as he applies it to "try it on." He does not bear down too hard—he even displays a seductive tentativeness toward his orientating concept, "Yet, while the sociological theory I used to frame the study initially was helpful, data soon suggested that alienation was (at best) only half of the conceptual framework needed to explain the experience of teaching." We realize that we are invited to join him in his search. So as you read, you too are free to weigh the concept he intends to apply and to ask yourself, Is this it? Does alienation adequately explain why these teachers are dissatisfied?

Does a single overriding concept even exist that can explain teacher behavior, that will help us to understand why in virtually every high school in the country (somehow, I believe that elementary schools tend to show less of it) and in every decade the same gripes can be heard? Why, he asks, have educational scholars endeavored to understand why those who work in public schools report acute dissatisfaction with various aspects of teaching? Is the problem created by too-attentive researchers plying their trade? Is it endemic to teaching itself? Is it perhaps due to the organization of schools (having one person designated the leader could be the problem, but having schools run by a committee seems to me to be far worse)? Or is it the nature of the task they set before them, an impossible one by any standard and only exacerbated by misguided efforts like the current No Child Left Behind?

My own hunch, after a professional lifetime of searching, is that if there is any one single factor, it may be simply the lack of *recognition*, a self-serving need for anyone who chooses teaching as a career to want to be recognized for his or her efforts. This is always coupled with the incessant drive of everyone external to the classroom to insist that regardless of the effort, education still fails to accomplish all it could. I don't know if that is *the* answer, but it is mine. Over and over, I hear the words of a wise and experienced teacher who reminded me, "Teachers are never told that they are doing anything right!"

In his effort to drain every ounce of wisdom from his interviews, not even the kindly and sympathetic observer in this study would have crossed a line to tell anyone that they were doing a good job. Presumably no parent or nonteaching administrator dared to reveal any weakness about letting teachers off the hook with such praise. (It is, of course, all right to let one's guard down for a moment to suggest that some *particular* teacher under *particular* circumstances did a good job in some *particular* instance.)

So heed Jeff's search for some broader concept to help explain what is going on and help to explain the serious problem of teacher dissatisfaction. If it isn't alienation, what is it? If it isn't some parallel concept, is there an overarching idea that holds the answer? If it isn't even that, how else explain how a group like these teachers manages to carry on year after year in spite of events that would seem to drive them out of a school, even out of their chosen profession? When all the forces we identify work so incessantly to make teaching difficult, what is it that keeps teachers at it? Jeff Brooks here poses his answer to that essential question. Is he closer than anyone has yet come? If the answer lies not in these pages, at least here you will find plenty of food for thought for contemplating the issue he addresses.

Harry F. Wolcott
Professor emeritus, anthropology and education
University of Oregon
January 2005

ACKNOWLEDGMENTS

I extend a special thanks to the teachers, staff, and administrators of Wintervalley High School. I am grateful for your effort, patience, and willingness to accommodate me during this study and I admire and respect your work with and for the students. I also offer thanks to the students, staff, and faculty of the Colleges of Education at the University of Missouri-Columbia, Florida International University, and Florida State University, in addition to everyone I worked with and for at the University Council for Educational Administration. In particular, Karen Cockrell, Peggy Placier, and Jay Scribner have been important to me as mentors, teachers, and friends. Thanks to Don Ranly and John Merrill, both of the School of Journalism at the University of Missouri-Columbia, for challenging me with wisdom, humor, and for demanding that I commit myself totally to those principles in which I believe. Thanks to Bill Ayers at the University of Illinois-Chicago, who through his words, life, and work reminds me that the fight for freedom, love, and compassion is the only possible agenda. Thanks are also due to many friends, mentors, and colleagues in the academic community who have inspired and supported me, but especially Michelle Young, George Petersen, Gerardo Lopez, Bruce Cooper, Lisa Delpit, Carolyn Herrington, Joel Westheimer, Greg Michie, Catherine Lugg, Roy Fox, Vicki

Rosser, Fenwick English, Jo Blase, and Margaret Grogan. I owe a huge debt to Tony Normore, Pam Flood, Stacey Rutledge, and Julie Gawarecki and several other reviewers for reading and commenting on previous drafts of this work. I extended thanks to Ulrich Reitzug, editor, and the editorial staff of the *Journal of School Leadership*, where some findings from the pilot study for this work were published. Thanks also go to Cindy Tursman and Tom Koerner at Rowman & Littlefield Education for their interest in my research and support in preparing this book.

Among academic friends, I am most deeply indebted to Harry Wolcott. Harry's insightful work has been a source of inspiration to me as a neophyte educational researcher, and in many ways this book would not have been possible without his contributions and influence. I am honored that Harry consented to write the foreword to this book and I bestow on his research the greatest praise I know to give; each time I reread one of his many published works, I discover schools and educators anew.

Thanks to old and new friends, family, and teammates, for allowing me to take some of the direct free kicks, lingering with me too long over bottomless cups of coffee, talking philosophy on the tops of parking garages, keeping correspondence alive, raising pints to toast camaraderie, and for telling me what I need to hear, for better and for worse, in good times and bad.

I acknowledge a great debt to Richard and Carol Raleigh, whose constant encouragement and support are two of the pillars on which my little family rests. You have taught me the strength of devotion, the power of determination, and welcomed me into your family with love. For all these things I am grateful. Thank you for your guidance, good judgment, humility, and humor.

Immense thanks are due to my parents, Anne and Brian Brooks, for steadfast commitment, assistance, and generosity. I have a deep respect for your effort and patience, and I feel the warmth of your love. You taught me to stand on my own feet (literally and figuratively!), and for that I am forever grateful. Thank you for remaining by my side and believing in me through everything.

While all of the people listed above have been important in supporting this work, I offer a most precious and heartfelt acknowledgment to my three daughters, Holland, Bronwyn, and Clodagh. You remind me that Seuss is just as important as Sartre and that we all need to dance, smile, and sing. In your bright eyes I see unlimited promise, in your smiles I find truth, and in your arms I find peace—I will always love, honor, support, and protect you.

I reserve the greatest thanks for the love of my life, Melanie Brooks. Melanie, you are the star, wind, and compass that guide me through this journey. You are my greatest friend, my closest confidante, and my most honest and loving critic. Your selfless heart and soaring spirit carry me through the crazy days and nights. My admiration for your wisdom, passion, intelligence, and kindness grows each day. I am proud and honored to be your husband and partner. I love you! This book is dedicated to you.

INTRODUCTION: EXPLORING THE DARK SIDE OF SCHOOL REFORM

Are educators captains or captives of change?

—Don A. Orton

Are you a teacher? Maybe you picked up this book looking for answers to some of the questions you face in the school where you work. If this is the case, you are in the right place. Well . . . that assertion comes with a caveat. The odds are good that I don't know a thing about your school, so from the onset I won't pretend that this is a book of *answers*, and you shouldn't read it that way. This is a book of *looking*. I invite you to explore problems and solutions in life and work that one group of high school teachers developed over the course of two academic years. On these pages you will read about the teachers of this school—referred to throughout the study as the pseudonymous Wintervalley High—as they teach, lead, laugh, and cry. As the name of the school is fictitious, the teachers' names are likewise withheld because interviews and observations were conducted under condition of anonymity.

The teachers you will read about in this book discuss their frustrations and joys as they interacted with administrators, peers, students, parents, and the content of their academic area. Beginning with the first chapter, this book relates findings from a research report focused on understanding how one school's reform efforts changed teachers' work and the teachers' attitudes toward that work. Accordingly, the central focus of this book is what happened between 7:30 A.M., when Wintervalley teachers were required to be in their classrooms, and 4:00 p.m., forty-five minutes after the bell rang to signal the end of the school day for students. Teachers were expected to remain on campus until this time. However, the day has more than eight and a half hours, and teachers spend the remaining fifteen and a half living the rest of life. They are partners, consumers, drivers, center midfielders, gourmet chefs, lovers, fathers, mothers, worshippers, sisters, activists, hikers, friends, and enemies. Certainly, this list could continue and fill a book by itself. Suffice it to say that teachers are more than teachers and those whom I met during this study were complex physical, psychological, sociological, political, emotional, cognitive, and spiritual beings. This is as good a time as any to reveal the first of many biases I bring to this research.

This book contains the results of a qualitative research study. In these sorts of studies, the researcher is conceived as the primary instrument of data collection and analysis (Bogdan & Biklen, 1998). Thus, it becomes important to acknowledge biases that may frame and limit "the instrument." I have an insatiable curiosity about human nature. In my research, I wanted to learn about teachers-as-people as much as I wanted to learn about teachers-as-professionals. I didn't stop the microphone or redirect the conversation every time a teacher talked about noneducational folks or events in his or her life. In fact, I often urged conversations in this direction if teachers seemed willing to discuss such issues. On these pages, you will find tales of teaching that involve spouses, sons, lovers, and daughters. You will find love and hate. You will find eloquence and common profanity. You will find value judgments and prejudice. I present all of this without omission because it was all part of the human side, the sociological side, of school reform. To me, ignoring the highs, lows, and supposedly nonacademic aspects of school reform would be like presenting a single apple and calling it an orchard. As the study commenced, it became apparent that there were few teachers who could draw a distinct line between their personal and professional lives, anyway; feelings and technique melted into one, public and the private were part of the same whole.

Public school teaching is nearly impossible in the worst situations, and still challenging for those fortunate enough to draw the best assignments. No one who has spent time with teachers in public schools needs me to tell them that. Teaching can be tough. It's so tough, in fact, that the profession chews up and spits out many teachers within the first three years of their careers. Yet even though teaching is difficult, it isn't all doom and gloom. Just as you don't need to look far to find struggling teachers, you also don't need to ask many teachers before you hear them describe their work as a calling, proudly proclaim theirs among the most important professions in society, and assert that despite the many challenges they wouldn't trade what they do for all the gold in the world. For many teachers, their thoughts about work are shades of gray between these extremes. It's not all bad and not all good; some of the work is wonderful, some of it contemptible. Why? What is it that makes teaching a paradox that alternately sends the spirit soaring and dashes dreams? Although peeking into both the light and the darkness of the teaching profession, this book mainly explores the shadows in between.

Are you a public school administrator? Maybe you are reading this to try and figure out why the last reform didn't work, what can be done with the one in progress, or what you might learn as you implement the next. You have listened to the gurus of educational change and school reform sing seductive songs, but you are not sure which is North Star and which is Fata Morgana. You may have tried, or may be tempted to try, any number of reform-related changes: restructuring the school day from (or to) block scheduling; revising curricula around measurable academic goals, multicultural principles, the needs of at-risk students, or interdisciplinary concepts; creating shared governance structures that involve teachers and other educational stakeholders in schoolwide decision-making processes; forming new committees or task forces to look into specific areas of student need; working with faculty to craft a vision and mission that properly reflects the values of the professional community; continuing your own professional development by learning or refining concepts associated with instructional leadership; distributing budgetary or policy-making power among colleagues; or increasing student and teacher accountability through high-stakes, market-based concepts. Of course, this list could go on and on. Administrators are besieged with an endless barrage of theoretical solutions to substantive problems, but which to choose and how long should a leader keep faith when an initiative seems to be failing? If you are interested in understanding some ways that conceptually sound, seemingly inspired, and data-driven school reforms can break down—as well as succeed—this book is for you.

Are you a parent? You may be concerned that your children are left behind in a "failing" school, or alternately proud that they attend a "successful" school. Certainly, the millennium has ushered in a new era of accountability. Student achievement scores on statewide standardized exams consistently receive top billing as a prime indicator of both institutional and educational value. Every year, districts, state boards of education, and even newspapers print aggregate scores of students in local schools and rate them using raw scores or various statistical formulae. Outcomes are duly judged, and the sentence is usually swift and conclusive. If a public school gets the equivalent of an A on its report card, the school is "good"; if the school receives anything else, it is inadequate. An F is a disgrace. By law, all must show adequate yearly progress toward excellence.

You may, however, suspect that these grades and scores are only a small part of the larger picture of what happens at the school. If this is the case, you are correct. Students can flourish in schools performing poorly on such tests, while other children can fall apart in the highest achieving academic environments. There are wonderful, and most likely dreadful, teachers, administrators, and staff at schools scoring on every part of the spectrum between A and F. If you believe there is more to a school than a single letter or quartile may indicate, I invite you to read on; this book is for you.

Are you an education researcher? This study took a qualitative approach to data collection and analysis and used a sociological theory of alienation as a conceptual framework. Although this is definitely not a phenomenological study, I used many data collection and analysis tools borrowed from grounded theory. Data collection began shortly before the Fall 2001 school semester and continued through the end of the 2003 academic calendar. During this time, I conducted a total of forty-two in-depth interviews with school personnel and completed seventy-two observations of formal instructional and noninstructional sessions. I also engaged in countless impromptu exchanges with teachers as we raced down hallways or stood outside a classroom waiting for the next group of students to arrive. These brief moments yielded some of the most powerful data in this study. I also gathered data via written and electronic texts. If you are interested in a more detailed discussion of research methods and theoretical orientation, I encourage you to read chapter 11 and the Methodological Appendix.

Are you an education policymaker? Whether a legislator, school board member, department of education executive, district official, lobbyist, or other educational stakeholder, you may be wondering what is happening in the schools and how you can help. While there has been interest in schools and school reform for at least over a century (Tyack & Cuban, 1995), the volume, intensity, and frequency with which the debate is engaged have amplified significantly over the past two decades, resonating most forcefully and recently in 2001's No Child Left Behind Act. Aside from federal legislative mandate, the cry for educational change is also manifest in state, district, and school policies. People are talking about schools, teachers, and administrators—and many critiques are harsh. Educators are ridiculed from the trenches to the ivory tower, from carport to Congress, from barrio to barroom, from Wall Street to Walgreens. In thousands of schools across the United States, adoption and implementation of comprehensive or programmatic school reforms are educators' responses. Various reform initiatives ask teachers and school leaders to reconsider, reconfigure, or realign central aspects of their professional work to accommodate a different vision of how to best meet their students' needs. But what policies are best? How can a state legislative body, school board, or district possibly meet the needs of every student? These questions are central to this book, but rather than consider teachers as an abstract plenum, the issues are here considered at the level of site-specific implementation. On these pages, I explore what school reform looks like in action, at one school. Policymakers may consider the trials and victories of Wintervalley's teachers as one example of the day-to-day impact education policy has at the school level. If you are interested in thinking about how policy actors enact mandates and programs crafted at higher levels of the system, this book is for you.

Are you a student? If you attend or ever attended a public school in the United States, you are affected by school reform. You may have noticed that your school is a place of motion, a place of constant change.

You might sense this most strongly as you move from class to class, but more than bodies is in motion. Programs and people come, go, and sustain. Your teachers try "new" lessons or approaches often enough that it is unlikely that students in their classes a decade ago had a similar experience. The school day or classroom may look different from place to place and time to time. You may talk with students from other schools and realize that their school is not at all like yours. You may have learned from teachers who used whole language, phonics, new math, lecture, experiential education, cooperative learning, or a host of other strategies to deliver instruction. In doing so, your teachers and administrators are not alone. Educators have been tinkering with the way programs, curricula, and instruction are delivered, designed, implemented, evaluated, and tested for over a hundred years hoping to better meet your needs, and the needs of students before you. No one has ever gotten it right and this experiment is likely to continue long after you leave school. In the chapters that follow, I invite you to take a peek into one of the 35,000 school-laboratories that continue the grand experiment of U.S. education.

Are you simply interested in or concerned about what is happening in schools? Whatever your reason for picking up and opening this book, you are invited to join the teachers of Wintervalley High as they find success and failure and try to make sense of one of the most difficult and rewarding professions in the nation—public school teaching.

ABOUT THE BOOK

This book features ten narrative chapters, followed by a chapter that discusses how this research connects to extant inquiry, and a brief methodological appendix that explains the approach to data collection and analysis I used in the study. Chapter 1 follows a single teacher as she goes about her work on a typical day at Wintervalley. The chapter details how Wintervalley's school reform efforts affected both the speed of the school day and also the school year. The pace of each day was accelerated by a host of reform-related initiatives that caused teachers to spend much of their time in a frantic rush. Moreover, as each day was a mad race, the constant implementation of new school reform measures and preparation for next year's efforts caused the entire year to pass in a flash. This had negative implications for all and left many teachers feeling disconnected from other teachers, administrators, students, and even from their children, spouses, and friends.

Chapter 2 centers on teachers' roles and duties with regard to Wintervalley's school reform efforts. Several teachers' voices are presented in this chapter, many of whom reached a point of professional saturation —a condition where they simply could not attend to all of the tasks they had been assigned or had accepted. The chapter explains how many teachers were forced, under threat of punitive action, to prioritize school reform initiatives above what they believed were their "core" responsibilities—instruction and care for the well-being and development of students.

Chapter 3 investigates ambiguity. As reform initiatives came and went at Wintervalley High, it became increasingly difficult for teachers to keep track of what policies were current and what procedures were to be followed at any given time. Reforms designed to facilitate effective communication among faculty and between teachers and administrators did the opposite. Policies, procedures, and expectations changed so often that there was great confusion among teachers as to what they were to be doing and how they would be evaluated. Many teachers, especially veteran teachers, responded to this lack of clarity by disengaging from extracurricular and extra-instructional tasks.

Chapter 4 is organized by teacher experience; it begins by presenting the views of several junior faculty members before transitioning to the voices of midcareer teachers and ending with two stories told by teachers with over thirty years of experience. As the study progressed, it became apparent that there were substantive differences in attitude toward school reform efforts that fell roughly along generational lines. Younger faculty seemed inclined to view themselves as progressives who needed to change a stagnant institutional culture, while veterans tended to adopt more of a cynical or been-there-done-that attitude toward reforms, even though many of their ideas were actually more progressive and innovative than those of the younger "progressives."

On paper, Wintervalley employed a shared governance structure to make schoolwide decisions and to ensure that all teachers had input on policies that impacted practice. However, an informal and powerful group of teachers exerted an inordinate amount of influence over both the principal and the executive council. This had a major impact on teacher performance evaluations, the distribution of funds, and many other important administrative decisions. Chapter 5, which investigated these phenomena, is presented in two parts. The first section emphasizes views of the school from what one teacher called the "Star Chamber," the school's informal elite. The second section presents outsiders' perspectives of the informal and formal power dynamics of the school.

Wintervalley was not a large school by urban standards. Nonetheless, the school's size increased rapidly during the previous two decades, and during the time of the study the school was approximately twice the size it was on the day it opened. Growth was accompanied by the usual responses: departments were created, the physical structure was expanded, and the number of instructional, administrative, facilities, and support staff increased. While most of these responses were borne of necessity, they were accompanied by new institutional norms—some of which were unwanted. Chapter 6 examines how teachers were isolated both physically and socially, how departments operated as antagonistic forces competing for scarce resources, and how many faculty members who worked in the same building for years have never met.

Chapter 7 centers on a single in-depth interview I conducted with a teacher who discussed his thirty-year attempt to find meaning in the teaching profession and in life. For over two decades, he was intensely committed to school reform efforts, but over the previous ten years his enthusiasm has been replaced by disillusion. He offers views on how the work teachers do is sometimes at odds with their own journeys as both educators and as private people. He explains that while his devotion to his students and to high standards provided moments of joy in the classroom, it also destroyed his family life and makes him long for a future he can never have.

Chapter 8 examines how some Wintervalley teachers have become dispassionate toward teaching. Teachers explain how *schooling*, the social processes of working in and attending an institution, can be antithetical to *education*, which centers on authentic experiences and learning for those who work at Wintervalley and attend the school.

Self-styled "progressive" teachers say that Wintervalley's mission and values continue to evolve as the school "tinkers toward utopia." Others feel that the school stands for nothing; that the work of teachers is blown by the winds of fate and guided by the whim of administrators, external funders, and district policy. Chapter 9 explores tensions that arose from the school's seemingly never-ending discussion about what they stand for and what is important.

Chapter 10 presents an odd paradox. Despite the overwhelming negative effects of school reform, nearly every teacher and administrator insisted that the work must continue. This chapter, the last narrative chapter of the book, ends by chronicling the school's end-of-the-year efforts to prepare for the next year's reforms.

Chapter 11 connects findings presented in the ten narrative chapters to extant research on school reform and sociological theory. The chapter concludes with a set of recommendations. Particular attention will be paid to reformers who seek to create more authentic schools for teachers as they undergo the work of reforming schools. Finally, a short methodological appendix is included for those interested in technical aspects of the design of this study.

While this overview has provided a peek into the contents of this book, it is also necessary at the onset to make a quick comment about the manner in which data are presented. In an effort to convey the mood of situations and preserve the cadence of conversations, I have evoked many literary tropes uncommon in the presentation of educational research. For example, in certain passages you will find ellipses to indicate pauses and midword hyphens to show interruptions. You will find a few stream-of-thought passages that roll over the page without indentation and other sections where sparse prose and staccato punctuation are used to impart a sense of accelerated speed. There are other literary devices at work here as well; some are overt and some are more subtle. But enough overview—let's visit Wintervalley High School and listen to the teachers.

❶

THESCHOOLDAYISFASTANDTHE SCHOOLYEARISFASTER!

Hurry! I never hurry. I have no time to hurry.

—Igor Stravinsky

When a person comes out of their front door at sunrise, he hits the ground running, catches up with his office building, hurries up and down flights of stairs, works at a desk propelled in circles, gallops home at the end of the day. No one sits under a tree with a book, no one gazes at the ripples on a pond, no one lies in thick grass in the country. No one is still.

—Alan Lightman, *Einstein's Dreams*

Wisely and slow; they stumble that run fast.

—William Shakespeare, *Romeo and Juliet*

Tape recorder? Check.
Tapes? Check.
Extra batteries? Check.
Yellow notepad? Check.
Blue "note-to-self" pens? Two.
Black "actual data" pen? Check.

Second 20-oz. Styrofoam cup of gas station coffee? Check.
Fatigue? Check.

It was early for a school day—6:18 by my dashboard clock. After years
of conflict with extracurricular activities, Wintervalley High School faculty meetings were now held before school, at 7:00 A.M. I made my way
across town. The wheels shushed arrhythmically over a dull sheen left
from last night's rain. The sky was flat and gray.

There was very little traffic in Owen City at that time. I passed a few
early-morning commuters, a milk delivery truck, and a van that adver-
tised "WE KILL PESTS!" At a red light, a police patrol car pulled up
behind me. We rolled along together—the only cars on the street—for
several blocks. Although I had done nothing wrong, I was nervous. I always get tense in those situations. Why? The worst crime I had committed was letting a baker's dozen of library books lapse into overdue
status. When I had received the library's e-mail I counted up the
stacks—between the university library and borrowed books I had sev-
enty-three, semiarranged thematically in not-so-neat piles next to my
desk at home. My wife, Melanie, gave me a hard time about the clutter;
but what can you do? My dissertation had moved in with us for the year
and needed a room of its own. At the next stoplight, I glanced into the
rearview mirror. The police car was gone. I was quite alone.

Wintervalley has segregated parking lots—teachers on one side, students on the other. Even though there are signs, you don't need them to
know who parks where. The students drive better cars and mill around
in the lot, which, for some, is the social hub of the school. Teachers
quickly park their late-model compacts and newer economy cars and
rush into the school, cradling reams of graded papers or dragging little
cream canvas bags full of books. They pick up those freebie bags at
professional functions; they are emblazoned with catchy teacherspeak
slogans like "Every Child Is a Success," "I ♥ Algebra Teachers," or
"Leadership for Learning, Learning for Leadership." They might also
bear the name of a long-forgotten conference, product, or a quizzical
acronym: "Teachers Summit for Data Driven Instruction," "CTB-
McGraw Hill and Teachers: Partners in Excellence," or "NCPBEA."
Like most of the programs and resources they advertise, the bags are not
built to last. The thin material usually holds out for about a year. The

bags and programs share another quality, as well—there is always another one when the old one gives out. The lot was nearly full when I arrived. I placed my temporary parking permit on the dash, gathered my things, and turned toward the building.

Wintervalley is primarily built of reddish-brown brick and is punctuated, at irregular intervals, by big, long, darkly tinted windows. Built in the early seventies, the school's style is Frank-Lloyd-Wright-on-a-budget. Its one tall story is nestled into the contour of a rolling green slope. There are no businesses near the school; the district owns an undeveloped acre on both sides. A basement hides under about half of the building. The school serves students in grades 10–12 and has an enrollment of approximately 1,400. The district reports the student population as 84.4 percent White, 9.8 percent Black, 4.3 percent Asian, 2.0 percent Hispanic, 0.4 percent Native American, and has a total minority population of 15.6 percent. Teacher demographic data were not reported by the school or its district in the two years of my study. I noted that it was roughly congruent to the student distribution.

By popular anecdote and according to many measures, Wintervalley is a successful school. Students perform well on statewide standardized achievement tests, the teachers and administrative personnel are energetic and decorated, and the relatively new physical structure is in excellent repair. Wintervalley is an affluent school that benefits from a well-heeled tax base. The school regularly wins large grants to supplement funding for everything from the school's fully operational planetarium to the up-to-date technology in the media center. All Wintervalley teachers have a networked computer in their classroom on which they enter grades into a schoolwide system, use Internet resources for teaching, and even respond to executive council meeting minutes, which are posted every other week. The school was even recently renovated and a new wing was added to accommodate a swelling population base.

Wintervalley is situated on the west side of Owen City, a town in the Midwestern United States with a population of approximately 85,000. Owen City expanded rapidly over the past few decades and, despite its modest size, houses a large state university, two small colleges, and three hospitals. Yet for all the town's amenities, it is still a community of haves and have-nots. There are marked differences between the "poor" and "rich" sections of the town. Wintervalley caters primarily to the latter and has a reputation among many in the community as the country club school; with its manicured grounds, impressive sports facilities, and arcing skylights, it indeed looks the part. This opulence is in stark contrast to the other large high school in the district, a much older school located in the city's core. Heskey High's building and grounds are in a perpetual state of disrepair and students are crowded together in classrooms with no air conditioning—a challenge through the hot Midwestern summer, late spring, and early fall. In the winter, heating problems are normal at Heskey. Wintervalley's students, faculty, and staff know no such discomfort. The school is saturated with modern comforts: central air and heat, vending machines, advanced audiovisual equipment, plush chairs and couches, and plenty of communal space for students, parents, and professionals to gather.

The school district has a total enrollment of approximately 17,000 students and governs schools in adjacent rural areas as well as Owen City proper. As a result, the 27 schools in the district range from urban to suburban to rural. The racial composition of the district's student population is reported as 25.4 percent minority (18.7 percent Black, 2.1 percent Hispanic, 0.5 percent Native American, and 4.2 percent Asian) and 74.6 percent White. Yet, as is so often the case, reality is lost on these aggregate statistics. This distribution is mirrored in only a few schools; minority populations either exceed 39 percent or fall far below 15 percent. Wintervalley is an example of the latter distribution.

Although it would normally be too early to sign in as a guest at the main office, which I was required to do, everyone was there for the faculty meeting. Although busy, Ms. Weems, the head administrative assistant, still greeted me with her friendly smile. Looking through the filing cabinet on the far side of the room, she nodded toward the open binder that was always on her desk. "Hi, Jeff. Crazy morning! You know the drill!" I signed the same way every time I entered the school—Name: Jeff Brooks; Time: 6:25; Destination: Research.

I was spending the day with Rachel, an English teacher. She had been teaching for eight years but only the last three of those had been at Wintervalley. She was slight, pretty, and looked young for someone with her experience. Rachel dressed conservatively, blond hair up, and always had a smile on her face and a bounce in her step. We had already completed three long interviews earlier in the semester and I had observed her in class on seven different occasions. She was an enthusiastic teacher and, for the most part, students responded well to her poetry-with-a-smile approach. A few sullen and subdued students seemed to resent her incessant bubbliness, but even they perked up from time to time in response to her zeal. Before I entered her room, I knew this morning would be no different than any other time I had seen her. From the hallway I could hear her loudly humming an upbeat tune. When I tapped on the door's frame, she looked up from paper shuffling and laughed warmly.

"Ha! I knew you'd have coffee."

"Second cup." I raised it toward her as if giving a toast.

"Yeah, if you're not used to it, I see how you could need a pick-me-up. Are you a morning person? Maybe I should take the notes today."

I'd been doing interviews with other teachers for a few weeks so we hadn't seen each other for a while. We chitchatted for a few minutes to catch up.

"How are the girls?" she asked.

"They're fine; thanks for asking. Everyone was asleep when I left this morning. How's Frank? Does he like the new job?"

"He's not sure yet, it's too soon." She paused, thinking, and then snapped her fingers as though she'd just remembered something. "Look—I have to get a few things done before the meeting. We'll talk more about all this at lunch, okay? I'm going down to the copier. You can come along or stay here; I'll be just a minute."

I looked at my watch—6:44 A.M. "Do you have time before the meeting?" I asked, but she was already halfway out the door. I followed.

When we entered the room, there was a queue at all four copiers. The smells of coffee and warm toner mixed in the air, and here and there teachers spoke to each other over the hum, click, and whir of the machines. Several teachers greeted Rachel and after she spoke briefly with each, she turned to regard the situation. Her chances of getting the copies done before the faculty meeting were slim to none. Everyone else had the same idea but had acted a bit faster. Rachel allowed herself to frown briefly at the back of a man who was running off a huge study guide for his chemistry students. It must have been forty pages long and according to the screen by his right hand he was making ninety-three copies. The machine was up to only eleven. Just above his head was a sign:

**Please Make Copies Double-Sided
And Limited to
One Hundred Total Pages.**

For higher volume copies, see Betty and we will send them to the district resource office. These will usually be ready in twenty-four hours.

Thanks!

Rachel pursed her lips, annoyed, but said nothing. Then she turned to me and waved a single sheet of paper in the air. "Hm, I needed to run off copies of this review sheet. I want to use it today." She shrugged. "Guess I'll have to do it after the meeting. Let's go."

We hurried back down the hallway . . . more people around now . . . more "hi's" to teachers . . . hardly any students yet. . . . We took a left at the dark and closed guidance center . . . then walked straight for a bit . . . a right and past the main office. . . . It was abuzz with activity . . . the administrative staff was in jig and reel getting ready for the meeting . . . but a quiet commotion . . . at least not out here . . . the walls facing us were glass . . . you couldn't listen to leadership on this side . . . some teachers called the main office the administrative aquarium or the principal's fishbowl. . . . It was true . . . you could see everything . . . but it was only a silent feature . . . at that moment it was like an old Keystone Kops flick colorized . . . so much happening! Excitement! A ballet without music! Assistants moved between desks! Deans shimmied around filing cabinets! An assistant principal negotiated crates of Scantron forms! Someone pushed her way past an unoccupied . . . copy machine!

"Hey," I said to Rachel, "why don't we use that one? Nobody's there."

She didn't even glance, but responded, "That's the Accelerated School's copier, we can't use it."

"What do you mean?"

"They bought it with money from a grant. Rumor has it that one time a teacher in a hurry went in there to use it and was told that she couldn't because it was the accelerated school's copier. I don't even know if that's true but that's what I was told, so I just act like it doesn't exist. Only the principal and his assistants use it."

When we reached her room again, Rachel skipped over to the shelves behind her desk and in one graceful maneuver grabbed a large green three-ring binder labeled "Faculty Meetings" and twirled back toward the door. She breezed past me on her way out. We were about twenty feet down the hallway when she asked, "Aren't you going to bring anything besides coffee?"

I looked down and realized she was right, I had left it all on the floor next to her desk when we left the first time. I was ethnographically naked! No pens, no recorder, no satchel, nothing! "Good grief!" I exclaimed. "I'll catch up, you go ahead."

"It's okay," she said.

I ran-jogged down the corridor . . . turned the corner into Rachel's room . . . where was my bag? There . . . just behind the desk . . . open one zipper . . . another . . . no time . . . dumped half the contents on the floor. . . . Books! Articles! Mints! Highlighters! All in a pile . . . where are the pens? I felt my pockets . . . back first, then . . . okay! There they are . . . one black, one blue. Good. Now . . . what about paper? Into the bag again . . . this was easier . . . found the pad straight away . . . ready to go! I stood quickly and the lid burst off my coffee cup . . . hot black spewed onto my wrist . . . yow! Flicked my wrist to get it off, but hey . . . no time for that . . . gotta go! Slightly scalded, looking a little more like someone with university legitimacy, I made it back to the hall. Rachel was there, tapping her toe. She turned as soon as she saw me.

"Sorry," I mumbled.

"Forget it." She grinned. "I just don't want to have to take notes for the absent-minded-professor-in-training!"

I tried to keep pace with Rachel as we flew down the hall, but by now she was in a serious rush. Although we were moving quickly, I tried to re-affix the coffee lid to the cup so I could avoid another spill. I managed to prevent a major catastrophe, but still got some on my pants. What a start to the day!

We passed the fishbowl again on our way back to the library, where they held the faculty meetings. I glanced over. No one was using the Accelerated School's copier.

In the media center, people were milling about. Rachel and I sat down with four other teachers from the Classics Department. Veteran Lisa Brindon had a stack of graded papers to the side of her left hand, and a dozen or so ungraded papers she was trying to finish before first period. Jim Finnan and Joan Wilkes were discussing a film both recently saw, and Thom Flannery tapped a red pen nervously on top of his grade book. I had spoken with all of them at one point or another and we all exchanged pleasantries. Rachel joked to the group that I was perfectly suited to academe, given my hopeless lack of organization and forgetfulness. We all had a good laugh, and after some more small talk we settled in for the meeting. It was 6:58 by my watch, but the clock on the wall read 7:04. Noting my confused look, Jim leaned over and whispered, "Don't you know that time runs faster in schools?" He winked.

Wintervalley's media center is impressive. Books fill shelves that stand some twelve feet high. Clusters of comfortable couches are interspersed between neatly lined aisles of up-to-date computers and scanners. There are magazine racks and long tables where students and teachers can spread out or collaborate while using the many reference resources housed in the Wintervalley collection. Busts of historically significant figures such as Nefertiti, Edison, Plato, King, Buddha, and Jefferson rest atop rows of shorter shelves near a section of reference books. Like the computers, printed texts are current and in excellent repair. There is a row of soundproof audio booths that students use when listening to books on tape, completing foreign language modules, or simply wanting quiet space. This is not the library of my generation, a place of shushes and whispers; on the contrary, during normal school hours the Wintervalley media center is one of the loudest spaces in the building. It is a place to connect with ideas and people, a place to gather resources and friends, a place to work among great works.

Except for the auditorium, the media center is the only room large enough to accommodate everyone who must attend faculty meetings. The Wintervalley faculty number in excess of a hundred full-time teachers, and attendance at these monthly meetings is mandatory. This was not always the case. Before the current principal, Dr. Benjamin Weleck, began his leadership tenure, faculty meetings were held on an as-needed basis. Usually, this meant dealing with crises or dispersing "hot topic" advice on legal and/or educational policy that related directly to classroom instruction or interaction with students and parents. Back then, meetings were short, infrequent, and to the point. When Dr. Weleck joined the school, he immediately changed the as-needed policy and instituted a regular schedule. In the interest of building school culture and fostering a sense of community, faculty meetings have occurred every month for the last four years.

Today's meeting, held in mid-March, began like the others I had observed. On one end of the room, Dr. Weleck stood before the assembled faculty, who were seated throughout, largely congregating as academic divisions. When he announced the topic of this month's meeting as the upcoming statewide standardized exam, the Statewide Assessment Program (SAP), there was little reaction. However, when he said it looked like it would take nearly two full school weeks to administer the test rather than the single week for which everyone had planned, an audible groan rose from the crowd. Instruction is put on hold during testing, and losing another week meant even more pressure on teachers to fit Wintervalley's ambitious curriculum into the academic year. Teachers had known about the exam all year and prepared their calendars accordingly, but no one was ready for this change at such a late date. Considering that many teachers already viewed SAP as an unpopular and unwelcome imposition, many were furious with the change.

As test administrators, teachers are given strict guidelines and scripted directions they must read verbatim. Unlike several surrounding states, the legislature and state board of education have not made this exam a high-stakes assessment. That is, students' scores have no bearing on their grades or graduation, and failures or poor performance come without any attendant consequences—they have little incentive to take the exam seriously. The test is a no-stakes assessment. Motivation is a challenge for teachers as well, who are not privy to test scores until well after the school year ends. This means that even if teachers value the test results, scores cannot be used to guide instruction for the group at hand.

A few eyebrows rise when the principal announces changes in SAP. There will now be a "teacher number" in the upper right-hand corner of each test sheet. This means that data heretofore aggregated could potentially be disaggregated to show how well a particular teacher's students fared. Amid concerned looks and more grumbling, the principal emphasizes that no such analyses will be run—student performance on SAP will not be used as an indicator of teacher effectiveness. Still, several teachers wonder aloud what such a policy could augur and question the veracity of the principal's assertion. After all, as Jim asks no one in particular, "Why put the number there if no numbers will be run?" It seems hard to believe.

The principal then asks if anyone would like to speak. Oddly, this is when the crowd falls silent. Nothing. People look in any direction but the principal for a few long moments. Then he says, "Next item, faculty recognition." Meekly, a French teacher raises her hand and singles out three of her peers for recent exemplary work. One went to a conference, one is about to finish the coursework for her master's degree, and one used a French newspaper for an especially creative lesson. These achievements elicit a smattering of applause, which sounds very small in a room filled with so many more hands. She sits back down.

A few moments later someone pushes a button and a screen slowly descends from the ceiling.

I notice for the first time that one of the teachers at my table, Ms. Brindon, had been scratching comments onto a paper she is grading, presumably for her first-period world history class. She glances up now and then, but clearly her intent is to make sure she can't be seen by the principal rather than to find out or engage in what is being discussed. As the lights go down, she whispers to the table that she still has nine 12-page papers left to grade. Her class will begin in twenty minutes and now she sits in a dark room lit only by the familiar blue background of the default PowerPoint template. The screen reads: "Learning the SAP: All Students Can Succeed!" Ms. Brindon removes the glasses from her face and presses her thumb, index, and pointer fingers into the area between her eyes, which are now closed. Her face is contorted into a wrinkled mass and her shoulders are slumped as she leans her elbows on the table. This is not meditation, it is frustration. She remains in that pose, her face all of one grimace, for the next fifteen minutes.

As the lights went on and the screen rose, Ms. Brindon gathered her things and made for the door—nine ungraded papers in her clenched fist.

And they're off!

The meeting adjourned about ten till eight with a "thank you" and a "see you next time.". . . I could see why so many teachers were clustered at the tables nearest the door. . . . They scurried out of sight like rabbits who've seen the fox . . . boom! Gone! And the other teachers, too . . . everyone pushed to get out . . . to get back . . . get somewhere! Help!

"My class starts in five minutes!"

"I'm giving a test!" someone yelled.

"I'm meeting a parent!"

"Me, too!" came a call from the other side of the mob.

"Hey, get off my foot!"

No one cared or made way . . . no one could move . . . except as a slow and collective lurch . . . and would they have stepped aside if they could? . . . Maybe, but there was little evidence of sympathy from the school-teacher mob on this morning. . . . Everyone had problems . . . a hundred agendas . . . and fifty-one escape routes . . . for a hundred teachers. . . . They might care for one another under other circumstances, but now? . . . For that instant, they were in conflict with each other . . . everyone a road block . . . everything in the way.

The classics teachers formed a little wedge and pushed their way through. . . . Rachel took the lead . . . Thom was just off her left shoulder . . . he was using the grade book to cut through the mess. . . . They've practiced the drill . . . and they're good! They mutter pleasantries as they pass . . . 'scuse me! . . . sorry! . . . see you later! . . . take care! . . . We make it to the hall . . . but once we we're there, all bets were off! Ms. Brindon cut off the left flank and disappeared past the guidance center . . . Finnan broke off to the right . . . gone in a poof of smoke! . . . The rest of us pressed forward . . . we wanted to push, but how? Where? Our momentum dissipated instantly. . . we hit a new obstacle . . . ground to a halt. . . . What's happening? Kids! A massive throng of students was clotted in the hall . . . they were waiting to get into the media center . . . or passing on their way to gym . . . to Spanish . . . band! If it was a battle to get out of the faculty meeting, the hallway was war! Adolescents everywhere! Every shape and size! An ICP hat! A Philadelphia Eagles jersey! Low-rider jeans! Ridiculously tight tank tops! Flip-flops! Hoodies! FFA jackets! It was all there . . . the fashions of the Middle American Public High School. . . . Suddenly, there was a little gap—Go!

We burst through the other side and into more students . . . but those were moving . . . toward classes . . . toward lessons about Kubla Khan . . . democracy . . . or quarter notes. . . .

I tried to keep up with Rachel, but I couldn't . . . she was lithe . . . nimble . . . and disappeared around the corner. . . . I was big and awkward in the stream . . . but then it started to thin . . . the bell must have been close. . . . Regulars in schools develop a sixth sense about the bells . . . pros can time it just right . . . crafty students hit their seats at just the right instant . . . veteran teachers begin their first sentence with the bell's echo still in the air. . . . I peeked at my watch as I made the turn into Rachel's room . . . I had long since synchronized my timepiece to the school . . . forty-five seconds to go.

The room was full of the din, smells, and color of high school sophomores. Fifty-five in all . . . mostly crammed into or sprawled over little desks . . . about six were standing in a huddle around Rachel's desk. As she fielded concerns about last night's homework, I cleaned up the mess I left from dumping my bag behind her desk.

"Ms. Price, I didn't understand . . ."

"Ms. Price, my dog . . ."

"Ms. Price, my parents . . ."

"Ms. Price, I lost my . . ."

"Ms. Price, my car . . ."

"Ms. Price, my television . . ."

Rachel tried to listen but there were too many and time was short. She waved them off and announced that the homework was due. "Please, all of you standing, return to your seats." It was the same nearly every day. Then, raising her voice and addressing the entire class, she said, "All right folks, pass your worksheet to the front. I'll grade them and have them back by tomorrow."

Rustling . . . groans . . . a laugh. The students had the drill down, but as they had from day one of the year, they poked each other and giggled at those who didn't have the assignment ready. In Rachel's class, passing in papers is a loosely choreographed educational moment with room for improvisation. Some papers were tossed over shoulders, other students twisted all the way around to receive assignments, while a few raised an open hand to the student behind them without looking. Whatever method, all completed work eventually made it to the front of the eleven ordered rows and was passed toward Rachel's desk.

The usually unflappable Rachel looked as frantic as I'd ever seen her. A strand of her neatly tucked-away bangs had come loose and waved down in front of her eyes, which were scanning the desktop for the handout we never managed to copy. She found it under a late assignment and turned to me. "Hey Jeff, would you mind . . ." Rachel stressed to me the importance of making the copies double-sided and only doing ninety-nine at a time. If no one was waiting, it would be okay if I did them all at once. I smiled and promised to obey the law. Before I left the room to make copies, I heard her begin.

"Samuel Langhorne Clemens was born on November 30, 1835, in Hannibal, Missouri. Clemens began his professional career as a printer's assistant. Later, he worked with his brother, Orion, editing a series of unsuccessful tabloid-style newspapers. It wasn't the greatest gig, but his experiences during this time proved invaluable, and allowed him to support himself as he traveled the country . . ."

I walked down the hall toward the teacher's lounge. My charge: 137 double-sided copies of the Mark Twain Discussion Guide. The Twain sheet would be that night's homework, due tomorrow. I needed to return quickly. On my way to the lounge, I passed the administrative aquarium. Rather than continue onward, I opened the door and entered. The office was much quieter than when I had seen it before, only two assistants at their desks. Soft Muzak was in the air. One woman looked up from her task at hand and asked pleasantly if she could help me.

"Hello. Ms. Price asked me to run off some copies of this study guide for her class, and I'm not sure where to go," I lied. "Would it be all right if I use this copier?" I pointed to the Accelerated School's copier.

"They're for Ms. Price?" she asked.

"Yes," I said. "Actually, she needs them for her class right now. She just didn't have time this morning and—"

She interrupted and responded by saying, "As long as it's for a teacher, you can help yourself." She smiled and then went back to her work.

When I returned, Rachel was well into her lecture. To accompany her narration, she put prepared overhead transparencies and was showing them on a projector.

[Sepia picture of a riverboat]: "In 1857, Clemens decided to go to New Orleans. However, on his way to the Big Easy, Clemens became so enthralled with the lifestyle of the men he saw working on the steamships of the Mississippi that he decided to try his hand at being a riverboat pilot . . ."

[Picture of the young Twain at a desk]: "Secession eventually closed the river, and in 1861 Clemens moved to Nevada in order to join his brother, who was now a prospector. This didn't work out though, and by the next year Clemens signed on with the staff of the newspaper *Feral Entrepreneur* as an at-large writer. His work with this newspaper represents his first use of the pseudonym Mark Twain . . ."

(Picture of Twain with an enormous moustache [in each hour, this slide elicited loud laughter and a smattering of shouted comments]): "Reinvented as Mark Twain, Clemens set the world of letters alight. He worked at various newspapers in California while building a reputation for having a keen sense of wit, humor, and bombast. His spoken-word tour was a great success. Upon returning to California, he became restless and persuaded the newspaper to send him to New York. This agreement was contingent upon his writing a weekly newsletter of his exploits. Upon arriving in New York, Clemens got the bug to travel again, and went on a tour of the Mediterranean . . ."

And on it went. In each of the first two periods, she concluded by explaining the heartbreaking story of Twain's later life, when he lost his wife and his eldest daughter, and spiraled into depression despite garnering worldwide fame.

Then Rachel announced, "Your assignment is to read chapters 1–3 of *Huckleberry Finn* and answer the questions on this worksheet. It's due Thursday. You have the rest of the hour to read, so I suggest you get started."

Whew, I thought, now she gets to collect herself for a moment. Right? Not a chance.

The second that Rachel made the assignment, she had to field a flurry of questions.

"How many pages?"

"Do we have to take notes?"

As she tried to answer, most of the students who had tried to plead their cases before class descended on her desk again . . . and new ones

. . . the old ones had unfinished business and the new ones were sure they couldn't read Huck by tomorrow.

"Ms. Price, I have a soccer game!"

"Ms. Price, my dog . . . !" Students clamored closer . . . they swallowed up her desk . . . she took each in turn, but they were impatient . . . the next spoke before the last was finished . . .

"How many points will I lose if I turn it in tomorrow?"

"What's my grade?"

"When is it late?"

She had fended off most of the sorties when—

Rrrrrrrrrriiiiiiiiiinnnnnnnnnnnnnngggggg!!! The bell!

Another mad scramble! Students grabbed their bags and pushed out the door . . . the race to second hour was on! Rachel's room was the starting point for some . . . the finish line for others. . . . Most from first hour were gone in an instant . . . lickety-split! How did they do that? Their system was better than the teachers' had been at the faculty meeting . . . but still, no time to reflect on what had happened or learn a lesson in crowd control . . . a new horde flew into Room 114 . . . new homework problems! Rachel hadn't solved the first batch . . . holdovers from first period competed with the new lot . . . some gave up and left . . . others stayed.

"Ms. Price, I left my homework at home!"

"Ms. Price, can I go to my locker?"

"Ms. Price, did we have homework?"

"Ms. Price, I need a drink of water!"

In a repeat of the previous hour, she waved them off. . . . She performed her Twain lecture . . . assigned homework. . . . She was swarmed again. Somehow, despite mostly the same action, second hour seemed to plod along very slowly . . . maybe because I had heard it already . . . but it was a surreal tempo . . . a quick film at the wrong speed . . . one of those reels where you see an exploding building in slow motion. . . . There was a tension throughout, dust and debris in the air, but it was somehow more distant . . . then unexpectedly . . . before I knew it, the bell sounded and second hour was finished. I waited for the students to clear . . . for the calm after the storm. Third hour was Rachel's planning period. Finally, we could pause. Right?

No! We raced down the hall to be three minutes late for a meeting . . . Rachel's planning period was filled with a meeting! . . . Committee

work . . . schoolwide teams of teachers . . . everyone on a team . . . each
assigned a different topic. . . . She was on the at-risk team . . . no one
could define at-risk . . . they'd been trying since February. . . . Is it the
kids getting Fs? The kids barely passing? Is there a difference between
academically at risk and regular at risk? Does it fall out along race?
Class? Gender? Are we talking about dropouts? What about the kids
who fall asleep at their desks? What do the guidance counselors think?
And the principal? What are we doing? . . . Writing recommendations?
Evaluating the current policy? John thinks "at risk" means X . . . he took
a class at the U last semester and that's what the book had said. . . . Mar-
sha thinks it's Y, and she's been here for twenty years. . . . Yolanda was
grading papers during the meeting and didn't look up the whole time!
Debate! Passion! And indifference . . . some people rolled their eyes
through the whole thing . . . they shrugged and couldn't care less . . . not
about at-risk kids . . . at least I didn't think so. . . . They didn't care
for the meeting . . . all a waste of time when they could be working on
hour four . . . seven teachers in the room and only three having a meeting. . . . Before they knew it, it was time to adjourn . . . the coffee was
cold! Some were happy . . . some leave with tasks for next time . . . bye!
See you later! Whew, I thought, time for lunch!

"The school day is fast!" I opined as I unwrapped my sandwich. We ate
in Rachel's room.
    "You should try it for nine months—the school year is faster."
    "Can you tell me more about that?" I clicked on the recorder.
    "Are you thinking specifically about the pace of our lives on a day-to-
day basis, or the idea of implementing new programs and new focus?"
    "Both. Either. All of the above."
    "I think everything happens very quickly at both levels. The irony is
that on paper we have made a less hectic structure for the school, but
my life and days are more hectic. Since we switched to block scheduling, most of us only see three groups of students a day instead of six or
seven like we used to. Not everyone likes it, but the switch to blocks allowed our department the freedom to restructure. We were able to
combine the old English and Social Studies Departments into the new
Classics Division and we now team-teach most classes in pairs. We could
never have done that in a traditional fifty-minute period. Now, not

THESCHOOLDAYISFASTANDTHESCHOOLYEARISFASTER!

everyone likes that either, but I do and I think most of our department faculty do."

Rachel paused and took a sip of ginger ale. She gazed upward for a moment, thinking about what she had said, and then continued.

"Still, the redistribution of time has come at a price. Since we don't see the kids every day, their sessions are jam-packed with activities. If you think about it, the students only get half as much instructional time in social studies and language arts as they used to because I only get to teach English during about half of the block period. Laura, my team teacher, has the same issue. We never get through all the material and we end up assigning quite a bit of homework. That's fine, mostly. I don't have a problem with giving homework, but I get frustrated when I have to say 'on your way out of the room, pick up this worksheet and do it by Thursday,' without more explanation. That frustrates me and creates a bad instructional cycle because most times we have to go back on Thursday and work through the assignment since some of them didn't really understand what they were supposed to do in the first place. I hate that and I find it happens a lot now. We try really hard not to do it, but we have material to cover if we're going to hit the state benchmarks and that's the only way sometimes. So, that's one thing, but it's not even the biggest problem."

"Really? What is the biggest problem?" I asked, without looking up from my notepad.

"Writing is a process of learning the tools of self-expression, and reading is about developing good habits along with critical skills. Right?"

I nodded. She continued.

"Both writing and reading are learned sequentially, progressively. Today you practice and build on the concepts and tools you studied yesterday. So, seeing the kids only twice or three times a week rather than every day slows their growth because their practice is interrupted. It's the same amount of time, quantitatively, but the quality of the time is compromised because kids just don't learn to read and write that way. They need daily practice—if they come to our class on a Tuesday-Thursday week, they won't see us at all on Friday, Saturday, or Sunday. There's a three-day break on Monday-Wednesday-Friday weeks as well. The only way we can try to compensate is by giving lots of homework, but that's not guided instruction. Like I said, we often have to go back over that stuff so we end up getting behind and then racing through other things to catch up. It's a vicious cycle."

"So, restructuring the schedule has had both positive and negative effects in terms of classroom instruction. It's bogged down the curriculum sequence. But that's day-to-day stuff. You said the school year is fast also. What did you mean?"

Rachel held up a finger to ask for a pause while she finished a bite of apple. Before she started again, another question occurred to me. "One more thing. Teaching is hectic, right? No one would argue that. But to what extent is the day and the year accelerated by reform efforts? What do you think about that?"

Finished with the bite, she began, "Well, it's funny you chose today to do this visit. Look at today's schedule. First there was the faculty meeting about SAP and then the committee meeting about at risk. Those are both externally imposed reforms and they took away two important parts of the day that I don't get back. Also, you heard the news—now SAP will take two weeks. I don't get that time back, either. If you had come another day it might have been an 'inspirational assembly' about the test, a department meeting, a professional development session, or an impromptu conference with the other folks who teach my subject. My mornings are increasingly consumed by this stuff. And it's not all *The Test*! It's the new or the next restructuring, the new or next district policy, the new or next gizmo that will revolutionize teaching, it goes on and on."

"Okay," I said, "but, Rachel, those things are not all reform. You're also talking about realigning curricula, adhering to administrative and state mandates, restructuring governance, and trying to learn about how a constantly changing accountability system measures achievement. Research tells us that there's a change process, which entails a period of adjus—" She interrupted me midsentence.

"Please stop, Jeff, I know about that. I've read Fullan's stuff too. I used to give a PD workshop on all that. Look, I honestly don't care about the difference between reform and restructuring. That's just a game with words. I'm talking about higher stakes, I'm talking about the kids. Here's what I know—my school day is considerably accelerated by things only marginally associated with teaching or with students. Call it what you will, but to me, that's reform; that's making a new form. My work is being changed and I don't have much say in how it changes. My professional development time, committee time, and even my 'free' time is now exclusively devoted to teaching test-taking skills, sharing SAP tricks, and reviewing content modules created by a test-developer in California. We're in the Midwest, what do they know about me or these kids? Those stupid modules don't deal with my reality. They act like I have a week or two to do some in-depth unit on Shakespeare, but I don't, I have a day, maybe two for the whole *Merchant of Venice* . . . if I'm lucky. So my time is gone and where does that leave me? Does anyone say: 'Rachel, here are a few days or a few hours off to catch up on grading?' No. They say, 'More and faster!' 'Do better or else!' 'Give us more time!' 'After school!' 'Before school!' 'During school!' 'And do it for free!' Planning and preparation comes out of our hides now."

She paused to catch her breath, and then said, "Look, I know teachers are a different breed and that teaching is a strenuous job. Who doesn't know that? We don't do it for money, but whether or not the district or the administration means to, they use that passion against us. They pile on the work and if we say anything, then it's 'Oh, this teacher refuses to teach' or 'This one doesn't care about the kids' or 'This one doesn't believe in the mission, they must be burnt out. Maybe they should quit and find another career.' I'm up past midnight most nights doing my grading and planning, and I'm no superteacher. Plenty of people do more than I do."

Rachel stopped and looked out the window. Like it had for several days in a row, a light rain began to fall. Without looking toward me, she started again wearily. "It's too much, too fast, and it compounds as the year goes on. Over a period of several years, even those of us who are most enthusiastic begin to wonder what we're doing here. Teaching is great. It's very rewarding at times . . ." Then her voice trailed off and she finished, "but those rewarding moments flash past me so quickly now, they are increasingly harder to enjoy."

As I finished scribbling my notes, rain continued to fall. You could almost hear it through the thick, tinted glass. Rachel stared at it in silence for a moment before the moment was shattered by the fourth-period bell.

RRRRRRRRRRRIIIIIIIIIIIINnnnnnnnnnnnnnnnnnnnngggggggggg!!!
Off again!

2

ADD DUTIES, ~~SUBTRACT DUTIES~~;
ADD RESPONSIBILITIES, ~~SUBTRACT RESPONSIBILITIES~~;
ADD RIGMAROLE, ~~SUBTRACT RIGMAROLE~~

Teaching and learning should be personalized to the maximum feasible extent. Efforts should be directed towards a goal, that no
teacher have direct responsibility for more than 80 students. To capitalize on this personalization, decisions about the details of the
course of study, the use of students', and teachers', time and the
choice of teaching materials and specific pedagogies must be unreservedly placed in the hands of the principal and staff.

—Principle Four of *The Ten Common Core Principles*
of the Coalition of Essential Schools (This appears in documents
and on posters throughout Wintervalley High)

MONA WARREN, CHEMISTRY

You don't connect with the kids by what you teach. Half of them hate
what you teach. My vision of the good school is one where you develop
those interpersonal, emotional relationships; a school where no one is
afraid to express himself or herself. And I'm talking about everyone—
teachers, students, parents, staff, counselors, and administrators. A
school where you have a lot of work, but it's work you want to do, and it
all helps the kids. That's what's important. Everything is focused on the

kids; we each take on our differentiated roles for their benefit and if any given activity doesn't contribute to the students' academic development, we abandon it immediately and either replace it with another activity with the proper focus or intensify our efforts in other areas with the time freed by dropping the old activity. It's weird, but I'm not sure I know how that would look. I've never seen it. Maybe no one has. I used to dream about that school a lot when I was a beginning teacher, but over the years I've given up on that dream. Really, that's neither here nor there; let's talk about *this* school.

"Public schools are not focused on academics, and Wintervalley is just like the rest of them. We have become a one-stop shopping mall of public services, some of which are outstanding and some of which are second-rate. Like a lot of malls, we have a few top-end merchants and we have some cheap stores that are a rip-off. Look around: we serve junk food in the cafeteria, yet there's a basket of apples next to the cash register; we provide after- and before-school child care in the form of clubs, sports, tutoring, and intramurals but depending on the completely random interest and skill of the coach or sponsor, the experience is meaningful, worthless, or detrimental; we teach democratic values in the classroom, but ironically many teachers don't even vote in school board elections. We also have little say in terms of what happens in this 'democratic' school, despite the supposedly shared governance structure, and we have absolutely no input into district policy; we have an academic honor code for students and a code of ethics for educators, but teachers routinely violate copyright law in their lessons and I wonder about cheating because I hear the students say they do it now and then, although all I can do there is ensure it doesn't happen in my room; we demand organizational skills of everyone, but offer no systematic training or instruction to develop them even though most everyone agrees that with those skills many more students would succeed in life than currently do; we give lessons daily on personal grooming, etiquette, multicultural sensitivity, nutritional awareness, social expectations, test-taking skills, ceramics, copy editing, flutter-tonguing, holding a tremolo, frog dissection, and how to appreciate a van Gogh, but some of the kids in those classes can't read or write the way they should be able to, and haven't mastered basic skills in subjects like math and science. The way we teach history ensures that most students forget the material within a few weeks of being introduced to it. And that's not even the half of it.

"Each of the people in the school has to march to the beat of a different drummer. Students have their own issues, teachers too. For us, it has to do with a lot of nonteaching rigmarole: filling out sheaves of forms every week; following procedures that don't have much to do, if anything, with instruction; keeping up with the latest trendy educational lingo from the word police; dealing with nonacademic issues concerning parents, colleagues, students, and administrators; coaching, conferencing, running off copies, going to noninstructional meetings, sponsoring clubs, taking tickets at sports events . . . it goes on and on. And those are just the extras! Those are things we do besides teaching, which now has to do more with jumping through lot of hoops and time-consuming obstacles than ever: aligning lessons with vague state standards, teaching for The Test, planning, grading, professional development, my own classes at the university, department meetings, faculty meetings, subject meetings, interdisciplinary task forces on achievement, tutoring, advising, calling home about student performance, all the usual stuff. Now, I don't have a problem with any of that, with teaching and the things I do related to teaching. What gets my goat is that other crap. It's all supposed to be a part of school reform, educational change, but here's what I know: I've reached my limit. I'm tired.

"It's just like a closet. If it's empty, you can fill it up, but you reach a point when there is no more room. I think all of those committees and all that work is well intentioned, but it seems like it might be better to just say this is what we want to accomplish and once we've accomplished it, let's not be meeting any more. I guess really that would be more the way a task force works than a committee, but maybe it should be more about task completion, maybe we'd be more committed if we ever sensed that something actually came to an end. We have to find a balance between all these things we have going on and what's really important—which is the kids in the classroom. That's the bottom line and increasingly we are losing that focus. We want to be better at instructing them, and this, that, and the other. We want to connect with them. Every teacher would say that. But if you have to constantly be working on PLTs [professional learning teams], on SPTs [shared planning teams], on committees, and all this other stuff, it's harder to make those connections.

"Actually, all of this goes against our charter—most of what we do. I don't know the exact quote, but it says something about keeping it simple, trying to do a few things well, and not serving too many students. We do the opposite. Hell, none of those things mean a thing—our mission, vision, covenant, and all that stuff are a bunch of words on paper. There's another thing in there, about how teachers shouldn't be asked to do all the work, that the burden should be shared. What a joke.

"And those are just issues *in* school, there's another dimension.

"When you're tired at the end of the day, you want a break from the school life. I go to the gym or I go home. I don't come back after school too often, so I miss what is most important to some of these kids, I miss their basketball games, their proms, their other interests. Of course, some teachers do those things and get involved, and they are important —some of those things are more important than anything I do in class— but I can't get out to meet the students that way, even though I recognize how important it all is. I used to, when I was younger. I found a lot of inspiration in seeing the kids in a different way, but that changed for me over time. I seldom see that spark in an academic setting, the way their faces come to life after three o'clock, and I grew frustrated that I couldn't evoke those sorts of responses in my classroom. After school it was all smiles, but during the school day I had undermotivated students who couldn't see that learning was a joy. If I blew up something they'd perk up, but for the most part I'm resigned to the fact that no one gets excited about chemistry but chemists. I don't know if teachers in other disciplines face that issue.

"Also, I began to recognize the cost of overcommitment. As I got older, I recognized what running around like that was doing to me. There's only so much I can do and I have to make choices. I could be a teacher 24/7, but at what price? You sacrifice the rest of your life. It's tough to do that. I've done it. Lots of teachers have. Look at some veterans, they're just shells—burned out. You run out of energy daily and you can sleep at night to regain that, but you also lose it over years and you can't replace that. You just run out and have to pick some things over others. And it never ends, there's always more to do."

SHEILA BRINDON, ENGLISH AS A SECOND LANGUAGE

"For teachers, the professional and the private become blurred. At the very beginning, I had probably been here for six or seven years, I can't put my finger on when or certainly how, being overbooked became less of an issue for me. I stopped saying no because I was worried that people had the impression I wasn't a team player. I did a lot, but I tried not to overextend, especially since I was a newlywed. But at some point, I guess I just came over to the dark side and just let those wars go. It seemed effortless because as a teacher you are always being asked to do something, but honestly, it was not a bright thing to do. I suffered for it. My husband suffered, too. I mean, teachers are like other people, you can get consumed by the job, but for us it's expected. If you aren't okay with taking on excessive levels of work, then you're not a team player, or you don't care about the kids, or you are selfish. Even though it's not in the contract to stay past four, if you say 'My husband and I have tickets to the 5:00 matinee," you get cold, hard death stares. And you can't ever bring up the contract! I did that once, and I think I'm still trying to live it down. People resent you for refusing to work unpaid overtime. One week I was tired and I'd stayed late every night at the school. At the last moment on a Friday they announced an 'emergency' meeting of my committee. It wasn't really an emergency and I told them it was too much, they don't pay me enough to stay late every day of the week. I left. The way people reacted, you'd have thought I tore up a picture of the pope! I later apologized, but no one heard me. It happened five years ago and I still get ribbed about it sometimes in meetings.

"I struggled to maintain a balance between two lives for a long time, one with my husband and our friends, and the other at Wintervalley. I worked very hard at keeping the two worlds separate, and that's a painful process. I'm a guilt-driven personality, so I was always guilty about something. If I wasn't worrying about shortchanging my husband, I was worried about shortchanging the students. It wore me down. I kind of just let the struggle go, and of course, now I'm involved in tons of extracurricular stuff. But while I've accepted more responsibilities, I've also changed my attitude and my schedule. Rather than doing a lot of fun things with my husband during the week, like going out to dinner or seeing a movie, we save it up for the weekends. Those are supposed to be just for us. No work. It never really happens that way, though; there is always a lot to do as you prepare for Mondays, but, hey, what can I do? I'm a teacher.

"When I stopped worrying so much about keeping things separate, I noticed that my school days instantly became longer and more full. I never left at four, which is when the contract asks us to stay, I was there until five or six. I usually draw the line if it gets much later than that, but even that is hard at times. We are even supposed to go to meetings before school, after school, during our lunch hour, and in our planning periods. So I put in more hours, but the day is shrinking. And this is my first year to be an assistant coach. For a few hundred bucks more a year, I have to run practices and go to the games. I've always loved soccer, and it's fun, but my days are even more full now and when we are in season, I even miss entire days if we are traveling to a game on the other side of the state. I chose that, so I shouldn't complain, but it's my reality. How does it work for me? Well, it doesn't work for me. I have soccer after school and then before school I have meetings. No one gives me a break because I chose to coach."

THOM FLANNERY, SOCIAL STUDIES

"I've changed a lot since I was first a teacher. I think I am a lot more relaxed in front of the kids. It wasn't that I was ever *not* relaxed in front of them, I've always been comfortable with kids, but I think I am more confident in my knowledge base and what I know. I'm a little more comfortable in making a conjecture if I don't know the exact answer based on what I do know. I'm not afraid to say, 'I don't know the answer to that question.' I wouldn't have said that the year I started. Also, my classroom management has become a lot easier. At least I think it has! I think that gets better all the time not only because I improve but because kids talk. The kids we have this year have heard about our reputation for a while so they know what to expect. I mean, the very first year Joan and I taught together, we established that this would be an open classroom that was going to have very few rules. But if you didn't follow those rules, there was going to be trouble. Kids know if you are fair or not.

Kids know if you really care or not. They pick up on it. Just like you can pick up on the vibe that they are learning, they can pick up on the vibe that you care. They may be pissed off at you from time to time, but generally, they trust you to do stuff in their best interest. So I've changed for the better, but of course, I am always learning new things: I've gotten a little more comfortable dealing with the parents, I've learned to let some discipline stuff go, which was hard to do. I let some grading pressure go, too. I'm trying to get more of a bigger picture of things. There are things more important to these kids' development than social studies. I've tried to really feel out the class and go with what I have rather than be too rigid because they are all so different. I can't pull out a lesson I did last year because it's usually not going to work without some tweaking. I have to adapt it, somehow. I think knowing that change is inevitable is how I've changed the most. I have to stay on top of that.

"But the biggest thing has been learning to juggle. We have so much to do around here, it's crazy! I've become a king of multitasking. It's unbelievable. At any given moment, I've got to get through my lesson and I still have a billion and a half things to do. Even as I speak with you now, it's tough for me to sit here and relax or concentrate fully on what we're discussing. I seldom have only one task at hand; it's much more common for me to be juggling tons of stuff. The tasks never stop. The administration does a good job of talking about needing to lighten the load on teachers, but it's not happening. I don't get any time to reflect, to ask myself, 'Am I the teacher I want to be? Am I the person I want to be?' There's no time, but it hasn't always been that way.

"We have early release days on the second Friday every other month. Those used to be a time to reflect. We would get together with other social studies teachers and discuss best practices, share good lessons, or ask questions about how others approached teaching a difficult topic. I remember going to one of those when we first had them and asking for help teaching the Vietnam War. Well, one of the other teachers was a veteran and he had these incredible resources. It was amazing and really helped me understand both the conflict itself and ways I could teach it to the students. That was wonderful, but it isn't that way now. Originally, the meetings were districtwide and focused on instructional issues, on teaching methods, and on content-specific professional development. Then at some point, it all changed. There was some concern from certain parents that the district was giving teachers too much time off—Ha! Isn't that hilarious? Anyway, I think the district mostly ignored those complaints, but within a year we were no longer discussing classroom issues. I think another thing happened as well. The district office realized that they had an opportunity for us to do some of their work—and all of the sudden, we were discussing districtwide problems and developing work plans for improving various things the district was facing. Instead of individualized professional development, we were doing the legwork for other people's success. Honestly, in the beginning that was all right, but the longer it went on, everyone became frustrated that we weren't talking about the kids anymore. A few teachers complained and so they disbanded the program. Now, when we meet on those days, it's only with people from our school and is almost entirely about school-specific reform issues. You know, learning about the 'Coalition of Essential Schools' or accelerated schools and all that stuff. They spend that time, which used to be reserved for professional development, on the latest-and-greatest reforms and I try to get into it, but it's hard. I feel the original purpose of those early release days, as I understood it, has been lost.

"I also have a hard time seeing the difference between the reform we just finished and the new one that's coming in. Sometimes they look different on paper, but it never changes anything on a day-to-day level, except for adding more work! There are always new forms to fill out, new procedures to follow, and new committees. More, more, more! It seems like every time we have free time, and I don't know if it comes from the board office or the administration or what, but there is this compulsion to fill up the time: 'Oh, teachers have free time, we have to have a meeting' or 'Oh, teachers have free time, we have to create this other project for them to do.'

"Now, don't get me wrong, it hasn't all been bad—but the craziness of school reform is that whatever is new becomes the most important thing happening for that year. People are buzzing about the newest and latest, which I think is good because it gets us thinking about different approaches to improvement. However, after a while we stop talking about it and you notice, 'Hey, nothing has really changed except that I have eight new tasks that I didn't have before.' Also, I think reforms look different if you are an administrator. I think they believe that things are actually changing, moving forward. Every time they ask us to begin a new reform we go through this 'taking stock' stuff where we talk about how things are going and where we'd like to be. Again, that can be good—I actually enjoy those discussions—but the real problem with it is that they don't want to hear anything negative and they get mad if you say that something is trivial or busywork. It reduces the authenticity of the effort."

JIM FINNAN, LANGUAGE ARTS

"I think our school, for very different reasons than a lot of other schools in the district, is on the verge of staff burnout on those people who are the leaders in the school in the sense that I would understand *leaders*. They are committed, but they are being pulled in the wrong direction, and that's away from the classroom. Extra-instructional activities are fine, but they take a lot of energy and they erode your sense of the joy of teaching because it's all outside the classroom and only impacts the students in a very indirect way. One of the reasons they are headed for burnout is that they receive no special training for being change facilitators. I think that's another burnout thing; at least, as I understand it, there is no real orientation for being a team. We try, like every other school, to put people in teams and on committees who can be successful and who are compatible with one another. There's no formal system that teaches you how to develop consensus, how to get along, or how to handle a certain problem. The leaders don't know how to lead and the followers don't know how to follow. It's a sort of being reactive rather than proactive, those things are decided on and remedied after a disaster happens. We've had a lot of team and committee disasters here at Wintervalley. We've had instances of people coming to the meetings and not even speaking to each other. It's not the norm, so far as I know, but I do know of a few instances where that happened this year. And some of it is ongoing, you know, some people refuse to work with certain other people, that kind of thing.

"The best thing about Wintervalley is the students. And for the most part, the teaching staff here is generally committed to the idea that the students are a priority and learning is a priority. I sometimes wonder if the administration feels the same way. Not in their hearts, but in their policies. I wonder how some of the things they ask us to do line up with what this school is all about. I used to ask those questions a lot, but stopped after a while when I realized that the answers were superficial, not substantive, or just plain lies. Who has time to chase a red herring? But I feel free in the classroom to do my curriculum and my lessons without somebody saying, 'You know you also have to add this.' Part of it is that I'm not part of the SAP test yet.

"If you want to get into leadership in Wintervalley, you make it known and for the most part, that's enough. For somebody who wants to do a particular area—for example, we vote every year on the executive council—and if you were a competent person, eventually you could get on it, then you could be active. I think it's kind of gotten big enough that you feel like you can't. There was a lot of stuff this summer; there was the meeting about PLTs, explaining what they were, but I never sensed that it was, 'Do you want to do this?' it was always, 'This is what we are going to do.' You get to pick how you are going to do it, but whether we are going to do it or not, it was not a choice. I'm sure they've gone through different levels of faculty input but, again, I don't know what sort of freedom people had to set that up. I think the planning groups were going to be that you could avoid faculty meetings because all that information would be presented in planning groups and everybody would be going to planning groups. But now we have planning groups *and* faculty meetings.

"Also, this is small, but it has ended up being part of the history of this place. There is no clerical help for teachers anymore. There used to be. We have mentor kids who run stuff off, but you have to track them down and compete for their time with the other teachers in your department and there are certain things they are not allowed to do. You can't have them run off tests and they don't do typing. You do have to be careful about what you give them. They are supervised, but not all the time. The concept is that the student mentors are learning to be leaders them- selves and they do learn from being in that. But that doesn't replace what we used to have, full-time departmental secretaries. The woman who used to be ours now works for one of the assistant principals. At first, it was a shared appointment, but she's totally the AP's now—there is no help for the Classics Division. No one. Before, Cassie, our old secretary, had all my stuff on a disc—for me and for everyone—she did a lot of stuff that really helped us out. She freed us to focus more on teaching. Even the department chairs have lost their clerical support, who have all moved to administrators.

"I'm sure I sound ridiculous, complaining that we don't have a secretary. I mean, really, that's quite a luxury! But now that I've been here a while, I realize that it's just one more form of support that has been yanked from us. I know that in leadership research they talk about the tension between pressure and support. Well it's not tension here, it's a one-way train. More pressure, more tasks, less support. Back then, we had secretaries, and when we lost them no one complained because we are just teachers and are supposed to be humble and take shots for the team. But the shots keep coming, one after the next. Some are real haymakers and the others are little jabs, but along with all the glorious success this school has achieved, there is also a history of taking away the things that are in place that ensure the success and adding obstacles and rigmarole.

Some of the things we are asked to do are done online or electronically, but they still take time and they are still just heaped on top of the pile rather than replacing a task that was removed. It does help in some ways that some of the daily procedures are handled by the computers, like attendance, but shifting it online hasn't saved me any time; it mostly helps the administrative staff with record keeping. We can also respond online to executive council meeting minutes, but I don't have the time.

"This school is fine, there are some truly amazing things happening here most days, but it used to be a much happier place to work. It was a joyful place to be and so it's sort of like—everyplace has ups and downs—but you had so many chances for renewal and so many ways to get excited about things; to connect with people; so many different ways to make a difference in kids' lives. It seems like those ways are fading, being taken away through formal and informal ways by people who don't give a damn about anything that made this place what it is today. I realize I sound like a cliché, the disgruntled veteran who is stuck in his ways, and you can write down what you like, but I don't think that's accurate. I would welcome change. I would love progress. I would pull my weight, and probably even more. I would lead. But it won't happen the way the school is headed right now. We are caught in a cycle of nothingness. We solve paperwork problems, not substantive ones; we stack bureaucracies on top of one another instead of eliminating unnecessary work; we add, add, add, and we never subtract.

"It's not like we don't know part of the problem. Part of the problem is the same problem we have in knowing students. The size of the school and the legacy of previous disappointments are working against us. We know that and there are lots of models out there to deal with the problems of practice we face, but you can't implement one of them at the stroke of a pen or pass a resolution from a single meeting, and we don't have an administration that has the stick-to-itiveness to do what we did when we went to the block schedule. We spent between eighteen months and two years doing our homework and bringing people from the community and parents and students, involving everybody, and educating ourselves in an ongoing way. We agreed to take some chances and see what would happen so we adjusted things as we learned. We can't sustain that now—that process of inquiry and experimentation— and it is driving me nuts. We could fix some of these things if we were willing to spend three or four years planning something like small learning communities or democratic governance and then implemented and tested them. But we're not going to, because that takes persistence, vision, and elimination of all these other distractions. We don't buy into that process because it is now all about product—about a test score, a ratio, or an average. This comes from the top, from the administration. They have pressure from above. They want it yesterday, because that's what their jobs demand. Numbers. And it doesn't even matter what kind of numbers. They can show growth over time, adequate yearly progress, or just be a shot in the dark. As long as it fits on a graph and makes us look good, we'll use it. Numbers are the currency of success in today's schools. It's all about numbers these days; whatever it is tomorrow, we'll produce that. I have no idea what it might be, but I guarantee this, we will be asked to do more tomorrow and nothing will be taken away. Always more."

3

TEACHING AS AN EVERYDAY AMBIGUITY: WHO IS DOING WHAT, WHERE, WHEN, WHY, AND HOW?

There is no such thing as a conversation. It is an illusion. There are interesting monologues, that is all.

—Rebecca West

A crisp Midwestern morning in October. As summer gave way to autumn in Owen City, more than foliage was falling. Teacher morale was in decline at Wintervalley High. It wasn't that the bottom had fallen out, but the initial enthusiasm and rush of institutional adrenalin that accompanied the beginning of the school year had faded and been replaced by routine. Many schools experience this dip in exuberance as the school year begins. It is not so much something to be worried about as it is a sign that folks are "getting down to business." Banners welcoming faculty and new students back from their summers are taken down and replaced by signs indicating upcoming events and meetings, induction processes and orientations are replaced by regular schedules, and high-spirited hugs and hellos between faculty and among students give way to silent nods and monosyllabic acknowledgments in passing. What was new becomes normal, and so it was at Wintervalley High.

It was hour two and I was observing a Team Tutor Program (TTP) planning session. Wintervalley's TTP was designed to help students who fall behind in their academics get caught up through additional work. Essentially, the way the program worked was that if a student's grade fell below a C average in any class or the student missed several days of school, he or she might be referred into the TTP by a teacher. The student then lost his or her study hall, and instead attended a more structured "guided" study hall, where students would receive help as they completed assigned work or just remained on task for the duration of the period. The guidance center facilitated the program and counselors staffed guided study hall sessions and acted as tutors. By many accounts, the program had been rewarding and frustrating at once. Originally, the TTP was to be a resource for students academically at risk, and at its inception there was a manageable ratio of student to tutors. However, this year, the program's second, had been different. A reorganization of faculty lines and the counselors' already busy schedules stretched the moniker "Team Tutor" into a misnomer. At any given time, a single "tutor" was overseeing as many as thirty students. And it wasn't just any group of students, either. Students referred to the TTP often had behavioral talents that enabled them to disrupt an entire classroom by themselves. The TTP brought several such students into the same room for what could be a challenging hour and a half for the counselor on hand. Through the referral process, teachers sent work for students to complete or counselors drew from archived lessons, organized by subject and grade level, to keep students engaged. Counselors learned what subject and lessons were giving students the most trouble and helped as best they could.

Counselors involved in the TTP met once a month to discuss the program. That day's meeting was the group's second of the year, and an air of agitation clouded the room even before all participants were seated. Many of the regular conference rooms were occupied and the team was meeting in a cramped space meant for individual consultations. Eight counselors were crowded elbow-to-armpit in the tiny room made for two. They pushed and wiggled politely in wool sweaters, heavy cable corduroys, and long winter skirts trying to accommodate each other and make themselves comfortable. It wasn't the luxury suite everyone would have wanted, but these were friends and they made the best of it. Little inside nudge-and-a-wink jokes flitted around the room:

"Hey Mark, you could stand to lose a few pounds. No wonder it's so tight in here!"

"I'm not the only one; us whales would need to become sardines to get in here!"

"I'm glad I didn't bring my planner, there wouldn't be room!"

"There isn't even room for the meeting agenda, and it's only one sheet of paper."

I participated in the premeeting shuffle too, twice giving up my chair to late-arriving TTP members. I tried to press myself as close to the wall as possible and eventually offered to leave so the group could have more room. They insisted I stay, even though my absence would have made things much more spacious and, save for my own study, there was no real reason for me to be there. That meeting was one of the times I acutely felt the imposition I made on the teachers. Not only did I intrude on their meeting, I also took their physical space as well.

I was closest to the door and the chairperson asked me to close it so the meeting could begin. As I did, the temperature seemed to rise fifteen degrees, either from the winter gear or the heat of passion. The TTP had problems.

Counselors were frustrated with what they saw as teacher noncooperation with the program. They lamented that teachers refused to supply them with adequate materials in a timely manner so they could do their jobs and help the students. Several tutors complained that they regularly had to track down teachers for work or simply to find out why a particular student had been referred. Increasingly, students arrived in the TTP room without the proper yellow forms the team had worked so hard to develop over the summer. Everyone recognized that there was an initial time of adjustment as teachers learned to use the forms, and they expected some confusion, but how long would it take? It seemed like students arrived empty-handed every day. As the meeting progressed, some openly questioned whether teachers were devoted to those students who were more academically challenged. Maybe they didn't really care about those kids and just referred them to the TTP to get them out of the room so they could concentrate on higher-performing students. That statement provoked others to nod their heads.

Lydia Smith, a fourth-year counselor, used the example of helping struggling algebra students to illustrate the program's issues to her colleagues. She suggested that she understood and could do the work—she could help the student get the correct answer—but she didn't know *how* the teachers wanted it done, so there was little point in helping because the problem would be counted incorrect for having used the wrong steps. "After all," she recalled, "that's always the problem with helping students with math—there were many ways to get an answer, but teachers always want only one of them." She was exasperated. "How could the program succeed if there wasn't more buy-in from the teachers?"

Her example was met by a hearty endorsement and an assertion that there were other similar issues in nearly all academic areas, not just math. That being said, several counselors agreed that math was especially problematic. Then the team discussed strategies for dealing with the situation:

Should they write a memo? No. Not everyone would read it and many would forget anyway.

Should they let it go? No. This was a real problem that needed immediate action for the students' sake and for the health of the program.

Should they reinstate the once-used policy of sending students back to the teachers' rooms if they arrived at the TTP room without everything they needed? No. When the program was first approved, teachers insisted that this stipulation be removed, as it could lead to continual interruptions if referred students reentered the room for materials or clarification of expectations. Counselors had begrudgingly agreed to a different policy. In cases where tutors and students were unclear as to what was expected, students were to complete worksheets from a district-provided file. They had asked the teachers for lessons and materials, but many were not interested in delivering a year's worth of material to the TTP. After turning to the district, the TTP received a set of academic study guides designed to increase student scores on the state's standardized test. These were "cross-referenced" with the state standards in their given subject. If no standards existed, there was a file of worksheets prepared by the subject area specialist.

Should they enlist the administration to exert pressure on noncompliant teachers? Maybe. Some counselors were convinced that a threat from above would be the best way to encourage program success. The TTP was a form of academic support, and if people weren't supporting the students, they should be held accountable. Maybe the TTP staff should keep track of which teachers were noncompliant. One team member got very excited about this proposition, but suggested it wasn't enough: "You know what, we've got to go and get Dr. Weleck on our side. We've got to get him to give job targets to those teachers who won't give us materials. That's the only way we're going to get their attention, if we threaten their jobs."

Other tutors weren't as excited about the idea of skipping more collegial appeals in favor of intimidation and antagonism, but admitted that some teachers probably didn't think highly of counselors and might need a gentle push from a stronger hand. The teacher who had advanced the job target idea originally concluded the discussion by asserting that "the only way you can facilitate change when there is no buy-in is to force it. If we don't stand up for the kids, who will?"

The group deliberated further and decided that the prudent course of action was to keep track of how many students arrived at TTP sessions without proper materials and paperwork, and also the names of the offending teachers. At the next meeting, they would look at that data and decide whether noncompliance was widespread or a problem concerning only some teachers. The matter was tabled for discussion at the next meeting.

As luck would have it, I was scheduled to interview an algebra teacher later that day. During her after-lunch planning period, she explained the department's approach to instruction (note the emphasized sentence).

"We decided about five years ago, as a division, that we weren't empowering our students to make the kinds of decisions they needed to make and weren't fostering their critical thinking enough. You know, looking at a problem and saying, 'Okay now, how can I go about this?' That's what we are trying to achieve—to use any of the tools we have studied in solving a problem. *We don't care how they solve the problem as long as they document the steps they use.* I think that this is extremely important—it guides everything we do. If the kids come out here and they can solve a long, complicated equation but you can give them some raw data and they can't do anything with it—can't find the relationship, can't do anything about projecting it into the future to determine something, then what have we given them? Nothing. They can manipulate variables in algebra class, but it means nothing to them as a tool to make their lives better. We want them to be able to do more, so we have to give them those kinds of experiences. We're very committed to that philosophy."

Though not always so immediate or profound, teachers and groups around the school exhibited similar characteristics. That is, they initiated unnecessary conflict with one another due to poor communication. People whose work would have been made much more meaningful and easier were not in communication and did not work from the same pedagogical orientation. Interestingly, poor communication seemed to exacerbate an extant siege mentality among the various working groups within the school. Almost every meeting in the school was marked by us-against-them language—some of which was fairly benign or in jest; some of which took on a combative tone; some of which induced frustration, dismay, or indifference. Institutional ambiguity and antagonism were more a norm than the common core principles espoused in the school's charter.

During one interview later in the semester, I explained what I had observed to Anson Yakubu, a veteran teacher who was also chair of the Science Department. Why did this happen? Couldn't a fifteen-minute conversation between the parties resolve these sorts of communication problems? Were threats of a job target or other forms of intimidation widespread or a tactic evoked by a ruthless few? He explained,

"You know, I am sure this has occurred to you, but one of the reasons for that kind of malicious response is not because that's the first time they ever thought of that, it's because it works. Some people do it all the time. They scream bloody murder and go to the principal, who then raises hell and calls "emergency" witch-hunt meetings. He does a lot of damage when he gets that way, to both programs and to individuals. I've seen him sweep away entire programs or hold a teacher's feet over the fire. And for what? Based on what evidence? None. He does it all with information from only one side. His passions are aroused and he doesn't get his facts straight. If he would do a little research and find out the facts, he might see things differently. Sometimes a leader has to pause." Anson paused.

"But look, every year some of our departments undeservedly acquire the reputation that we are out to flunk kids, which is kind of an interesting thing. I mean, are you kidding? What teacher is out to flunk kids? It's stupid, but I hear it every year. That's the mantra some counselors speak to parents and students because they don't understand what we're trying to do or what we have changed about our instruction from the previous year. Since they don't understand, they don't like what we do. Improvement without communication breeds contempt. They never spend any time observing or talking to teachers, they just try and placate parents who are upset with a kid's grades and they tell them anything."

"But, are you sure?" I asked. "Couldn't it be the case that they are also trying to help the kids in some way and you don't exactly understand their methods and motives? Couldn't this be a two-way street? A communication problem rather than a problem of conflicting interest?"

"Maybe." Anson lingered on that thought. "But, hell, we are the teachers. Counselors should come to us first. We're on the front lines! What am I supposed to do, call everyone in the universe when we do anything? They wouldn't pay attention anyway, everyone is too busy. Let me give you an example."

"Shoot."

"Last year around the end of September, I was called into a meeting with Weleck, and it's about all these kids who are flunking science."

"Midterm grades?" I asked.

"Right. He looks at me and says, 'What are we going to do about this?' Of course, he forgets that we have had the same meeting every year for the last four years. And, just like each of those other years, I have to go down to guidance and pull all these permanent records and spend two or three hours running analyses on the files. After I've gotten a printout of all the kids who got Fs from the secretary in guidance who handles all that stuff, I segregate and disaggregate the data to identify the kids who are only flunking . . . Biology I, let's say. That's a good example, because the administration is always concerned about the tenth graders. And for good reason. It's a very difficult year for a lot of kids. Incidentally, many teachers have never taught sophomores and don't realize why we spend so much time focusing on them rather than the other years. Some people complain about it, but not me. I taught sophomores for years. It's a very difficult year and the administration has nailed this one. I'm not sure if the actual support programs we have now are the right ones, but since Dr. Weleck has been here we've made tremendous strides forward in sophomore retention and achievement. They have shown me that they understand and are committed to the kids." He voice trailed off and for a moment he was alone with his thoughts about sophomores.

"Anyway, then I identified the ones who are only failing Biology I. It's a very small percent. Maybe there are fifty or sixty sophomores failing anything in the entire school. Maybe ten of those are failing Biology I. Maybe twenty of them are failing math, because math is tough for a lot of them, and the rest of them are failing multiple courses. Then I go back and run the longitudinal study: I use their file to go back to the sixth grade and I go through their permanent record and find that *this* kid has a history of failing multiple core classes. I notice that *this* kid has always struggled with science and has also always struggled in English. One of the things I look for is whether or not students do well in all other classes but have problems either only in science or in math and science. It takes the same kind of thinking, the same kind of analytic skill, the same kind of discipline to succeed in those courses, so if they do well in English, or social studies, or history, but they have a dip in science and math, that gives us some direction. That kid might need some help with problem solving, organization, and step-by-step processing. Some kids are great writers or readers, and that will get you far, but it takes more to excel in math and science.

"Another kid might have a really fat file because he's been in disciplinary referrals. He's been thrown out of school. He's been in four different schools. He's been in five different school districts. His parents are divorced. It's all in the files. Now, some years are different than others, but in roughly three hours, I've got a profile of the kids that flunked tenth-grade science. So I turn around and give Dr. Weleck a little report. Maybe it gives him something to tell those kids' parents or the counselors, I don't even know why he has me do that. At first, I resented it because I thought I was being made to do the counselors' job. But when I got over that, I realized that I could take my little report and discuss it with the students' teachers. I think it helps. But . . ." Anson frowned as he paused.

"I try to be positive, but I don't know what the guidance people are doing. Last year I went to a meeting with all the department chairs and the guidance folks. At that meeting Dr. Weleck asked the guidance people if they could do something similar to what I had done for each student—whether they were low or high performing. I thought it was a brilliant idea. It could really change what we do in the classroom." Anson searched for words.

"They balked at the suggestion. They told him it takes too much time. What else do they do? I mean, I know they work hard and I respect them. They meet with students on important issues and work with parents more than most teachers, but I have to wonder . . ."

When he continued, Anson asked a rhetorical question that brought Wintervalley's communication problems full circle.

"Do they really care about the kids? Do they care about the students' academic success? Maybe it's just a technological issue. Maybe the district doesn't have the right technology to run those sorts of analyses easily because there's no districtwide system and our stuff doesn't interface with data systems from the middle and elementary schools. Nevertheless, if I could do it for ten students in two or three hours, they could do something like that for the rest. They have six administrative assistants, six gals that—surely to goodness, before they start jumping our case about their remedial programs, they could do their own homework rather than make me do it every fall! The fact is that thought never occurs to any of them. It's always about pointing the finger at somebody else. And there's something wrong with that." Anson paused again.

"Look, I'm sure there are things we could do better to make their work more efficient, maybe there is something wrong with the way we do our work. Maybe there is something wrong with us if the guidance people are always pointing their finger at us. I'm not shirking our responsibility to do a better job. But the bottom line is that we, the teachers, are down here busting our asses on the front lines and they are there to support the students, and really, to support us. But obviously we are not working together because we really don't communicate properly. They do their thing and we do ours. The right hand doesn't know what the left is doing and that's likely both sides at fault."

Later that month I met with Becky Swales, a fourth-year history teacher. We were scheduled to meet in one of Wintervalley's conference rooms. I was early, and as I waited I paced the room and looked around at the many posters hung on the walls. There were the requisite eduposters (the kind with pictures of neatly groomed and smiling teachers plying their trade to eager, happy, and engaged students with "just the right mix" of ethnic and gender diversity) and even a leaderposter (these usually have a dramatic picture and a caption of motivationspeak. The

one before me had a picture of a mountain climber and read
LEADERSHIP: THE PATH TO PEAK PERFORMANCE). In be-
tween these was a smattering of institutional documents, blown up to
poster size. I stopped in front of one and read,

Wintervalley High School Mission
Wintervalley High School is committed to helping every student develop
the knowledge, skills, and attitudes that will lead to a satisfying and productive life. Students will:

- Acquire and process information in order to become lifelong
  learners
- Think critically and creatively to solve problems
- Communicate effectively
- Express creativity and aesthetic awareness
- Be healthy, productive and socially responsible citizens of a global
  community

Just as I finished, Becky entered the room. "Hi," I said. "Listen, Becky,
I've prepared about a dozen questions to ask you about communication,
but I want to set them aside and ask you about these posters."

"You mean the Mountain Man?" She laughed. "We always joke about
that thing. Look at it—is he going to get to the top and plant his flag or
is he lost and stuck? I wonder the same thing about most of our meetings, too. Will we get there or are we lost?" She placed a stack of papers
on the table and flopped into the chair at the head of the table. "I'm just
kidding, really. We've done some good work in this room." A copy of
Will Durant's *The Story of Philosophy* rested on top of her pile of material. I nodded toward the text. "Great book."

"Yep," she said. "I use it all the time."

I pointed at the poster I had been reading. "What's this third bullet
about? Communicate effectively—what does that mean at this school?"

"Okay," she began. After a long, tall drink of Diet Coke from an enormous sixty-four-ounce jug, she continued. "I imagine Wintervalley is like
a lot of schools. We communicate with each other in formal and informal ways. We have a school newspaper that the Journalism Club puts together, and they do a good job. It's obviously very student focused, but

there's a feature in each edition where they interview a teacher. It's mostly about some hobby they like to do outside of school. They interviewed me a few years ago and asked me about hiking. I don't do it much anymore, but I used to get out to the park fairly regularly. Anyway, there are other institutional-type publications that are just for teachers. Some of them are internal to the school, like memos, departmental bulletins, and such. Others are meant for the outside world, like when teachers write notes for the parents, or organizations send out newsletters. There are also tons of flyers posted around the halls that advertise various clubs, performances, and events. There are a lot ways to get the word out in print, but I guess we also communicate through e-mail and in meetings. Some teachers are tech savvy and have websites for their rooms. Not many, but a few of them do some cool things."

"How much of the printed stuff do you read?" I asked.

"Me? Not much. I don't have time. If I'm meeting someone for lunch in the teacher's lounge and they're late, then I'll look through the paper if one is lying around. But I don't really read the articles or anything."

"Okay, so there is a lot of printed material at the school, and you don't pay it much attention. What about the other teachers?" I asked.

"Ha! It sounds awful when you say it that way, but I guess I really don't read that stuff. Is that bad? I read the more important bits, the professional memos. But for the most part, I think whoever produces the stuff pays attention and the rest of us are too wrapped up in our own business to notice. There is so much going on around here, you can't keep up with what's happening down the hall."

I crossed the room and pointed to a different poster, titled *Wintervalley High School Vision*. It read as follows:

Wintervalley High School Vision

To ensure success for all students, Wintervalley High School will be a place that:

- Fosters purposeful learners and problem solvers who respect others
- Exercises individual and social responsibility
- Strives for academic excellence
- Encourages community involvement and democratic decision-making

"There's nothing here about communication, but what about this fourth point? I mean, if you are encouraging community involvement and democratic decision making, doesn't there have to be effective communication? How does that work?"

Becky took another swig of Diet Coke, and answered. "Well, we have this shared governance structure that involves everyone in the school. So that's democratic, right? Everyone serves on a committee, and then each committee reports to the executive council. That's how we participate democratically."

"Wait," I said. "I think I have something about that . . ." I rummaged in my things for a moment and then placed an orange sheet of paper in front of her. It had been passed out at a meeting near the beginning of the school year. On the paper was a diagram that showed the interaction and process for cross-disciplinary teams.

"Yep, that's it, the orange one. Last year, we made our cross-disciplinary teams by getting together with folks from across the school. Teams were formed by a marriage of convenience depending on when you had your planning hour. It was fun to see people I don't normally see, but the model didn't really work for us, in terms of helping us communicate or engage as a democratic entity. I don't even think we use that anymore. It's a work in progress, that model, but as a means to facilitate democratic interaction, it clearly doesn't work. It just puts us in different little silos. It doesn't break down communication barriers, it just made new ones. I think somebody complained, because they've changed how we meet, when we meet, and whom we meet with. It's all different this year. But if this is the way we are supposed to communicate, to put democratic principles in action, we are no democracy. I still don't know what people around the school think about key issues, and I'm not sure I ever will. The school is too big and communication is difficult."

"What about this one?" I asked as I gestured toward a laminated list of bullets that read:

Common Commitments of WHS Faculty and Staff
- We will promote authentic learning and pedagogy.
- We will provide students with the support needed for higher achievement.
- We will participate in focused professional development to improve student achievement.

- We will cultivate a safe environment that promotes freedom with responsibility.
- We will communicate with students, parents, colleagues and the community.
- We will collaborate to promote student achievement.

"This one says, 'we will communicate with students, parents, colleagues and the community.' Does that happen?"

"Hm," Becky hummed low and thought for a moment. "Sure. We communicate with students every day. As far as communicating with parents, that is more of a teacher-by-teacher thing. Some of us are better than others about it. We have parent-teacher conferences and all that, but anything more is usually up to the individual. I don't send home many notes, but some people do. I communicate with my colleagues all the time. We have a good team and we have to get together so we can find out what is happening in each other's classes. If we didn't do that, it would be a mess. We get together over the summer and plan for the year, too, so I think we communicate effectively. As far as community communication, I have no idea what that means. I assume it's an administrative function. They handle the press if they come around, and I know Dr. Weleck is often at meetings at the district offices, or with parents, or even our Partners in Education liaisons. I don't know if he does a good or a bad job, but he works hard." Becky tapped the table three times and then continued.

"The thing we don't have is good communication across departments. I have no idea what most of the people in the school are doing. I don't know what they think, what they do, if they are good, if they are bad, or anything. For all I know, there is a teacher down the hall whom I should be working with because we teach similar or relevant things. How would I know? The curriculum isn't aligned across disciplines. When do I have the time to talk with social studies, art, music, or anyone else about what they are doing or what I am doing? It doesn't happen. I communicate with the people I work with the most, but not many other people."

"Well," I said, "maybe that's all right. Maybe as long as your unit is doing well it's okay to not have much interaction with other folks."

"No," Becky's countenance changed and she retorted, "I don't think you quite understand what I'm talking about. For one thing, like I said, we can't function as a democracy if we don't communicate, so you can scrap all this talk about shared governance. We spend a lot of time talking about that and rearranging the chairs on the deck of the *Titanic*, but it doesn't really change. Second, last time I checked, I don't work in a *unit*, I work in a *school*. I don't know for sure, but I would guess that we are missing some great opportunities for collaboration and for learning because we are siloed off in our departments. At the department level, it's efficient, but when you step back and look at the whole school, we are fragmented. I think that's an interesting paradox; we are efficient and inefficient at once because our communication is great with our closest peers and nonexistent outside of our little circle. Also, aren't we missing a chance to make the whole thing a lot more interesting and meaningful? I've been here for several years, and I would like to hear some fresh ideas and see some new faces. But because of the way things are set up, I am denied the opportunity to interact and communicate with most of the other teachers in terms of content and method. My department works hard, and we do a good job, but I think we are on our own. It's us against the world."

Becky gestured toward another poster. "We went through 'Coalition of Essential Schools' a few years ago. Look at that one, it presupposes excellent communication. None of those ten principles can work at all without sound communication, and none can work for school improvement unless they work well. I've thought about this quite a lot, and I am pretty certain that's why the coalition never really changed the way people work at Wintervalley. We were all sort of broadly in agreement about those principles, but after the initial conversation, the dialogue stopped. We never went through the process of operationalizing those principles as a school. We talked about them here and there, but really, it fizzled pretty quickly. That poster is all that's left of what could have been a school-changing reform." It read:

The Ten Principles of the Coalition of Essential Schools

1. The school should focus on helping adolescents learn to use their minds well. Schools should not attempt to be "comprehensive." If such a claim is made it is at the expense of the school's central intellectual purpose.
2. The school's goals should be simple: each student is to master a limited number of essential skills and areas of knowledge. While

these skills and areas will, to varying degrees, reflect the traditional academic disciplines, the program's design should be shaped by the intellectual and imaginative powers and competencies that students need, rather that necessarily by "subjects" as conventionally defined. The aphorism "less is more" should dominate: curricular decisions should be guided by the aim of thorough student mastery and achievement rather that by an effort merely to cover content.

3. The school's goals should apply to all students, while the means of these goals will vary as those students themselves vary. School practice should be tailor-made to meet the needs of every group or class of adolescents.

4. Teaching and learning should be personalized to the maximum feasible extent. Efforts should be directed toward a goal, that no teacher have direct responsibility for more than 80 students. To capitalize on this personalization, decisions about the details of the course of study, the use of students; and teachers; time and the choice of teaching materials and specific pedagogies must be unreservedly placed in the hands of the principal and staff.

5. The governing practical metaphor of the school should be student-as-worker, rather than the more familiar metaphor of teacher-as-worker, rather than the more familiar metaphor of teacher-as-deliverer-of-instructional-services. Accordingly, a prominent pedagogy will be coaching, to provoke students to learn how to learn and thus to teach themselves.

6. Students entering secondary school studies are those who can show competence in language and elementary mathematics. Students of traditional high school age but not yet at appropriate levels of competence to enter secondary school studies will be provided intensive remedial work to assist them quickly to meet these standards. The diploma should be awarded upon a successful final demonstration of master for graduation—an "Exhibition." This exhibition by the student of his or her grasp of the central skills and knowledge of the school's program may be jointly administered by the faculty and by higher authorities. As the diploma is awarded when earned, the school's program proceeds with no strict age grading and with no system of "credits earned" by "time spent" in

class. The emphasis is on the student's demonstration that they can do important things.

7. The tone of the school should explicitly and self-consciously stress values of certain expectations ("I won't threaten you but I expect much of you"), of trust (until abused) and of decency (the values of fairness, generosity and tolerance). Incentives appropriate to the school's particular students and teachers should be emphasized, and parents would be treated as essential collaborators.

8. The principal and teachers should perceive themselves as generalists first (teachers and scholars in general education) and specialists second (experts in but one particular discipline). Staff should expect multiple obligations (teacher-counselor-manager) and a sense of commitment to the entire school.

9. Ultimate administrative and budget targets should include, in addition to total student loads per teacher of 80 or fewer pupils, substantial time for collective planning by teachers, competitive salaries for staff and an ultimate per pupil cost not to exceed that at traditional schools by more that 10 percent. To accomplish this, administrative plans may have to show the phased reduction or elimination of some services now provided students in many traditional comprehensive secondary schools.

10. The school should demonstrate non-discriminatory and inclusive policies, practices, and pedagogies. It should model democratic practices that involve all that are directly affected by the school. The school should honor diversity and build on the strengths of its communities, deliberately and explicitly challenging all forms of inequity and discrimination.

She continued, "I mean, look at that list; it's teacher friendly. What teacher wouldn't buy into those things? We had a few preliminary meetings where we discussed this stuff, but I have no idea what happened after that. Sooner or later, we weren't talking about the coalition anymore. Of course, that's not all bad, we take some good from each of those efforts and those coalition discussions weren't a total waste. But although we are still generally talking about the same things, about the kids and about our beliefs, the language always changes around here so it gets confusing. What's more, over time I have realized that implementing reform after reform without clear articulation of what we are keeping from the old one and what we are leaving behind tends to disillusion folks and they disengage from discussions altogether. Even teachers who would die for their kids just throw their hands up when they hear terms like *mission, vision,* or *taking stock.* At one point we were going to be a 'learning community' and somewhere else along the line we were going to be an 'accelerated school.' What happened with that? I'm sure there were dozens of things before that and there will be hundreds after. None of it has taken hold. It's not because we don't have committed teachers or engaged administrators or good parents or good kids, we have all of that. It's because those good people don't talk to each other and when they do they don't listen. When we do get together, no one is certain what language to use and what to emphasize in the conversation. Reform has put a communication barrier between us rather than make things more fluid. Since no one has any idea what is happening down the hall from them and they don't have a common language to describe it, our communications structures are inoperative. Every time we take on one of those big reforms, we are really starting fresh instead of building on what we have. It happens over and over and over again."

Becky and I concluded our interview shortly after. Later that night, when transcribing the tape from our discussion, I took a break and found my own copy of *The Story of Philosophy.* I hadn't looked at it in years, and the highlighted pages had little scribbles in the margins. In no particular order, I thumbed through, picking up long-forgotten stories about Aristotle's huge and crazy collection of things from around the world, Russell's philosophic explosion after freeing himself from the shackles of logic, and Voltaire's acute sense of hopelessness. I finally stopped when I came to an underlined passage in the Plato chapter: "Every form of government tends to perish by excess of its basic principle. Aristocracy ruins itself by limiting too narrowly the circle within which power is confined; oligarchy ruins itself by the incautious scramble for immediate wealth. In either case the end is revolution" (p. 19). Revolution? I reached for another book on the shelf.

In 1971, Neil Postman and Charles Weingartner cowrote one of my favorite education books, *The Soft Revolution,* which is a blueprint for engaging, and disengaging, an evil or inflexible system with social and interpersonal dexterity. The book is designed to encourage students, teachers, parents, and administrators—really, anyone who recognizes a need for institutional change toward greater social justice and individual authenticity—to oppose inflexible and insensitive public school systems by starting their own after-school programs, classes, and even schools. *The Soft Revolution* suggests that to become empowered in schools, students and teachers need only understand the school system and local political community—democratic schooling offers everyone the means to facilitate substantive change. I wonder if Becky would agree?

4

THE "OLD GUARD" VERSUS THE "NEW WAY"

It is the malady of our age that the young are so busy teaching us that they have no time left to learn.

—Eric Hoffer

When I first interviewed Jackie, she was in her second year at Wintervalley. Before coming to the school she spent a year teaching science in a rural high school about forty minutes outside of Owen City and, by her own account, "had a bad experience." Although she lived only a few miles down the road from the school, Jackie explained that she had never really been accepted as a member of the community, and was instead treated as an outsider "from the city." By her account, teachers, students, and the administration at her old school viewed her as a short-timer, regardless of her espoused and authentic intentions to remain at the school for several years. As a newly certified teacher, Jackie had been crestfallen that her colleagues and students refused to respect her as a professional and constantly reminded her that they had seen "girls like her come and go." At first she was determined to prove them all wrong, but eventually she tired of eating lunches alone and enduring the "silence of the commute," which seemed to grow larger as the year progressed. After that February Jackie decided enough was enough and sent her application to Owen City. She was hired over the summer and never returned to her old school to say goodbye or even to retrieve her instructional materials. Wintervalley was a new start, and although things weren't perfect, she was one year wiser and was ready to put the lessons from her previous school experience to good use. As she began her work at Wintervalley, she surmised that the keys to survival as a high school teacher were (a) listen more than you speak, (b) document everything, (c) don't expect anything from fellow teachers, and (d) avoid administrators at all costs.

Jackie decided all that bunk she had been taught in her teacher preparation program about collegiality and learning communities was just that—ivory tower rhetoric that had little to do with the social reality of the schoolhouse. When she left her university program, Jackie was excited to work with other people to effect meaningful change in their school. She was ready to help parents, students, and administrators to be part of the creative environment she hoped to generate in her classroom. As she said, "I bought into all that teacher-prep crap. All of that pie-in-the-sky bullshit: Teams! Collegiality! Shared this and community that! My experience in schools has been very different. I don't think working in schools is about sharing, it's about competition. It's about individual accountability, not group accountability. It's about figuring out who the power players are in the school and it's about learning unwritten rules." She concluded our first interview powerfully: "Professionalism is about meeting contractual obligations and strategic avoidance of the silent demands of the job. It's about knowing the boundaries of your contract so you can fulfill them and then being free to leave and live your life. I don't let them take any more of me than they pay me for. Now, of course, I don't say that stuff to anyone here. You have to be politically savvy. For the most part, if you have a smile on your face, loan people paper or pens when they need them, and don't piss off the parents, you are okay. The key is to remember that even though some people pretend like Wintervalley is one big, happy family, they would turn on you in a second if they could benefit from it somehow."

Jackie reported that, so far, defensive professionalism and politically astute maneuvers had paid off at Wintervalley. She mostly cloistered herself in the classroom, focused on the students and her own lessons, and was largely silent in meetings. Jackie was cordial and warm to everyone, but guarded with her time and not looking for friendships at school. She arrived on time each day and hustled out to her car quickly when contract time was over. She was an efficient instructor and hit all the state benchmarks over the course of the year. Luckily, as she explained, she was teaching the same preps (and the same lessons) at Wintervalley that she had taught in her old school so unless she was reassigned she figured she could continue in that manner for the foreseeable future. As far as her professional future, she would continue to teach until something better came along. Maybe she would become an administrator "for the money." Maybe she would go back to school for an advanced degree "to get a better paying job." Maybe she would sell insurance, like her friend "who makes a killing." To Jackie, teaching was something between a task and a chore. And, like a child who has learned to shove the mess into a bedroom closet to fool his or her parent in order to collect allowance, she has sat, listened, and observed the official rules of the Wintervalley game, but has also paid special attention to the unofficial ways the game is played. To Jackie it was important to use the language of the official rules but to practice only the unofficial code. However, Jackie's vision of professionalism was not shared by all of her younger peer teachers.

Sam explained that new teachers at the school gravitated toward one another for a variety of reasons. "Teachers connect at Wintervalley through teaching philosophy, gender, race, and a bunch of other things. I think those things are true whether or not a teacher is a veteran or a newbie. Age is certainly a factor, too, but not the most important one. When a group of teachers comes in at the same time, you certainly notice them. At the beginning they sit together in meetings or eat together. After a while you settle in with your content peers but often you retain those bonds with the other new folks. There is a New Teacher Committee here that helps with induction and orientation. I went through it last year and I thought it was great. I'm not a new teacher, per se, but I'm new to Wintervalley. I used to teach across town at Heskey and they have a committee like that over there as well. I think that's a huge factor in keeping new teachers, even though this school has a reputation for losing new teachers. Induction creates an instant support system and I think a lot of people, especially new teachers, need that. We can get this 'deer in the headlights' look, and if the orientation is done well, a group like that can help people get through. I also find teachers who go through that stuff together tend to hang around together as best friends. So induction is an important time.

"Some of the other teachers in my group from last year are my best friends at Wintervalley. And, although I never really thought about it this way, most of the friends I have strong social bonds with outside of school are the teachers I met during induction at Heskey. Hm—" Sam paused, thinking about his fellow Heskey inductees. "That group was atypical. When I was hired at Heskey there were five other English teachers hired at the same time. Basically, the whole department was replaced. It was an early retirement/buyout kind of thing. You know—a whole bunch of teachers retired at the same time and left, for whatever reasons. I don't know why that happened all at once, but we all came in at the same time and we became friends. That was interesting because we were a variety of ages and backgrounds. Three of us were fresh out of college and in our early twenties, and the other two came to teaching later in life. It wasn't an issue at all, really, we were all learning the ropes at the same time. I think that if you come in and teach the same subject at the same time, you build solidarity because people are experiencing the same thing, whether or not you have other characteristics in common. Those other things I listed are important: age, race, and gender. But there are other ways people connect that can be equally meaningful: induction date, years of experience, a common disciplinary interest, an extracurricular hobby, religion, sharing a room, a planning period, or a lunch hour with someone, marital status . . . this list could go on and on."

I asked Sam to expand on his thoughts about how people in the school connect professionally. "Some of those things you list are formal, like the New Teacher Committee, and some are informal, like sharing an interest in hiking or in watching films. Is the formal connection solidified because there is a set of common experiences? Certain professional development or in-service training activities? I suppose what I am asking is, how much do people connect through planned activity and how much is serendipity?"

Sam responded, "Actually, I think that for my new teacher cadre—that's what they call them—it was that we were all new to the English

Department. We got together and spoke about behavioral issues, subject-matter problems we were having, and stuff like that. Real teacher stuff. We talked a lot about how much writing and reading to assign, what to grade for, and how classes might build on one another. I suppose we were inventing a new curriculum. We all knew what made a good paper but, ironically, if you teach English, you can be your own worst enemy. We all agreed that kids need to write a lot to become good writers. Yet the more writing assignments you give, the more you damn yourself to grade them. It's a tension for most teachers, but especially English teachers. And so we talked a lot about things like that.

"We also talked about the students who hated us and our classes, and how we were going to make it through the year with them. When you talk about the thorns in your side, you form strong bonds. To have a group of people you can sit with and say, 'You won't believe what so-and-so did in class today,' that's huge, to have that kind of confidence. Hopefully, you follow that up with, 'What should I have done differently?' In my experience, asking that question is the difference between a bitch session and a serious professional discussion. You need to have an open dialogue in a safe space. You need to be able to say, 'This is what I did, but I don't know if I did the right thing or not.' I don't think that's unprofessional. I think it's hugely therapeutic for teachers to get together and talk. Obviously, those conversations should stay within their group. That's a huge thing, again, that bonds teachers—trust. That kind of trust builds confidence and rapport. You need to be able to say 'I can't believe this. I really screwed this up' and know that it isn't going to come back to haunt you. That's huge for teachers. I have those conversations with my younger peers, but some of the veterans don't buy into that attitude. They don't have much patience with it and they want to do their own thing. I think most of them are afraid to change what they have done for so long. An open conversation can be threatening if you aren't secure about what you are doing and I think some of the older teachers know they are just coasting by; if they open up, they are scared they will be exposed."

"Really?" I asked. "Tell me more about the differences between veteran and less experienced teachers."

"In this school, maybe in most schools, there is an Old Guard and a New Way. I notice that there really is a difference between people in my generation of teacher preparation and older generations. The older crowd is afraid of innovation. They don't understand that students, administrators, and the world are constantly changing. I think you always have a group that is sometimes called the 'Old Guard,' which I suppose is a negative term, but you know what I mean, right? Teachers who have been here for twenty-five years or more. They all hang out together and they're stuck debating stuff that's been dead for decades! They may not always like each other, but I guess like us there is a shared experience."

Sam laughed. "I sometimes think those veterans are like an older married couple—there's a shared amount of experience together even if they don't agree with each other. It's interesting every once in a while to hang out with them, but I don't do it too often because it brings me down to hear too much negativity. I've sat at those tables in the lunchroom before and listened to their war stories. It's tired old stuff. I guess they are bonding, too, but they need to step aside and let the new generation lead. We have innovative ideas and could move the school forward, but ironically and unfortunately they hold all of the leadership positions. They know how to make things happen, and they know how to prevent things from happening."

I asked Sam, "Are the veteran teachers at Wintervalley burnt out?"

"Well, I wouldn't say that they all feel that way. Not all teachers who have been teaching twenty years feel that way. I don't think that's the case. I do think that if a teacher starts to feel that way it is very important that he look for something else, even if he is a veteran. They should be thinking about how the job is no longer healthy for them. I think that especially after teaching for lots of years, some of them come to a belief that, 'I can do this, and this, but I can't do *everything* and I can't change *anything*.' I guess you could call it burnout. They don't think anything will work. They are regressive, not progressive. Stuck in a rut. I'm sure their students view them as apathetic, and maybe they are, but I don't think that's entirely accurate. In my more generous moments, I think they have just found a clear delineation. I sometimes think they are maybe ultraprofessional. I mean, a lot of the veteran teachers here put in all these extra hours so I would never suggest they don't work. I even see teachers working at night in coffee shops downtown sometimes when I'm out with my friends. They've been at school all day and then they're there all night. It's nuts! I'm a committed teacher but I'm, 'like, get a life!'"

I thought about that. About how many nights I had spent staring at a cathode screen in some nameless midnight coffee shop while my wife and kids slept at home. Did I have a life? I had followed a similar path to the one Sam described. When I entered graduate school I was the one who was out with friends. I met Melanie in a Philosophy of Education class. Despite having our initial conversations mediated by a book neither of us liked, *Habits of the Heart*, a romance blossomed. It must have been all that Nel Noddings stuff about caring that finally brought us together. We courted throughout classes called Free Writing, Media Literacy, and Silly Lesson Plans 101 before eventually marrying and having children. Now here I was a few years later—getting researcher's pallor from spending my days under incandescent lights in a library or a schoolhouse. No time for love or health! What was I doing, spending the days and nights away from my wife, away from my children, away from familial duties and responsibilities in pursuit of the graduate sheepskin? Was I selfish? Stupid? Were my values misplaced? Was it worth time away from the love of my life and my little girls at crucial and tender ages to learn more about teachers? Was personal alienation the price of my pursuit of teacher alienation?

I sighed and came back to Sam. "Is that a common transition for people who become teachers? Is it common for them to become consumed by the job?"

"Absolutely." Sam continued, "They stay so late and give their time. They're totally committed to some aspects of the job but they don't understand some of the newer concepts that inform teaching nowadays. You know, cooperative learning is not just group work, it's very different; authentic assessment is not just writing essays, it's different; accountability is a good thing, not bad, because it provides data we can use to guide instruction; experiential learning is not going on a bunch of field trips or 'digging holes in the backyard' as a veteran once said to me. Learning new ideas would mean change, and veteran teachers are often reluctant to change. They've taught the same book or lesson for twenty years and that's just what they do. Even when we switched to block scheduling last year, some of them kept doing exactly the same thing even though we talked and talked about how it would mean a shift in pedagogy in addition to a shift in schedule. What can you do? Maybe you can't teach an old dog new tricks after all. They aren't willing to buy into new things and new ideas. I'm sure that's why our reform efforts fail, veterans won't give anything a chance and they have a lot of the power."

Jack had been at Wintervalley for six years. In the parlance of teacher-speak, he was a "midcareer professional." A classics teacher, Jack taught mainly junior-level language arts together with a team-teacher, Janet, who taught world history. Jack was an anomaly at the school in that he was a Wintervalley graduate. After he finished high school, he earned his teaching certificate at the local university and was immediately hired back at his alma mater. In his teens, Jack had been a star basketball player and an active member of the student government. His portrait was in several of the school's trophy cases striking various athletic poses. People joked then, and now, that Jack was "Mr. Wintervalley." In my third interview with him, he described his view of the school's culture.

"Teachers express themselves in their dress, certainly. I don't know if it's the same in middle or elementary schools, but in high school I think fashion matters. I profess the belief that even though I am no fashion maven, if I can try and dress as near to 'hip' as I can and get away with it—now, I don't want to be too hip—but to be comfortably approachable and not looking like, I don't know, the ultimate teacher dweebs you see in those *Ferris Bueller's Day Off* movies, then I can better connect to the kids. That is an important expression in itself. I think dressing well helps me connect to the kids a bit better. High school kids are very self-conscious and since they are obsessed by their own looks, they notice what the teachers wear and it matters. I mean if you go through the art department, the art teachers have great clothes—you know what I mean, it's important. They are a very expressive lot and the kids love them. I guess that's what you'd expect. I mean art teachers are also cool because they do all that nonacademic stuff and everyone gets an A for throwing some clay in an oven. New teachers dress well, too, as a whole, and I think it is part of the reason you see such a strong bond between younger, newer teachers and the kids. Some veterans have that but as they get older they become more removed. I think that clothing is an expression of self and maybe also of what you do on your off time. I mean, I go straight to the gym after the final bell so some days I wear sweats."

"So," I asked, "are clothes like a uniform of some kind? Can you tell a social order by looking at who is wearing what?"

"Hm. I'm not sure what you mean by 'social order,' but there are definitely sets of people, cliques, and they wear the same kind of clothes. Among the kids it's very pronounced. You have those kids who wear all black and are into acting depressed, you have the preppy kids and all that, you have the jocks. Also, it's not that simple. There are tensions around the most unlikely things within each of those groups: The ICP kids hate the Eminem kids because the bands have a feud; the Goth kids and the skaters kind of look the same, but they are totally different cliques; there are also differences between the really popular crowd and the wannabes. Some kids are really into high school and everything that comes with it. That's how I was; I got a lot out of it because I went all out. To kids like that, these are the best years of their lives. Others resent the formal culture of the school but I think that's a silly way to live your life. You know, there are the prom-haters, the sports-haters, the kids who skip assemblies or sulk around between classes and all that. They don't care for it and they cause tension sometimes by not actively participating. High school is about having school spirit and it bums me out when people don't have it."

Although he was bright and positive, imbued with the glow of school spirit, I suppose, there was something sad about a person who admitted that the highlight of his life had passed. Mr. Wintervalley continued.

"Like I said, those are the obvious things. The kids wear their clique colors like a badge. But teachers do the same thing. Some of them wear nice clothes and some of them wear those awful teacher clothes. I don't have any teacher clothes."

"Good grief, Jack," I finally said. "You're making me feel like I'm back in high school myself! Does it take a toll to be so self-conscious every day?"

"That's high school, being self-conscious. For teachers and students, too. The subcultures of the school are the same no matter whether you face the chalkboard or have your back to it. Some people get it. They understand that high school is a special place. They buy into what is happening around them and get involved, while others are wallflowers. It doesn't matter if you are a veteran or a new teacher, what really matters is the image you project to your peers and the students, and that should be an image that they recognize, admire, and respect. You also need to get on board. Everyone knows who is a team player and who isn't. Now, just like back then, the team players rise to the top and the individuals get left behind."

Just down the hall from Jack, but a world away, was Deirdra. Deirdra was a special education teacher who had worked at Wintervalley her whole five-year career. We met for lunch one day, her with a bagel and cream cheese, me with a coffee and an apple. After she made a joke about me bringing an apple to an interview with a teacher, I asked her about differences between veteran teachers and new ones.

"I think it comes down to control. For all of us here in the school, there are things we can control and things we can't. Veteran teachers have learned how to operate that way and newer teachers haven't. Look at this, I keep this inside my daily planner." Deirdra leaned forward and opened her thin red book to the first page. A frayed piece of paper was taped inside the cover. It was a familiar prayer:

> God grant me the serenity to accept the things I cannot change,
> The courage to change the things I can,
> And the wisdom to know the difference.

She explained, "I'm not really a religious person, but there's something to that sentiment. Veteran teachers understand that concept as the fundamental truth of the schoolhouse. Newer teachers are all about action without understanding or are paralyzed into inaction and a lack of courage to change what they can. That is what defines those two groups. Now, I understand that some teachers are movers and shakers and that some are more laid back, but every veteran has come to grips with the way power and control work in the schoolhouse. They may not like it, but they know.

"Take my situation. Are the special ed. kids at this school getting short shrift? You bet they are. They do in every school, especially in schools like this that send them from their general ed. classrooms to a pullout situation, but how should I handle that? When I was younger, I would tilt at the windmills. I would make a fuss thinking it would force people to change policy. Later I learned that even if policy changed it was more important to change behavior, and people resent it when you force them to change through mandate. Teachers are like everyone else, they want respect. Policy is about control and seeking to control others is showing them you don't respect them. I learned to shut up, to look for things I could change, and to heighten people's awareness. That is a result of my maturation as a teacher. I'm becoming a veteran where I was inexperienced."

Jonathon was a veteran teacher. One day during his planning time, we discussed some of the many initiatives in motion at the school.

"How is the electronic system working out?" I asked.

"I love it. You get the executive council minutes by e-mail every time they meet so you can read what happened. You can respond to the council. You get personal e-mail too regarding what people have said and how people plan to address certain things. I think it's great. I'm all for the electronic communication."

"And you're doing grades online?"

"Grades, parent e-mail, I have my own website, the whole deal. It's been very helpful. I'm old, and don't know if I'm wise, but the electronic stuff doesn't intimidate me. It's part of the process. A lot of young people—we have many of them now who are very good people because we have hired carefully and we had a chance to snap up some good people—are in the crisis of realizing a fact of teaching, this idea that one day you will arrive. They think there is a professional destination out there called Best Teacher Town. In Best Teacher Town you are all things to all kids. You save the world thirty students at a time. You don't know how, but when you are younger you are sure that you can *get* there. You are certain you will arrive. Some of us who have been at it longer see that journey differently because we recognize after a time that you always see more things you could be doing or ways to do things better. You may improve, but you never really get to a place where you reach every kid. I still try hard, but I know that what I do just doesn't work for some kids."

"Right," I said, certain that I didn't really understand what it meant to have that sort of experience. "I imagine it's tough, but you keep going. In another interview I did this morning, another veteran teacher brought up mastery learning—"

Jonathon interrupted me, "Jeff, please use the term 'experienced' or something. I actually am a veteran of the armed services—I was in Vietnam. That term 'veteran' means something very different and special to me. It's more than anything that has ever happened in Wintervalley."

"Okay," I said. Jonathon's eyes glassed over, and for just a moment he was in a distant country as a young man. "Sorry for bringing it up," I continued, "my father was there, too. Do you want to talk more about that?"

"No. Forget it. Let's drop it. Mastery learning? When that came through, it was the big thing that was going to save education. Well, it was going to save the school anyway. In fact, mastery learning looked a lot like what people are calling the new accountability, only it was an everyday thing we dealt with rather than some test we prepared for that only came around once a year. What ended up happening when we implemented it was that students had to pass these benchmark tests, and if they didn't they went into this remedial mode. They couldn't pass a class in remedial mode so they had to work their way back to the classroom proper. If they didn't make it back, they failed. It's really not much different than what we do now with the team-tutoring stuff, but then it was based on hard numbers, not a subjective referral, and there were consequences. It wasn't the teacher's call; it was a schoolwide high-stakes pullout system. It was okay in principle, but it failed for the same reason that team tutoring doesn't work—students who went into mastery remedial also had to keep up with the pace of the rest of the class. It stuck some of the weakest students in a loop where they were forced to do twice as much work as the better students, and in a sense they had to finish it in half the time. When we abandoned it, it was a very practical decision because we were facing a logjam of held-back students. Teachers realized pretty darned quickly that it was a mess, but there was administrative commitment to mastery being the 'saving grace' or whatever, so it was a disaster because it lasted much longer than it should have. I brought up our problem with mastery implementation when we started the Team Tutoring Program, but I was quickly silenced. One young teacher even went so far as to ask whether or not I was committed to the 'at-risk' students in the school, so I gave it up. Why fight that kind of ignorance? I've led so many progressive and radical charges in this school. Some have failed and some have succeeded. I am the institutional memory of the organization, and if they won't listen I'll just step back and let them experience the same problems I did back then. Hell, sometimes you have to give 'em enough rope.

"I've been at Wintervalley since the day it opened. I was a new teacher, and as luck would have it I quickly became department chair for social studies. Back then, we were on an aggressive search for innovative ideas. We went all over the country visiting great schools and listening to big ideas. What a time! The first trip I went on for the school was with the principal and the other department chairs. We went to Chicago for a huge education conference. I'll never forget. There was this one speaker who really had our principal. You know, really took his ear. 'Mastery learning.' They had these huge wall-sized posters that laid it all out. I have to admit it was impressive. Anyway, our principal thought mastery was something that could be implemented in any classroom without a lot of planning or whatever. I disagreed, mainly because I thought that it would be difficult to establish benchmarks in certain subjects and I wondered about focusing student learning on competence and mastery at the expense of higher-order thinking. I was into helping kids broaden their horizons and this looked like something headed in the opposite direction. The principal and I had a—even though it was my first year as a department chair—he and I had a real donnybrook at the conference over dinner one night right in front of the superintendent and the other department chairs because I could not get him to understand that you cannot go back and say to individual teachers: 'You will do those things that the student will master' and then hold them accountable for that stuff without a lot of collaborative decisions about what is worth mastering. That was a big part of it. Mastery learning was about adopting their benchmarks, and what the hell did they know about our kids or our school?"

"Well, the principal could not understand this. He saw a nice and neat package and I saw a Big Brother curriculum. That struggle wasn't confined to our dinner table in Chicago, it played out in the school when we returned. Many people who jumped on mastery with his encouragement or exhorting ended up having kids 'master' the same mindless, pointless stuff. It was robotic, and I'm sure we lost a few teachers who might have been great during those years. When you take it from a mastery approach, you get this situation where you are asking kids who can't function at the pace you're running to do double work. What's more, it was pointless, soul-crushing, and mind-numbing work. Worksheets, worksheets, worksheets. Mostly irrelevant. So there was no buy-in. We underwent this total restructuring as part of joining mastery, and although we had a lot of materials, we received no training about how to use them. This is all playing out again, by the way; the state tests are in the same cycle, just like mastery and most of the other reforms that have come down the pike.

"Mastery marked the beginning of my interest in assessment, because in those days, we taught Western civilization through world history, which is one of my main threads, and kids always struggled with that because they saw no relevance and because it was 9,000 years of history in nine months. An inch deep and a river wide. I started a lot of experimentation with tests. In those days I gave tests that were predominantly multiple choice. No written stuff. That's how I learned to do it in my preparation program. But I discovered pretty quickly what I think the psychometricians probably already knew. That is, results on those sorts of tests are very small indicators of learning. What's more, if you take a bad item that mistests understanding or recognition of a particular factoid and then you tinker with that item in any way—change the choices, change the stem, the order, whatever—there is no guarantee that the kid won't still miss it again. You can change the way something is presented, but no matter whether you put the cheese or the meat on top, the sandwich tastes the same."

"You lost me, Jonathon," I confessed.

"All I'm saying is that multiple-choice testing is only one way of finding out if someone knows something, and it's an extremely limited way, at that. I've been playing with those tests and reading about test-item construction for decades and now my whole career might depend on how my kids perform on a testing form whose limitations I feel I've explored for thirty years? It's not only absurd; it's an insult to me professionally. Anyway, I pretty quickly recognized that you have to be very careful about how you assess. And if you really want to encourage learning or mastery, you need to change the whole format of your assessment to something that really tests what the kid knows. Something holistic, something authentic. That's kind of where I am now. I have created my own marginally sustainable system of assessment as a part of my own learning process."

"So, you don't think much of the state test, or the way it is being used?"

"It's nonsense, but what should I do? Stand up on the table? Go on strike? Fighting that fight just demands way too much time and energy." Jonathon paused. "For one thing, it will pass within another decade or so, all this testing. For another, it's late March and I'm entering the burnout phase of the year, where now I am really struggling to keep up with the paperwork and the kids are losing interest, especially the seniors, because they are all beginning to lose it, to burn out. We're still two months from the tests, approximately. We're entering the most crucial time of the year, and we're all kind of on a ragged edge.

"But getting back to your earlier question, my career has been an odyssey of experimentation. We haven't even scratched the surface in this interview. I've read John Holt, I've read Ivan Illich, I've read Paulo Freire, and hell—I taught through the early seventies and I lived the sixties. If you don't think we were about putting progressive and radical ideas into motion back then, you have no sense of history. Now, not everyone was, but I was a bit of a radical. I had my own personal revolution going on and, of course, my life was a lot simpler then so I had the energy to press and push. I had few obligations. But I managed to get some support from the district level and through some of my colleagues here and we did some great things. That was kind of the beginning of where we are with classics now, that we began to look at the reality of what's worth mastering and at what is the best way to make the assessment part of a holistic learning process. Some of the younger teachers think that because I don't publicly slag the test and suggest that it can tell us a little something about our kids that I'm an old-fashioned stick in the mud. They have no sense of institutional history and they have no sense of what I'm all about. We must work within the existing system to change the system. Beating on the walls from the outside doesn't get you very far. The Trojan horse brought down Troy, not an all-out frontal assault. Anyway, you use that test as a layer of learning and then you build up, around, and on top of it to get toward something meaningful. We need to be reflective and consider what we really want to diagnose about our instruction and what we want to track about student performance. We are a long way from having it any place where it ought to be, but we're much further down the road than we used to be."

"Jonathon, what do you think about the way vet—er, experienced teachers are perceived by their younger peers?"

"I'm nervous. I'm very nervous as I near retirement because the school is caught in a spiral of repetition and the younger folks haven't learned the lessons that us oldies have to give. We have chances now to move forward but it doesn't seem to happen, and it seems less likely as I watch the younger teachers make the same mistakes we made twenty years ago. Every decade or so the same reforms come back around but are renamed. Do you think accountability is new? Or standardized testing? Do you think that we didn't do what they call experiential learning back in the sixties and seventies? We've been there, we've done that, and to be honest, most of the time when reforms come around the second time they are a shadow of what happened before. They are echoes of the former reform, all style and rhetoric, no substance, no teeth. I'll tell you, there are a lot of uncertainties in the district and in our building and the new teachers around here are ill-equipped to move us any direction but backward. I worry. I worry because now I know that teachers can't swim against the current of the reform whirlpool and I see that newer folks don't recognize it as a whirlpool. I suppose it's a form of alienation that I have become less willing to keep an open mind about certain things that are coming to the table, but I fear that they are always driven by a series of disconnected agendas, programs, and half-baked ideas that don't turn out so good because they failed a long time ago. We are constantly reimplementing our failures.

"I don't know if you've noticed this in your interviews, but I've observed younger or brand new teachers for thirty years, and I've actually worked with five or six versions of teacher induction programs that served the school, the district, and even different parts of the country—there is now a different understanding of professionalism. People of my generation kind of expected to be exploited when we became teachers; we kind of feel this guilt. It's like Catholic guilt, but it's teachers' guilt. If we are asked to do something above and beyond the call or the contract, we feel a need to do it. It is always couched in terms of 'the school needs this' or 'the kids need you to do this' or 'I need you to do this for the school, for the kids.' I think all teachers are asked to do things that way, and teachers of my generation tend to respond. There is always a certain percentage that are resistant, but most veterans have been pretty responsive. Especially in this building where you are either terrorized by the possibility of being cast as that-guy-who-doesn't-care-about-kids or the-one-who-won't-pull-her-weight. Alternately, some people really feel they are part of a special change that is happening and they are personally invested in the success of the school.

"A lot of younger teachers feel invested in their students and feel passion, but they have a much different and sort of disjointed picture of professionalism in the sense that they think they can and should maintain very strict limits on their involvement. They decide how much of their time outside school they are going to devote to teaching. They are not going to do extra things without extra pay; blah, blah, blah. I have a mental image of some teacher standing up in a meeting and saying to some administrator or master teacher, 'I'm doing your goddamned job. Why am I doing this?' Actually, last year I had a teacher say something like that. I was watching her during this committee meeting. She was just so upset the whole time, fidgety, not paying attention. The committee had something to do with at-risk students. After the meeting I went up to the teacher and I said, 'Are you okay? You look so upset.' She said, 'I'm so angry because a couple of nights ago I looked up the principal's salary. I know my salary. And I'm in this meeting doing his job.' I guess I understand that frustration, and I've probably felt it, but her response after that was to disengage rather than get on with it or find a different way to make a positive contribution. It's a different vision of what it means to be a professional.

"Ironically, even though I don't share it, I have a great deal of respect for that vision of professionalism. I think those teachers are partially correct because you have to protect yourself. You don't want to be a victim of the system. The fact is that some people take advantage of teachers, as they do professionals in every walk of life. There is tension particular to teaching because we don't punch a time clock, because some people may leave early and some late, or because we 'only' work nine months of the year. I'm sure I put in more hours in those nine months than most nine-to-fivers do in a year. Anyway, as a teacher you're not in that assembly line or factory mode if you are a professional. Certainly that has meant that some of us do a lot of things above and beyond the call, but at least I felt like I was a part of something special. I had that investment. I still do a lot of things that are probably above and beyond in the mind-set of these younger people. I know they think that. But, while I respect them for that mind-set if they can hold the line on it, I just don't know what's going to fill the gap. Won't the kids suffer if no one steps up to fill it in? We know how the public is going to respond if test scores aren't there. Schools continue to be criticized for not teaching individual values in the community. We're havens for drug abuse and all that kind of thing. You know we are not going to get any more money to run this place. Basically, you have to have money to run the school and we don't pay people enough where we can actually have high standards. For a long time I thought there was nobody going into the teaching profession who was worth a dime because when we had a vacancy and we did an interview, everybody you could drag up to interview was a just a dud. I can be kind of harsh about that, but I know what is required for intellectual engagement and when I ask you what is the last book you read and you don't have an answer, or it ends up being *Reader's Digest* or something, that tells me something. Or when you are a coach and it's all over your resume but you don't show me any sign that you understand that the techniques of coaching are every bit as valid in the classroom as they are on the practice field and on the ball diamond, I know what that tells me. So I thought nobody who is going into social studies education is worth a dime. Well, it's kind of changed. We've been lucky to find some good people. They deserve to be paid well, they deserve to be respected, and they deserve not to be expected to do a lot of crap in addition to their normal duties, but guess what?"

"Yes?" I answered.

"Teaching is not about respect. It's not about being paid well. It is about doing a lot of extra stuff—that extra stuff is what makes an education worth a damn. That extra stuff is what separates an average school from an extraordinary school. The extra stuff is what changes kids' lives. Teachers who aren't here to change lives are not criminals, but to me they are less than teachers."

"What are they, Jonathon?"

"I'll borrow a term from my past. Teachers unwilling to go the extra step are . . . unfit for duty."

5

SNAKE CHARMERS
IN THE STAR CHAMBER

Man was born free and everywhere he is in chains.

—Jean-Jacques Rousseau, *Du Contrat Social*

It's often safer to be in chains than to be free.

—Franz Kafka, *The Trial*

In early October, I made an appointment to see Joan Wilkes, a social studies teacher in her sixth year at Wintervalley. Being a member of the Classics Division meant that she team-taught all her classes with a language arts teacher. Joan and her partner, Thom Flannery, had been together since the merger of the two departments four years earlier. They shared a large room, instructional materials, grades, syllabi, and about fifty students per block-scheduled hour. As a team, they were responsible for seeing that around 250 students walked through the streets of Ancient Rome in its heyday and sailed the seas with Jason and the Argonauts.

I had seen Thom and Joan teach several times. Their idea of teamwork was something more akin to sprinters in a relay than a well-coached soccer team playing one-touch total football. Thom or Joan would begin the class, work for approximately half of the period, and then pass the baton to the other teacher. There wasn't much interaction between them in terms of presentation of material, although I knew they worked hard coordinating assignments, assessments, and lessons in the summer and during their planning periods. In front of the students (two sections each of sophomores and juniors, and one class of senior "honors" students), they rarely delivered instruction together. When one was addressing the students, the other would be getting ready for the next time he or she was on center stage. The teacher not teaching would generally shuffle papers, check their overhead slides, or be grading assignments as the other expounded on the difference between Plato and Lao Tzu's ideas about government. Their primary interaction during instructional time was the kind of playful repartee you might expect from coworkers whose professional lives were completely enmeshed. They would add a point here or there, make obvious a connection to an earlier assignment, or just rib each other good-naturedly.

According to other members of their division, Thom and Joan were one of the best teams in classics. They respected each other and tried to be sensitive to sharing space and content with another teacher. For the most part, I had interviewed and observed the pair because their peers cited them as an example of successful team-teaching. However, when I entered their room, Joan was in no mood to discuss pedagogy or teamteaching methods and instead pointed our discussion toward the way schoolwide decisions were made. She was slouched over a flayed pile of manila folders, spread out on the circular table where students usually picked up graded work. The folders were as organized as any overgrown rainforest. As she turned, I could see a calculator resting near her elbow. She was, in Wintervalley lingo, "doing her grades."

"We have a networked grading system. Fully online, and we each have a computer. In some respects, it's great—you can put things in and when it's time to calculate grades you update the information and send it electronically. No paper, no mess. Convenient, right? Wrong. It frees up some time because it figures the grades, but you feel controlled. On the dates when we turn in grades, this midquarter report is due by 8:00 A.M., and if you don't get it done, by God, the sky is going to fall. We get these memos that threaten fire and brimstone. The administration and guidance counselors get very irate if you haven't exported on time. 'How can we do our jobs if you don't do yours?' and all this. We have to export every midquarter and it's basically like doing grades eight times a year."

Joan looked down again at the pile. She blew a puff of air upward in a well-practiced maneuver that made her bangs flip out of her eyes. She continued.

"When the proposal to switch to this system was on the table, I remember them asking, 'Do you want to do it that way?' Pretty much everybody said no."

"Why?" I asked. "It seems to me that doing it all through a computer program would help expedite the process as long as you got in the habit of entering grades regularly. Were people just scared of change?"

"It wasn't that at all. Mainly, we were worried that having to get the grades done so often would be time consuming in spite of the technological convenience. Computers in schools—well, at least in this school, never work the way they are supposed to. The servers always run slowly and if there is a problem with your machine, it can be days before someone comes and looks at it and if you need a new part or your problem is too complicated, it can be weeks. Lack of technical know-how is always a wrench in our efforts to improve technology. Also, they never replace the whole system. I have a brand new computer, but the server is so slow that it seems to be twenty years old. It's fine for word processing, for PowerPoint, Inspiration, and all that but getting online or on the network? Hopeless. Anyway, regardless of our concerns, when we showed up that fall, there it was—somehow it sort of snuck in."

"So, how has it worked?"

"We were right," she responded. "We really were on this one, it's been a mess and what's more, this 'innovation' has changed the way a lot of people go about assessing the students. They're rearranged their calendars whether it is appropriate for their course or not. That system has really changed what's happening in the classroom and I don't think the administration understands that."

"How do you mean?"

"It used to be that midquarter was a time to take stock of where the kids were. It was a time to reflect and exercise professional judgment. We could decide on an individual basis what a student needed, a kick in the pants or a bit of warm encouragement. But now, since we export, it's like a formal grade in a way. That takes the decision out of our hands, even though we know the students best. The grade card gets mailed, and e-mailed, to the parents. The counselors call home if a student is performing below a certain benchmark. It's traumatic—and it's all about the number, the grade. It used to be that at midquarter, if you saw a kid in trouble, you could tell him, or his parents, that if he did this-or-that by the quarter, he could pull out a decent grade. You could be gentle or hard as the situation demanded. The midquarter was not a permanent grade, so to speak. And it still doesn't go into their permanent record, but when you export it, they get the feeling that it is permanent—they panic and get consumed with grades rather than the topic we are studying."

Joan excused herself to fetch her Evian bottle. I had never seen her walk into the class with a new one, she refilled the same old bottle from the fountain in the hallway. That bottle, once splashed with primary color, had faded to a blur of muted pastel. The plastic itself was scratched. She returned to her seat.

"As a teacher, I feel out of control—particularly around grade time, which is every month or so now—because it all has to be done, and on someone else's schedule. If the computer screws up, you are still in hot water. And it's not only a problem if it crashes the week grades are due. The server is down or slow constantly, so trying to enter grades is hit-or-miss. Sometimes, I have to sit down and enter weeks' worth of grades at a time. That takes hours. But you have to do it somehow. There is no going in and saying, 'My computer screwed up.' It still should have been done.

"When we started all this last year, a lot of people were in trouble because they didn't know how to teach around the system. For example, last year it happened first quarter that I was ready to give a big test a few days after export day. That test was worth enough points that it really affected grades. So, what happened? We had only done a handful of assignments to that point and among those were the first two."

I frowned. "Okay, but shouldn't the students' grades reflect their achievement levels regardless of how many points were available or when grades were added up? I mean, I understand what you said about the server, that's a big problem. You've been asked to implement a new practice and the support is inadequate. But put that aside. Why does it matter when grades are exported and what's special about the first two assignments?"

Joan shrugged her shoulders while nodding her head and taking a drag on the water. She leaned toward me and pointed her index finger onto the table in front of me three times for emphasis.

"No. No. No. You don't get it yet. Have you ever heard of Harry Wong?"

I nodded. "The *First Days of School* guy?"

"Right. Well, Wong says that you have a short time at the beginning of a school year to establish behavioral and achievement expectations, and I agree. I found that if I grade those first several assignments extremely hard, *very* hard, it serves as a wake-up call for the kids. I never give an A on those two assignments and I seldom give a B. Thom and I talked about this a lot when we started working together. It has a tremendous effect. It gets students going. We show them that they can't produce mediocre work in this class. They can't drool on the desk and pass the class. It sets a tone for the whole year and I am sure that it elevates the overall work we see as the year progresses. What it also means is that their grades are lower than they would be for the first month and a half."

"And?"

"So when Export Day One rolled around, all our kids had these low grades. The best had low Bs and most had Cs and Ds. There were some Fs. Up to that point, the most points they could earn was about 100, including those two assignments which were 30 points each. The following week, we were all set to give a 200-point exam. No matter, we had to export, and we hadn't anticipated that. Partially because we only heard about the new grade system at our preyear planning retreat the week before school began. We gave much lower grades than students would have otherwise received and we got in trouble from the administration. They had to field a bunch of phone calls about us. We explained ourselves, but they were upset at having to take so much flak."

"They didn't support you, even though you had a sound explanation?"

"Well, I wouldn't say that. I wouldn't say the administrators and counselors are not sympathetic, there is just too much going on. There are competing timetables—mine in the classroom and theirs in the offices —and they win because they have the power to threaten us. That system is in place to make their lives easier. It makes mine harder. I don't have a problem with trying a new system, especially one that is technology based. Of course, we need to move forward in that area. But I resent the way the decision to implement the thing was made and I have a problem with how they ignore complaints about the thing. They keep saying 'it takes time.' But it's taking my time, not theirs."

Hearing this made me feel guilty for doing the interview during her planning time. I wrapped it up as quickly as I could so Joan could finish her work and left.

A few days later I spoke with two teachers as they ate lunch. Scott, a second-year biology teacher, opened a transparent plastic container that held a tiny iceberg salad he had purchased from the cafeteria. The green was garnished with shredded carrot and two tomato wedges that all looked too pale and sickly to be fresh. No matter; when he drenched it in iridescent orange Catalina dressing, any description of color was rendered moot. Scott ate with his friend Mona, who taught chemistry. She ate the same salad but flavored it only by squeezing a dry lemon over the leaves. Eating lunch together was one of the highlights of their day. Depending on mood, they ate in one of each other's rooms. I asked them about the way decisions were made at the school.

Scott and Mona explained that although they had a great deal of freedom to shape the curriculum as a member of their division and engage students with whatever instructional methods they chose, they had no input—or their input was ignored—on some school policies or programs that directly affected their work.

Mona explained, "Sometimes potentially important decisions are made for me. Especially with regard to all these school reforms Wintervalley is involved in. Take Golden Apple. It's a program intended to help kids who won't go to a four-year college. If they keep their grades above a minimal level, reach a certain attendance benchmark, and act as good citizens, whatever that means, then they get a partial scholarship to attend a two-year community college or trade school. Nice idea . . ." She paused.

"I hate it. It's a nightmare. Don't get me wrong, I'm all for giving kids as many opportunities as possible. But the result has been tracking, and I don't believe in that at all. Those kids now stick together. It segregates students in the classroom into classes of people. You can really tell a difference between the Apple kids and the others. Apples have lowered their standards and are watching their points. They only have to get Cs and a few Bs to qualify for the program, so when they know they're safe they stop trying. It's awful."

It is important to note that while Mona's comments were directed toward a particular program, other teachers reported a similar sense of powerlessness in relation to having a voice in the adoption and development of other initiatives. These teachers felt as if they were not able to influence either the formal or informal political machinations of the school. Scott picked up on Mona's point by explaining that he failed to see a connection between the time, effort, and recommendations he and his colleagues put forth in Shared Planning Team work and school policy.

Scott continued, "I honestly feel like there are times teachers are asked for our opinion, we give our opinion, and then the school just goes a completely different way. Anything that goes on outside the classroom, outside these doors, I don't feel I have much control. I get in here and I do my thing, but outside? A good example is the school's credit recovery program. It does absolutely nothing in line with what the Science Department is trying to accomplish. In the credit recovery program, students do only mechanical work. We are trying to teach higher-order critical thinking. But there, they fall asleep in a guided study hall and answer a multiple-choice test from McGraw-Hill. If students pass the test, which we didn't create, they get the credit. We didn't approve this program, we said it was a bad thing, and we didn't like it, and yet we're still doing it. How is that possible? The department says, 'This is not what we want to do, it is not what we are about. It goes contrary to what we stand for, which is deeper thinking and not just rote memorization.' Yet, they're still doing it. How did that happen if we are engaged in democratic governance—shared governance? I hear that crap at meetings and it turns my stomach. Some people think it's a great program. I think the guidance counselors love it and I've heard the administration brag about it as a success here and there. But the people who know the most about the content were purposefully ignored—our beliefs and pedagogy were ignored."

Mona chimed in. "I don't remember at any point voting on whether we wanted to do that, or any other of these 'reforms.' I don't remember ever voting on any of them. When do we get to vote on these things? When is our say-so? I do this PLT thing, I do the Apple thing, I refer

kids to credit recovery, and go to my SPT. I don't remember being asked
about any of that. It was a done deal. I showed up in the fall and all of
the sudden my professional development time was gone. I was learning
about Apple schools.

"To me, it's all confusing about power and control. I don't think I have
much of that, other than what I have in the classroom, the way I conduct
myself with the students, and with other teachers. Even my control in the
classroom is waning. We are going to spend two weeks this March taking
the state test. Three years ago it was one week. Will it be a month or the
whole school year soon? Maybe. Also, I am exporting grades all the time
and running this way and that to meetings. On those issues I am powerless. I show up at the meetings and they tell me what has changed. I'm resigned to it. I, myself, am the only thing over which I have even partial
professional control. Classroom autonomy. The only power I have is to
stay here or leave. To teach under these conditions, leave Wintervalley, or
leave the profession. To quit. Some freedom, huh? To quit what I love doing, to quit on these kids, or buy into a farce."

She gestured toward Scott. "He's new, but I've been here for a while.
I still believe in that ghost that was Wintervalley. I once overheard
someone from classics describe it well. I don't fully understand what this
means, but I think it's true. She said something like, 'Us old-timers probably still operate under the old Wintervalley Republic as opposed to the
new Wintervalley Empire.' Like I said, I don't really understand that,
but I think I get the point. I think people like me remember the republic days where we were all in this together. It's changed. The administration has kept enough of the republic language around so that it
sounds like we are together, but we have become an empire. Little people in empires have no say; there's a dictator and that's it."

After a bit more, I left them to their lunch and reflected on the two
interviews. Each seemed to describe something similar. There was a
marked difference between the amount of power teachers experienced
in the classroom and the amount of powerlessness they experienced
when engaging in beyond-the-classroom activities. Particularly, these
teachers, and many others, felt they had only a phantom voice in the way
schoolwide decisions were made, even though they had strong opinions
about them. This was interesting to me, and it seemed important—yet I
was certain I had only part of the story.

It would be hasty and inaccurate for me to conclude that all Winter-valley teachers felt powerless beyond their four walls. After all, I had watched SPT and PLT meetings where teachers spoke passionately about schoolwide issues. I had witnessed faculty meetings where teach-ers were asked for feedback on initiatives. I had been to meetings where teachers studied data they planned to analyze and use to form policy recommendations. On top of all this, there was a formal structure in place for making these decisions and a central component was teacher input! Was I listening to a disgruntled few? It took me two years to find the beginning of an answer.

The longer I studied Wintervalley, and the more access I gained, it became apparent that the paper bureaucratic structures described above (SPT, PLT, etc.) were impotent and that schoolwide decision-making power resided in two groups. These groups were the formal executive council (EC) and another informal group that one teacher called the "Star Chamber." The operations of these two groups had a direct impact on teachers' sense of powerlessness in schoolwide deci-sion making.

At Wintervalley, the EC is an elected committee with rotating mem-bership. It is comprised of six teachers chosen by a popular vote of their peers. EC members serve a two-year term, the tenure of which is stag-gered so that each year two new council-members leave and two new ones join the group. According to Wintervalley's organizational chart, the EC sits at the top of the schoolwide decision-making hierarchy. The principal, Dr. Weleck, is a permanent member of the EC, but only in an ex officio capacity. Just below the EC are each of the SPTs. Every teacher in the school is required to participate in a SPT. The minutes of these meetings are delivered and reviewed by the EC. This creates a conduit for participation between the EC and every teacher in the school. Officially, the executive council represents the voice of teachers and indeed, many meaningful decisions are made here with their inter-ests and perspectives in mind: allocation of grant monies, approval and/or disapproval of proposed classes, creation of task forces, concep-tion of public relations strategies, and professional development plan-ning. The EC convenes weekly, and meeting minutes are distributed to the faculty via e-mail. Teachers are encouraged to comment on them or contact an EC member if they have a comment on or criticism of proceedings. However, most teachers suggested that a second institution exerted more influence.

Wintervalley's Star Chamber was a small group of teachers who exerted a great deal of influence over the principal. They were publicly committed to supporting Dr. Weleck, and in meetings often spoke on his behalf and evoked the school's covenant or charter when dissent was in the air. Certainly, there is nothing wrong with supporting a school leader when he or she is absent. However, Star Chamber members seemed to exert an inordinate amount of power over a group and rather than enter a situation as an equal participant, they clearly were feared for their power.

For example, during one SPT, a debate ensued about whether or not the teachers should approach Dr. Weleck and voice their opposition of a recently implemented school policy that seemed minor at first, but had added a great deal of paperwork for teachers. Factions developed and teachers quickly took up sides: one group argued that the policy would provide useful data and keep people connected, while the other side was sure that there was no intent to use such data at all. Tension mounted, and then one Star Chamber member spoke up. "We have to support Dr. Weleck on this one. He's a great leader with a vision and we have to give him the power and the data so he can make things happen. We can't debate every little thing to stalemate. Besides, in the charter it says that we are committed to effective communication and this new program is clearly an improvement."

This statement had the dramatic effect of utterly and immediately quashing the dissent. It was as though an invisible hand had descended over teachers opposed to the policy and held their tongues. They simply ceased speaking. After an uncomfortable silence, one teacher grudgingly said, "Next topic." I was unclear whether or not the Star Chamber member's comment constituted an implicit threat. Indeed, as the first year came to a close, I wondered if I would ever understand this. Although I saw over a dozen meetings with a similar dynamic, teachers were largely reluctant to discuss episodes like this after they happened. After the meeting described above, a teacher with whom I had established a fine rapport would only say this through gritted teeth, "Now you've seen how it works." As the second year commenced, I realized that such dynamics were not isolated incidents, they were a regular occurrence at the school. The Star Chamber was a systemic elite of "yes men," though certainly that gender-specific term is misleading. It became apparent that many of Star Chamber members were women.

Mr. Barnes, a veteran vocational education teacher, described the effect that these people had on the school when we met one morning over coffee. "People don't feel safe. The other day a first-year teacher came to me and asked if I would go to the administration with them to bring up an issue about which they were concerned. It didn't even have to do with them. They were worried about a student. But they were *more* worried it might reflect poorly on their teaching if they admitted they were unsure how to handle something. They were very afraid. Now, some people are always intimidated by authority figures, especially new teachers. But it's not just the administration they are scared of. It's also people who are under this blanket, this in-group, and not even necessarily even the executive council. In fact, not the executive council at all; this group has more power than the EC and they use it to make others feel powerless and afraid. That kind of thing more than anything else bothers me right now. I mean, that teacher is scared to try and help a kid because he is scared for his job!"

We were in his room alone with the door closed. But before continuing, Mr. Barnes got up and walked to the door. He stuck out his head into the hallway and glanced both ways before returning to his desk. He took a nervous sip of coffee, glanced down at the rolling tape recorder, and continued.

"I think the administration may identify potential leaders on a different basis than what they tell us. One more utilitarian than democratic. There are two processes going on here at once. Of course, there is the democratic process by which we elect EC members. People are nominated and then if elected they accept or decline the position. Very straightforward stuff. But there is an informal process here as well. There is a network of people willing to tell the 'in-group' what people say about them in the classrooms, teacher's lounge, and in the hallways. The in-group gathers information to make decisions this way. After a while, you figure out who you can trust. At least I think I have it figured out. Sometimes I don't know but you can tell pretty clearly when resources are distributed. I think that if you aren't part of that network, that circle, you are politically powerless and you don't get what you need. That's most of us. That informal process makes Wintervalley a school of *us* and *them*. A school should be *we*."

Where is the principal in all this? Importantly, Mr. Barnes (and most other teachers) did not solely blame the school's most powerful political figure, Principal Weleck. Mr. Barnes characterized Dr. Weleck as a victim of his own strengths. "He has the best intentions, and a great vision of success. Have you ever heard him describe his ideal school? It's beautiful. I'd love for the school to be that way. A vibrant and trusting community, great resources and parental support, and students and faculty involved with high-level decisions. His strength is in the vision; he's a big-idea guy. But I think his failure is that he does not know how to get there. He's a lousy judge of character when it comes to choosing people who can deliver the goods. He surrounds himself with people who tell him what he *wants* to hear instead of what he *needs* to hear. They pump each other's egos.

"I'm close enough to him and I have been in on the decision-making process long enough to know that it's not so simple as saying he's Machiavelli or he's naive. It's not that simple. He's not just a son-of-a-bitch. He's not just a martinet. He's not just a fool. It's none of that. It's a combination of essentially good qualities put into a school and situation that makes him a loose cannon. He wants to help, to do good, but it's all undone because of those people who have his ear. They have a snake charmer's effect on him and anything they say suddenly becomes 'his' belief."

We both took a sip of coffee at the same time, understanding the gravity of what he was suggesting made us both a bit paranoid. I shifted in my seat. He glanced toward the tiny window in the doorframe. It was twenty minutes before his first class was scheduled to begin. Students peeked in every so often. To acknowledge them, he raised his hand in a little half-salute.

"The alarming thing is that, in some cases, these snake charmers in the Star Chamber are very self-serving and in other cases they are just as uninformed as he is because maybe they haven't been at the school very long and have never taken the trouble to find out what makes this building special. And so they don't try to work within the system. They are in the same place that he really easily gets, 'I'm going to change the system because it can be better.' It *can* be better, but not by tearing it apart—not by manipulation and not by sneaking around with a hidden agenda. Not by pretending to involve teachers in schoolwide decisions. Not by tearing people apart. It's been very sad and very frustrating because I remember that my voice, and the voice of all teachers, used to count around here. Everyone sees what's happening, and some are turning that to their advantage." Mr. Barnes suddenly looked me squarely in the eye.

"Look, I know your next question: what does this have to do with reform, right? You want to know if any of this is directly related to the reforms we implement. Well, let me tell you. These reforms are the vehicle for the Star Chamber. These reforms, built around a mission, a covenant, and values, have destroyed the school community, ripped it into an in-group and out-group, and thrown out twenty years of compassion and togetherness. Am I a bitter veteran? Yes. These reforms have turned my colleagues into a Gestapo and helped put in place viciousness and mistrust that wasn't here five years ago. Damned right I'm bitter."

There was an urgent knock at the door. We both turned and could tell students were queuing up outside, eager to get settled into their seats for first period. It was 7:58. Mr. Barnes rose from his seat and headed to the door. I gathered my things quickly so I would be out of the way when class began. The teacher turned the knob and greeted each student with a smile as they poured into the classroom. I waited for the last to enter and then headed toward the door myself. Our eyes met as I passed through the open doorway and my "thank you" was acknowledged with a nod.

The bell rang and I stood in an empty hallway looking at the door of Mr. Barnes's room. A poster of Dr. Martin Luther King covered the side opposite the window. It was a familiar picture of King exhorting the crowd on the steps of the Lincoln Memorial.

"I have a dream, that one day . . ."

So many unrealized dreams.

So many snakes.

So many Star Chambers.

6

STRANGERS IN A STRANGE SCHOOL: ISOLATED INSTRUCTORS, DIVIDED DEPARTMENTS, FRACTURED FACULTY

Sometimes you get so alone that it just makes sense.

—Charles Bukowski

I was warned there'd be days like this—and weeks, and months, and probably years. Before I ever started the Wintervalley study, Bill Ayers, a member of my dissertation committee, gave me a word of caution over an early morning Chicago-conference coffee: "You know, the type of study you are planning to do will demand that you spend a lot of time alone. The most important aspect of that for you is that it will mean sacrificing time with your family. Don't make them victims of your decision to be a qualitative researcher. Take time and do good work, but give it back also. Stay up until five in the morning to get the stuff done if you have to, but give the days to your wife and kids." Bill's advice sounded very reasonable, even inspiring. I remember floating out of that Starbucks thinking that I could do it all. I could be a solid researcher *and* a solid father *and* a solid husband all at once! My priorities were straight! Now I could focus on the work but keep a broader perspective! Pep talks are great. They might even be necessary at certain key moments in our lives. But while that half-hour rendezvous sustained me for the duration of the conference, the shelf life of my elation wasn't long. I quickly discovered what I had always suspected, and most of my friends and family must have known about me a long time ago—I'm not reasonable, I'm obsessive. I'm very good at taking, not so good at giving. Whether or not it was true, I felt the study needed the day *and* the night. Even when I wasn't physically writing, my mind was in front of the computer screen or I was mulling over the last chapter of some largely forgettable school reform book as I pushed Holland on the swing at the park. My hands could rest or play or cook, but my brain was always writing.

What's more, Bill was right. Conducting the study meant long hours in the library in addition to time spent interviewing, collecting, transcribing, observing, and analyzing. Still, while I did spend a lot of time alone, I came to think that doing a literature review was a lot like dating. Both processes are a needle-in-the-haystack search for that one thing that will make the whole opaque mess crystal clear, the only difference being that the literature reviewer chases ideas, not partners. I went on a lot of promising conceptual dates as I conducted this study. I read sophisticated analyses about locus of control, disaffection, anomié, deskilling, and burnout. I learned about existentialism, communitarianism, and professional community. I came to know more about closed-door autonomy, organizational silos, and professional bureaucracies. I worked through utopian, dystopian, and empirical school reform literature that suggested the promise of change, if change was implemented properly. I even read poems and novels about loneliness, isolation, and alienation, trying to make sense of the stories teachers related to me in the field. Yet each intellectual dalliance, no matter how promising or seductive, failed to satisfy. Each explained part, none explained whole. I kissed dozens of concepts on the cheek at the end of each night and started the search anew in the morning. Like my experience earlier in life with dating, I learned a little bit more through each near miss and failure.

Although I never found my theoretical soul mate, I did begin to recognize a familiar theme that connected much of the literature. The philosophers thought we were alone, the sociologists thought we were alone, and the education researchers thought the same. The poets and novelists were right there as well. Each of us is isolated in our own way. What varied among orientations was whether or not aloneness was seen as a problem, observed as a curious phenomenon, or celebrated as part of the foundation of personal liberation. Plenty of education researchers, such as Michael Apple and Sonia Nieto, thought that schools failed in part because teachers do not form cohesive and meaningful professional communities. Schools, argued reformers of their ilk, were fractured by unfocused leaders and incompetent followers, and fundamentally undermined by lack of vision, scarcity of necessary resources, externally imposed and irrelevant standards, cultural hegemony, a clash of educational and societal mores, and incessant attacks on teacher professionalism. Until reforms were in place that provided a more stable and meaningful foundation for students and educators alike, teachers would spend most of their time sticking their tiny fingers into the cracks of a bursting dike. The work of teaching was ever more demanding and educators were asked to produce more with less.

Other educational pundits, such as former assistant secretary of the Department of Education Chester Finn and American Enterprise Institute director Rick Hess, eschewed these "soft" school revolutions, sociological excuses, and touchy-feely mumbo-jumbo in favor of tough-minded reforms based on open-market principles such as instructional and managerial flexibility coupled with bottom-line accountability. These folks sought to reinvent the status quo by restructuring and reinventing the entire U.S. public school system through incentive systems, a focus on core subjects, decentralization, and data-driven instruction. Although these two camps of reform found little room for agreement, both bemoaned (or at least noted) the isolation of professional life in schools and pointed to closed-door autonomy, rigid bureaucratic machinations, and a lack of substantive and meaningful collegiality as a pox on the house of education. Despite their differences, these ideological opponents held hands to cry: We must come together as a collective to solve the riddles of education! We must share expertise, resources, and governance! We must fulfill our moral obligation to students and facilitate better learning experiences as measured through higher student achievement! All students must succeed!

The philosophers weren't too sure about all this, especially the loosely connected band of thinkers called existentialists, which included the likes of Jean-Paul Sartre, Simone de Beauvoir, Albert Camus, and Friedrich Nietzsche. Broadly speaking, they thought people (read: teachers) should acknowledge that loneliness is impossible to escape and that everyone should explore ways to achieve self-actualization and joy on his or her own terms. Who were teachers to define success for students, and who were policymakers to define success for teachers? Life, explained Nietzsche, was about rejecting the shackles of convention by molding yourself into a personal vision of Superman. Now, put bluntly, Nietzsche was racist, elitist, and misogynistic. He wrote of the Über*man*, not the Über*woman* or Über*person*, which is the way I choose to interpret this idea. To my thinking, the way Nietzsche represented women, disadvantaged peoples, and non-Aryan ethnic groups renders offensive some beautiful thoughts centered broadly on the pursuit of individual happiness. Sartre and Beauvoir later amended the brutish force of Nietzsche's thought by marrying his strength to a sensitivity that was apparently beyond his capacity. A Superman (Superteacher?) couldn't care less about society or community—which by their natures promote mediocrity and conformity—but is instead an authentic being buoyed by indomitable willpower. Although it is hard to imagine the brooding and turtle-necked Sartre joining anyone in song, I often imagined these philosophers in chorus: Be yourself and reject the madness of the crowd! You know what is right and wrong; identify it and act! Be a slave only to the tyranny of your own conscience, not the will or whim of others! Be your own new, fresh, and never-before-seen philosophy!

Although today neocommunitarianism, teamwork, group decision making, and shared governance are all the rage in schools of education across the land, these existential exhortations made more sense to me than "groupism" as a way to navigate the teaching life. After all, teaching is a profession that includes people from all perspectives and walks of life operating in ambiguous institutions in which power is unevenly distributed. Teachers make ethically laden decisions every day, but are not guided by anything like a Hippocratic Oath and can rarely even find the codes of conduct that supposedly guide their work as an employee of a particular district, much less recite them or explain how such dicta guide their work. Teachers in secondary schools often work without a common knowledge base in terms of content or method and the scope and sequence of their curricula is random, even if formal institutional documents suggest otherwise. Teachers spend much of their time in professional, if not physical, isolation. As a profession, teachers are without a unified instructional agenda, and dispute the aims, objectives, and goals of education itself. Why shouldn't they embrace the idea of the Superteacher—a self-actualized professional, a willful and bold ethicist, a fiercely autonomous instructor who advocates for her own and her students' educational rights and interests?

Sociologists have been curious about loneliness for quite a while. Through the later nineteenth and early to mid-twentieth centuries, Émile Durkheim, Max Weber, Georg Simmel, and others tried to discover why people felt lonely or removed from society. Most sociologists studied the phenomenon as social isolation rather than loneliness, and defined it broadly as an individual's lack of affinity to others or an individual's lack of identification with community norms, values, and goals. Certainly, one group may be isolated from another as well. This interest in the relationship of individual to group sustained, and helped produce, powerful insights that even appealed to a wide readership. Throughout the twentieth century, the likes of Eric Hoffer, Erich Fromm, David Riesman, José Ortega y Gasset, and Karen Horney produced engaging works that entreated nonresearchers to look inward and around to explore the social, cultural, and psychological elements of their modern condition. Yet, for all their contributions and the intrigue they provoked, social scientists remain in the dark on key questions: Are loneliness and isolation bad, good, or do they matter at all? Why are some people alone but not lonely? How can people feel socially or psychologically isolated in the midst of a group of people with whom they share much in common, such as coworkers or family? While interesting ideas have emerged, sociologists seem set to wrestle these issues for another several centuries.

On one particular evening near the end of my study, I was high in the stacks at the university library. I had managed to claim one of a few large oak tables located near the education section. My blue- and pink-highlighted interview transcriptions were spread wide over scrawls of graffiti, and were commingled with research journals, books, and barely legible notes scribbled onto crumpled yellow legal pads. At the beginning of my work session I was surrounded by other students, but as the hours passed they gave in to fatigue, obligation, task completion, or boredom and receded. By 7:00, I had been there for three hours and the carrels were still mostly full, but thinning. I should have been reading LeCompte and Dworkin's *Giving Up on School*, which was the closest thing I had found to an education study resembling my own. However, at that moment I was entranced by the new translation of Camus' *The Stranger*.

In *The Stranger*, Camus painted the portrait of Patrice Meursault, an intuitive man blown from situation to situation by winds of fate. He was unmoved by his mother's death, enthralled by nothing more than tactile pleasure in his lover's arms, and when ultimately convicted of murder, he remained dispassionate, an outsider in a society whose reasoning and values he could not understand but blithely accepted. To Meursault, life was not about philosophizing, reflection, or erudition but was instead a parade of doldrums between interesting physical sensations. Unmoved by spiritual or intellectual affectations, Meursault floated into, through, and out of the physical world. I had read the book as an undergraduate ten years earlier and vaguely remembered enjoying it, but was utterly rapt as I swept through the pages this time around. Were teachers like Meursault? Were they lost and wandering aimlessly through their careers without authentic reflection or engagement? Were they alone in their work and just marking time until the end? As I thought about those questions, I removed my glasses and massaged closed eyes. "The Rub" was a habit I had developed during my short time in graduate school. I did it when I experienced data shock—when there was too much information and I couldn't get my mind around it all. Frustration! I didn't feel like I was getting anywhere, and how could I justify reading a novel when there were so many articles to get through? I leaned back in the creaking library chair and waited for the lightning bolt of insight. Nothing. After a long pause I lowered the front legs to look again at the interviews. There was something here . . . could I find it?

Maybe I had been looking in the wrong place. Maybe it was the teachers, rather than the philosophers, researchers, or novelists, who had the answers. I reached for one of my transcriptions, which peeked out from under a bound volume of the *American Educational Research Journal*. Mrs. Parker, a second-year geometry teacher, had said,

Many of us are the ostrich. We put our heads in the ground. We shut the door on our domain. And the students are *my* kids. We are trying to do the best job we can, and rather than face the politicking within the teacher communities and between our communities and the administration, the teachers, the students, and the parents, we face certain fights that seem to be worth the fight and ignore the rest. It takes so much time and energy to fight for everything and you have only so much time and energy.

This wasn't Meursault's voice, but there was a familiar echo of Camus in the way Mrs. Parker described her resignation from community outside the classroom. She wasn't lost or emotionless, but beyond those four walls she couldn't be bothered. She had self-selected a sort of political isolation. Her decision to avoid politics might come at the cost of losing one kind of influence or social capital, and she accepted that. I read the next passage of her interview.

Being a teacher is like being a member of a wonderful church. People have a faith. They are there for a common purpose. But when you get active in your church you see it in a different way. You get to the politics of it, and it tests your faith. For some people, the political aspects of the school ruin their faith in teaching and they quit or continue, but without their idealistic or optimistic spirit. Both those paths are sad, and I have friends who have gone down each. I'm on the second path, with respect to politics, and that's okay. I love my students. I love what I do. But I basically shut the door as soon as I see some kind of politics involved because it just seems to remove so much from what I'm trying to do. I don't get involved. I don't say much in meetings and when I'm forced to weigh in on something political, I try to be noncommittal if I can't be silent. I'm not always good at it, but I try to focus on the kids and let the rest wash away.

The church metaphor made sense and over the course of my study at Wintervalley, I heard plenty of teachers complain about political isolation. Church and religion are not one and the same—one is a formal organization of like-minded believers, and the other is belief itself. It occurred to me that this was very much like the relationship between school and education. Wintervalley was the school, a brick, mortar, and glass shelter where education was intended to happen. Among other things, school also entailed the particular formal and informal ways people in

the building communicated to each other and the common experiences
and events they shared. But education, like religion, was individual and
knew no bounds. You don't walk away from education when the three
o'clock bell rings. The teachers, students, administrators, and staff of the
school continued to learn long after the school day ended and were at it
long before the students arrived at campus. Some lessons were designed,
while others were spontaneous and unexpected. People learned
in lunchrooms and administrative offices, in parking lots, bowling alleys,
bedrooms, and video arcades. They grew as much over the summer
and during spring break (or more) as they did between August and
April. So while teachers like Mrs. Parker continued to believe, they
were uninterested in the church due to politics and accepted a form of
isolation. In addition to Mrs. Parker's self-selected political isolation,
there seemed to be at least one other type of political isolation in
Wintervalley.

Teachers routinely described that they were disenfranchised when
members of a political minority. This feature of democratic governance
was identified by Alexis de Tocqueville centuries earlier, but was sitting
like an elephant in the lobby of this modern American schoolhouse.
This was all well and good, but did teachers experience other forms of
isolation?

I picked up two transcriptions that were paper-clipped together. A yellow Post-it note taped to their front read "Isolation, Physical." I didn't
remember writing that, but there it was; no doubt about it, that was my
scribble. I had even dated it, 2/22, about a month earlier. I twisted the
lid off my coffee and took a look in the cup. I had brought it in with me
and it was cold as a fish, but I swished it around anyway and forced down
a big nasty gulp. Ugh. Awful, but I apparently needed the caffeine to jog
my memory. I leafed through the interview, which I had conducted with
Mr. Jakes, another geometry teacher. When the "2/22 Jeff" had coded
this earlier, he had highlighted a section on page three in blue:

> We're all down here—the math division—people don't even know we ex-
> ist. Some of the parents and kids not involved with our classes don't even
> know there is a basement. They take a tour of the school and don't even
> make it down here. I do think we are isolated. That has been both bad and

good; we are able to focus on ourselves, but we aren't part of the whole school community.

In the margin next to this passage I had written "Theme 1: The Paradox of Proximity."

Common sense and quite a lot of educational research told me to expect physical isolation in a school the size of Wintervalley. In the first place, the layout of the building did no favors for random friendship and spontaneous togetherness. Wintervalley's architect had designed a strip mall and called it a school. The building hugged the ground in a way that appealed to Frank Lloyd Wright's aesthetic orientation, but demanded long sprints down twisting labyrinths between classes, created distance between departments, and meant that in many cases teachers rarely left the cluster of classrooms on their wing of the building. Some teachers explained that they seldom left the area immediately surrounding their rooms. I met one teacher who had been there for four years and had yet to set foot in the basement or the East Wing of the school; she simply didn't have the time or a reason. "After all," she said, "I'm here to teach, not sightsee." So physical proximity engendered a kind of isolation and that was bad, right? Not so fast and not so easy! Most teachers, in fact, had mixed feelings about this proximal isolation, and suggested that while it contributed to their sense of political isolation and created about a dozen or so little schools-within-the-school, it was actually good in that it increased solidarity within academic fiefdoms. The little boats might all be at sea, but at least the crews knew each other well. Still, while teachers felt connected to their department-mates and the other teachers with whom they shared a given hallway, proximal isolation came at a price that extended to other forms of isolation.

Veteran teachers in particular explained that distance and lack of contact between academic divisions meant that they increasingly assumed a siege mentality toward other departments, and an antagonistic "us against them" or an "us against the world" stance was becoming the norm for intradivisional encounters. Over the past few years, veterans said collaboration with folks from other departments was in decline and many faculty members were now distrustful of colleagues' motives from other parts of the building as a result. Physical isolation may not have been the sole reason collaboration was tricky at Wintervalley, but it helped set the tone for many schoolwide endeavors, which often had the feel of turf wars, waged for whatever stakes and resources were in contention.

Interestingly, the building itself also contributed to another form of physical isolation, as I was reminded when I turned to the second transcript in the pair. Gretchen was Wintervalley's media specialist. I recalled sweeping gestures as she pointed out the architectural features of the media center, which she codirected with Chance Lawson:

"We refer to this, affectionately, as the 'Bat Cave.' We really don't know what is going on outside unless it begins to hail. We can hear that. But if ping-pong-ball-sized ice doesn't pelt the roof, we are insulated from the world. We have these sort of pseudowindows. I've often looked at those and thought, 'Why on earth didn't they just install regular windows and let in natural light?' We have what we like to call 'ritzy' light down here. Broad spectrum. They are supposed to be good for us, but sheesh—I don't know."

I looked up at the humming incandescent lights above my head in the library. There was no way they were engineered for my health or comfort, but I saw what she meant. The dimness made the space seem tighter, smaller. Now, Wintervalley's media center was much better lit than where I was sitting, but it was true that neither space received natural light. Both gave you the sense that you were in some kind of educational submarine. Gretchen had continued,

"I used to teach English over at Heskey, and they don't have air conditioning. I had a room—this awful room—that they had to evacuate when it got too hot. I swear it would get to be 115 degrees in that room. You could have fried an egg on the chalkboard. It overlooked the parking lot and the heat would bounce up into the room. It was horrible. But at the same time, I had a window that went the full length of the room. There was nothing fuel efficient about it. It was a huge window."

As Gretchen had wistfully described her old room, I remembered wondering if she would cry, despite the fact that she had nearly melted there.

"The window went from the shelf, which was about waist high or a little higher and all the way to the ceiling. It had six sets of panes that ran all the way to the top. The room was flooded with light. In fact, we had to pull the blinds down during the day or I would be blinded up there at the front of the room. As the day passed, it was the students rather than me who would have been blinded. At the time, I hated that room because of the heat. It also got really cold in the winter. You could see your breath and the kids wore heavy coats. At the time, I hated that room because it was so lit up, so bright, and so hot or freezing."

I recalled a dramatic pause before she finished.

"When I looked into this job, I walked into this beautiful library and was really impressed. But I have to tell you, I asked my husband to walk through the building with me and we talked about the fact that there are no windows in here. It never even occurred to me to work in a place without windows. I don't have access to any windows, actually—unless I look down that north hallway. I don't spend much time in the commons. We talked about that. That became an actual factor to me, thinking about this joint. It doesn't get me down normally, but over the course of the year, it gets to me. I notice the times when I'm alone or isolated much more in March than I do in September. The walls are a little closer then. So I think you could actually talk about windows—that could be another study."

I leaned back, pictured Gretchen and Chance in the media center, and went into The Rub. I found that at times it was easy to get caught up in the literature, in the phenomena of the study, in "The Study," that I forgot that it was ultimately more about the teachers, the people, than it was about alienation or isolation. People are physical. They are affected by light and darkness, by space and time, by food and drink. Isolation was not only political, but physical as well. What else?

I looked at the table and picked up another book, but I was getting tired. I began to notice how big the silence in the library had become. It was nearing 11:00 P.M. and I was the only one in sight. The place closed at midnight. It was getting late, and a cascade of loosely related thoughts about isolation began to flood through my head. I thought about Virginia Woolf's (1990) essay *A Room of One's Own*, which chronicled a woman's life, her inner promise and literary potential unfulfilled, stifled by violent societal conventions. Living under the weight of such institutions eventually compels the main character to take her life. Due to the syllabus my Freshman Comp. professor used so many years ago, Woolf's piece is forever linked to Charlotte Perkins Gilman's (1991) short story

"The Yellow Wallpaper," the chilling tale of a woman whose life spirals into dementia via psychological and social forms of isolation and alienation. I also thought about Bardamu, the main character of my favorite novel, Louis-Ferdinand Celine's (1934) epic *Journey to the End of the Night*, who was ultimately forced to accept that society has nothing to offer the individual. He surmised that most people lived life as a foolish and unattainable pursuit for meaning, reason, and companionship in a vast nothingness. Then there was Kafka. In *The Metamorphosis* (1996), he wove an absurdist tale about a man whose life is so meaningless it hardly surprises him when he wakes one morning transformed into a cockroach. It was his way of expressing the everyday insanity and isolation of modern life. While not as fantastic, Kafka's *The Trial* hit closer to home, as it is all about organizational madness. Here, the main character, Gregor Samsa, is summoned to defend himself at a tribunal despite having no idea of what crime he has been accused, who his accusers are, or what recourse he has. But teachers weren't cockroaches, and while some committed suicide, the study wasn't about that. My train of thought was derailing. Maybe it was time to stop for the night.

I began The Rub in an effort to make one last push before the end of the night. I leaned into it. Social isolation. The characters in these stories all felt the loneliness of the crowd, but they could only be a point of departure, an inspiration. What did the educational researchers have to say? I took a quick glance at my watch, set aside the books, and dug into a pair of *EAQ* articles that dealt with isolation. In 1978, researchers Arlene Zielinski and Wayne Hoy found that teachers' social isolation from individuals in positions of power, friends in the organization, and respected coworkers were related to each other, and were also "significantly related to a failure to feel intrinsic pride or meaning in teaching" (p. 40). Okay, so particular forms of isolation bred (or developed alongside) other forms of isolation and corroded the intrinsic value of teaching. I had heard some of that from the teachers and from educational philosopher Maxine Greene, who had written a few outstanding books that explored existential themes as applied in education. Zielinski and Hoy's assertion was an empirical reification of philosophic assertions Greene had made in her classic *Teacher as Stranger* and further explored in *Existential Encounters with Teachers*.

In the second article, published two decades later, a trio of researchers looked at how teachers were isolated or included in school communication networks (Bakkenes, Brabander, & Imants, 1999). Their study rested, in part, on the assumption that teachers could be classified into three distinct kinds of communicators: isolates, group linkers, or group members. Based on these distinctions, they posited that social communications networks in some schools worked better than others and that some teachers needed to learn new collaborative skills to better engage their peers (p. 196). I heard some of that, too, but the Wintervalley teachers told much more complex and nuanced stories than either of these articles had captured. Isolation was much more complicated, and to their credit, each of these articles acknowledged as much but left me searching.

I put them down and picked up the green book in the center of the table. It was pregnant with Post-it notes. There must have been fifty or sixty hanging out in every direction.

In 1991, two researchers, Margaret LeCompte and Anthony Dworkin, published one of the more detailed works on alienation in education, *Giving Up on School*. Although they included a bit on isolation, it was more an acknowledgment of the concept than a study of it. Although this book was so helpful in other areas of my research, it was of little assistance here. I sifted through for the nth time and eventually put the book down out of frustration; there were only a few sentences here and there. Time to look elsewhere—what did the teachers have to say?

Teachers spoke of the ways they formed meaningful relationships with one another. Bonds were formed along common characteristics: age, gender, race, entry date, experience, teaching philosophy, teaching content, physical proximity, extracurricular areas of interest, marital status, and degree of micropolitical activity. Some teachers conjectured that absent these characteristics, a teacher would be socially isolated. Beth Thompson, a teacher with a dozen years of experience, explained, "You notice a group of new teachers. There is a New Teacher Committee here, which is great. They help with induction, and I think that's a huge factor in ensuring new teachers don't feel isolated. There's a good support system in this school. And so I find that those teachers hang around together as best friends. In fact, my two best friends at the school are people I came in with and the three of us were all different ages and had different levels of experience and backgrounds."

But . . . "Certainly, teachers in any scenario or school situation, it's just like in any workplace, there are going to be groups that form and some groups ostracize others. That is not always intended. It sometimes happens . . . and not always in the obvious ways you might think, like people sitting together in the lunchroom or the teachers who hole up in their rooms. For example, I can think of a teacher who went through a divorce and then she and this other teacher became such close friends that they became isolated from the rest of us. They had this intense and supportive relationship, which may have been good for therapy, but it impacted the professional community and both of their personal lives. It got to the point where it created serious problems for the other teacher, who was married herself. In the beginning, she was providing professional support in the classroom, you know, helping her prepare lessons, grade things, and all that. Very nice, you know, selfless. But then it extended past the classroom and became personal rather than professional. That might be fine normally, but this person was very needy and demanded quite a lot from that one person. It got pretty weird, and although they were isolated as a couple, the details of their relationship became a public soap opera. Teaching is so intense and the personal relationships can become very strong, but that can be good and detrimental."

Beth finished off that interview by speculating, "Teachers are isolated in many ways. There are the obvious things and there are the less obvious. Everyone knows about the closed-door autonomy of teaching. We all know about that kind of isolation and work hard to overcome this through collaboration. That's hit-or-miss, but since we are all aware that it is a possibility, it gets a lot of attention. The problem is that people tend to think teachers are isolated in only that one way, when there are many ways we are isolated. For example, I feel isolated when I work on some days more than others; I feel isolated when I work in some teams, but not others; some days, my friends seem to be strangers and other days they are very familiar. And, most importantly, I experience isolation in a very different way from everyone else."

Bingo. Social isolation was different for each person; each teacher was a stranger on Thursday and a friend on Friday. It was a dynamic phenomenon that changed at the rate of personal change, institutional change, and in relation to physical proximity. Reforms did contribute to some forms of isolation because they impacted the already unstable and fluctuating social currents of the school. Each teacher coped with bouts of isolation in his or her own way. Some retreated, while others were proactive. I made a few notes in a yellow pad and silently acknowledged what I thought was a "eureka moment." Of course, I had a lot of work ahead to iron this all out, but it felt like I had taken a step forward.

I looked at my watch and hurriedly began the nightly shuffle and sort. I placed the most important transcripts, articles, and books in my backpack, and began to collect the other things. Maybe it would all come together, after all.

I rolled up to the circulation desk with a trolley load of philosophers, sociologists, poets, and educators. The clock read 11:58 and the librarian on duty was visibly annoyed by the size of my haul. Still, he scanned in each bar code, rubber-stamped a date into each, and placed the books in a pile to his right. Then another pile. Another. And another, for an eventual total of five; each was about a foot tall. When he finished stamping, he looked through me impassively. "They're due in sixteen weeks." Before I could acknowledge understanding, he turned and disappeared into an anteroom with a few other workers. I looked around and wondered to myself about how I would carry all this stuff. A little roar of laughter and good fun rose from the librarians' area. I peeked behind the counter, but didn't see any spare bags that might help. Damn.

It took me three trips to cart all the books from the desk to the front steps of the building. I stared at the piles for a moment but knew that wasn't going to produce any telekinetic magic. I was on my own and I had to transport everything to my car. I still hadn't come up with a solution when the chimes from the bell tower began. By my watch, they started at 12:08. Okay—time to move—now, get to it.

Load 'em up! Fully stuffed backpack on my back! Bursting canvas tote swinging from the two smallest fingers of my left hand! Arms straight down with the wrists flexed at ninety degrees, I held the top of the swaying stack in place by stretching my neck at an awkward angle and holding the mess in place with my chin. A few students passed me on either side and laughed or made half-heard sarcastic comments. I shambled along carrying my tower. I was sweating. I was absurd. I was headed toward the parking garage, ready to fall at any instant. Teetering over the precipice. My back ached. Fingers set to burst. Finally, the clock on the bell tower was only a reverberation of echo in the stillness.

Then it was silent. Only my groaning. Huffing. Sweat rivulets cascaded into my stinging eyes. But . . . I could see the steps! I was going to make it!

Then came the fall. Boom! I think it was my right hand that let me down. It all went south right in the middle of the intersection, about forty feet from the entrance of the garage. Erich Fromm was splat face down on the road opened to page 88. Karen Horney was in the gutter with Henry Levin. Rousseau was under Diane Ravitch. Tyack and Nietzsche's pages were interlocked and dancing motionless in a grimy puddle. I was as relieved as I was frustrated—I'm not sure I could have made it up the stairs anyway. I picked up each book and began to stack them neatly on the sidewalk. I could see rhythmically in the flashing yellow lamp that swung over the intersection. There were no cars, but as I was about halfway through the clean-up job, I felt that I was being watched. I got that slow burning sensation of paranoia when in a strange and dark place and a strange and dark situation. Was there a posse of frat boys laughing at me? Were the librarians making fun of me from the window? Was some drunk leering at me from the shadows of the bushes? Who was it? I swirled around—left? Nothing. Right? Nothing. Behind? Nothing. No wind, no cars, no people.

I was alone.

7

THERE'S NO "I"
IN THE WORD "SCHOOL"

The deepest problems of modern life derive from the claim of the individual to preserve autonomy and individuality of his existence in the face of overwhelming social forces, of historical heritage, of external culture, and of the technique of life.

—Georg Simmel, *Sociology*

real
loneliness
is
not
necessarily
limited
to
when
you
are
alone

—Charles Bukowski

As I entered the coffee shop, it started to rain—just a sprinkle, but the sky promised more. I was early, 7:15, and I couldn't see all the way to the back, so my quick glance around the place didn't tell me if Jim was there yet. Our interview wasn't scheduled until 8:00, so I assumed I had at least a few minutes to settle in before he arrived. I put my things on a little table by the window, walked toward the register, and ordered. I'm not adventurous when it comes to coffee: black, usually in the largest size available. I drink too much of the stuff—three or four venti-sized cups a day. I paid and then scanned the rest of the room.

There he was. Seated in back, Jim was already there and by the looks of it had been for a while. He sat at one of a dozen small, circular tables directly under a portrait of Miles Davis. Miles was blowing hard, cheeks puffed wide, wailing to eternity. Jim's cheeks might have been equally inflated were he blowing a horn, but he was grading papers. I approached from one side, but it wasn't until I had drawn near that I saw the enormous pile of what looked to be term papers on his table. The stack reached about a foot and a half upward and teetered absurdly over the edge. Even a modest gust would have sent the semester tumbling.

Ah, I thought . . . the bane of the high school language arts instructor. Other teachers accepted quickly assessed projects or proctored tests, but the LA teacher wades through reams of paper. Over the years, I had known more than a few who gave up teaching English for that very reason. It occurred to me that Jim was smart to have them due two weeks before the end of the year. I was wrong.

"Rough drafts," he said as I peeked over his shoulder. "They need extensive revision, and the only way to make sure the kids engage the writing process is to do it with them. Peer editing only works for the best students. I collect them and make corrections. They have to address them on the final draft. I'll read all these papers again when they submit them for a final grade in a few weeks." He took a sip of something that looked like hot water. "You're early. Where are you sitting? Give me a few minutes and I'll come and join you." He was nearly finished with the page he was marking, page 14, with a running head "Tupac, Poet of the People." It was streaked with red and lined with cursive notes to a sixteen-year-old would-be author. I knew from our earlier interview that Jim had about 160 students. Each wrote a twenty-page term paper. Over the next two weeks he would read 3,200 pages—twice. Later, I found out that he also met with each student individually before or after school to discuss the first round of edits so that no class time would be compromised and his expectations would be clear. That was at least another 160 early-morning or late-afternoon hours of intense one-to-one work added to the busiest weeks of the school year. And it wasn't just once a year, either. A similar assignment was also due just before Christmas, so you could multiply each of the numbers listed above again by two. And that's only two assignments; there was a lot more packed into Jim's classes.

I walked back to my table at the front and began to unpack my bag. Two books, one for the study (Richard Schacht's *Alienation*) and one for pleasure (an old book of Charles Bukowski's poetry that was new to me). I had now carried the latter around in my backpack for three months without reading a word, hoping to find a moment. I flipped it open to a random page and read the first stanza:

starting fast

we each
at times
should
remember
the most
elevated
and
lucky
moment
of
our
lives.

Pretty uplifting for Buk. But I couldn't finish—no time for poetry, I had to get ready for Jim. I unloaded a few pink-highlighted journal articles and tossed a paper-clipped transcript of our last interview onto the table. We did that one at the school and had gotten through most of the questions before the 3:00 dismissal bell signaled the end of our interview. I sipped hot Kenya AA and reviewed the transcript. Along with my other notes in Jim's file, I had a decent portrait.

Jim's first love was organic chemistry. He had always liked history and political science and was an avid reader, but his parents demanded that he pursue a "serious" career. Becoming a teacher had not been an option. In Jim's family, serious meant making money or at the very least pursuit of a degree that would lead to a prestigious career. Teaching was hardly imbued with the necessary prestige. Teaching was a blue-collar union job, and a degree in education was a waste of time and money. Jim enrolled in state college and entered a program in chemistry. He took history and "social science things" to fulfill requirements. The course work in chemistry held his attention, but getting a degree in the field meant advanced work in calculus and inferential statistics. The science was interesting, but mathematics and statistics took the wind from his sails. After a great deal of self-doubt and agony, he decided to become an education major. Despite his interests in history and the social sciences, there was never a question his degree would be in the area of English.

Jim Finnan was born in a small, rural town of northwestern Missouri and grew up on a soybean farm. His youthful experiences with most of the English teachers in that community were encouraging, if not inspiring. English classes were not the most popular offerings at Jim's childhood schools. He remembered mainly worksheets, vocabulary lists, and sentence diagrams—boring stuff. Literacy was low and many of his peers hated that "writin' crap," but Jim enjoyed the books and short stories they read, if not the poetry. When he changed his career path toward education, part of his motivation was to instill the love of reading lacking in his own classroom experience. He would teach better than he had been taught. Jim set his goal at becoming a high school or junior high school language arts teacher, but somewhere near the end of his course work, an advisor suggested that he consider graduate work. "After all," his advisor had said, "you can always go and teach." He was counseled that it would be prudent to work on a master's degree before he got married and had a lot of other responsibilities.

That sounded good to Jim. Despite his academic preparation and desire to teach, he couldn't shake a fear of going into the classroom borne partially of his upbringing and partially of self-doubt. He enjoyed being a student, and went for the graduate degree. But, he insisted, he always saw that as getting more tools to do the job in public schools. Over time, that declaration became more platitude than reality. He did some teaching in college and thought teaching in college might not be too bad a career. Jim received a master's degree in English literature and met and married Ellen as he began PhD coursework. However, an initial frustration with how poorly college professors taught grew into an intense disdain for the entire profession. For a few years, he persevered unhappily. Then Jim saw two of his friends get "carved up" by the tenure process because they paid too much attention to teaching. That was enough; Jim reached his breaking point.

His decision to leave academe and go into teaching coincided with a new imperative. Ellen was pregnant and the young couple didn't have any insurance. Suddenly, Jim was acutely aware of his strengths and weaknesses as a job candidate and also as a provider. He found himself with plenty of education, but no teaching experience at the high school level, which made him an atypical applicant at many schools in 1971. His first job was a two-year stint at a private school (to get experience) and then after interviewing at both of Owen City's public high schools, he made the leap to the district's "new" high school, Wintervalley. At the time of our interview, he had been there for over thirty years and had taught essentially the same three classes for twenty-eight: senior English, sophomore English, and an honors class in composition. Jim had received tenure long ago and had won many awards for his teaching and his devotion to both school and student.

Jim is a powerfully built man, and at sixty-two he looks fit enough to guide a plow and harvest wheat, two things he hasn't done for four decades. In front of a classroom, he is in command of his professional space. His voice demands attention and he not only knows his students by name and nickname, but also by intimate detail. He knows who likes tap and who likes rap, he knows who is active in church and who sleeps until afternoon on the weekends, he knows who uses action verbs effectively in writing and who has a fear of reading his or her work in front of their peers. For fifteen years he has required students to begin each class period with five minutes of journal writing. Students may denote any pages they don't want him to read or any entries to which they want him to pay particular attention. His lessons incorporate free writing, lectures, films based on novels, concept mapping, and quite a lot of individualized instruction. There is heavy emphasis on the writing process. Jim believes that learning this process, which to him includes brainstorming, research, outlining, and multiple drafts with accompanying revisions, is most effective for a majority of the students. "Even if they don't learn to write, they learn to think." Still, despite strong beliefs, Jim doesn't think good teachers are inflexible in their delivery and he tries to accommodate different types of learners. "There is always someone who needs something presented or structured differently," Jim proclaims, but demands rigor of all. To him, this means any flexibility must still remain within the general framework of the writing process. "If someone wants to write a poem or a collage or do a painting to express his brainstorming phase, that's fine, but he must brainstorm."

Experience is etched into Jim's temples and he furrows his brow quite a lot when he speaks. He rarely gestures, but smiles, laughs out loud, and makes more than a few self-deprecating jokes throughout the course of the day. Pressed shirts and khaki pants are his uniform, and occasionally he sports a "teacher tie," one of those seasonal jobs with jack-o-lanterns or an ice-skating Snoopy. Ties last Jim about two decades. He wears comfortable shoes that have never been in style.

As I looked through the transcript, I made notes in the columns: alienation. . . . powerlessness . . . normlessness. . . . Jim spoke implicitly about most of the sociological constructs I was looking for in the study. Still, while that should have made the researcher in me excited, it made me tired. Speaking with and observing him as much as I had over the year, I could feel some of the weight Jim carried on my own shoulders. The enthusiasm Jim described from his younger days was very pale—he had lost some of the teacher's passion. His eyes only sparkled when he spoke of the past. As if on cue, Jim appeared beside my table as I finished jotting notes in my tablet.

He looked into my cup, "Coffee?"

"Yep. Black. How are you doing? Done with the papers?"

"No. I'll finish them later tonight, maybe tomorrow. You want to be careful with that coffee. Caffeine is a problem, and all the chemicals they put in there. Makes your teeth yellow. I quit years ago. Don't drink too much of the stuff—it'll give you kidney stones. I *know*." He laughed.

"Thanks," I said, "you're probably right. Maybe I drink too much." I took a glug of black, which was now lukewarm, put a new tape in the recorder, and cleared the seat next to me. "Ready?"

"There's no 'I' in the word 'team.' When I first got to Wintervalley, the principal used to say that all the time. It sounded like coachspeak to me then, but to be honest, I wanted to believe that teaching was all about people coming together to help kids. All for one, one for all. I came in as what I would like to think of as a confident instructor on the college level and somebody who was pretty focused on the clientele, the students, even though all my training had been focused on content rather than how students actually engaged that content. I came into a school that, at that time, had about 800 students and had been built and staffed for this very student-focused "whole student" kind of approach to education coming out of the 1970s. The staff here was inculcated in those beliefs and the administration had opened this building so it really reflected the principal's philosophy. Even though the school was new, there were a lot of veterans who had transferred in from Heskey High and other schools. They really taught me what it meant to be in a professional community. I got into team-teaching fairly early on, we did interdisciplinary kinds of stuff, and I worked with some really outstanding people. We had the district coordinator of language arts here who actually started that job as district coordinator the year I came in. That opened some interesting doors. I worked on a lot of district-level curriculum development projects and got to know some district folks in addition to my Wintervalley colleagues. I really learned to teach—and how to be a teacher—in this building. So it has been the making of me professionally and also, consequently, personally because I am the kind of person who is all-or-nothing. This job has been a part of my life for a long time, so it has shaped my character, probably in more ways than I realize." As Jim paused to take a drink, I scribbled furious blue in my little yellow notebook, trying to keep up.

"Jim," I said, "that last bit. What you said about how working at Wintervalley impacts your personal life, what do you mean by that?"

"I know for some teachers it's that way from the very beginning, the job and home life get blurred. To be a teacher, even a bad one, you have to put in many hours outside the school day: grading, prepping, whatever. For me, it was doubly bad because I desperately wanted to be great. That created tension. Great teachers don't work a nine-to-five day, they are at it every waking moment. If I wasn't in the classroom I was doing the pre- or post-work, researching new lessons, finding resources, running off copies, and all that. I went to all the district professional development workshops and read up on pedagogy and practice. If I wasn't doing those things I was thinking about it, lost in thought.

Ellen would tap me on the shoulder or say my name and I wouldn't even notice sometimes. That was a tough time. I wore myself out physically, emotionally, mentally. There wasn't much left for Ellen, or for Eddie. There was a lot of friction. Some of it had to do with becoming parents; some of it had to do with beginning a new working life. All of it was very tense and intense. That first seven or eight years nearly killed me. I mean it."

All the while Jim spoke, he stared at the rain, which had thickened into a steady shower. It would have made a very solid and peaceful shushing sound, save for occasional cracks of thunder that shot through the storm and rattled the windows next to us with a BOOM! The glass quivered in the wake of each strike.

"At the very beginning, I was consumed with the job. After a while something just broke in me, even though it was probably too late." Jim made little quotation marks in the air when he said, "I guess I just came over to the 'dark side' and started cutting corners as a teacher so I could enjoy my family. I returned papers later and a few of my lessons became stale, mediocre. If I had something solid, a unit or a lesson, I just redid what I had done last year and stopped continually revamping everything. I just let those 'continual improvement wars' go, which is not altogether a 'bright' thing to do. Unfortunately, we had been married for a while and in some ways were set in our ways." He continued, "I mean, my wife is a professional woman and she's upper-level management with one of the big pharmaceutical companies here in town. She's in that business out of necessity. She got an office job when we moved to begin my PhD work and then was promoted through the ranks. She's very successful, has a real aptitude for it. No passion, it's just a job to her, but she's damned good. It took her some effort to get a job when we first moved to Owen City, but once she got it she never looked back. She's like me, very much a workaholic. In that way our personalities are similar, but in one important way we are different: she can leave her job at work and I bring mine home. As I became a better teacher, I became a more distant husband, an absent father. I woke up one day and my son was nearly ten. I think I saved some of my relationship with him, but there's lingering damage." He hesitated for a moment, unsure of how to continue. His eyes followed rivulets of raindrops running down the outside of the pane. "I need some more water. Excuse me."

I paused the tape as Jim rose from his seat. He made his way toward the island that held the hot water dispenser and I tried again to catch up on note taking. My hand ached, but I was managing to get much of what he said in shorthand if not word-for-word. At least I had the tape to check for accuracy. Jim returned and sat down.

"Hey, I apologize for unloading all this personal stuff. I'm sure you don't want to hear about my problems. I know your study is really about the school."

"No. The study is about you; the study is about teachers, in and out of the school. This is helpful." Then, without thinking, I crossed a line: "Tell me more about your relationship with Ellen."

Jim's face changed. A flash of anger (or was it annoyance?) lit across his eyes, though only for an instant. He fixed his gaze directly on me rather than out the window for the first time in our conversation. He studied me for a moment, and then almost visibly quelled whatever had risen in him. The emotion was gone as quickly as it had appeared, and he asked a threefold question in low tone: "What did you just say? Why would you want to know about that? How is that part of the study?"

There is at least one aspect of interviewing they don't teach you in school: the art of backpedaling when you've gone too far. I found instantly that I lacked any talent for this skill. Stammering around, I fumbled out something about trying to understand how work life impacted personal life; about how I was trying to go beyond "typical" studies that treated people as though they were only teachers and not wives, fathers, bowlers, knitters, lovers, or deacons. I don't know what other nonsense I said. Shit. Had I just ruined the one of the best interviews of the study? "Sorry, Jim. Can we continue, or should we forget it for tonight? Maybe it's just too late and I'm not thinking this through clearly. I apologize."

He studied me in a way I hadn't been examined since offending my own high school English teacher by saying that I hated Shakespeare. I had forgotten that teachers are often highly skilled inquisitors and interrogators. Uncomfortable, I now remembered.

After what felt to me as an incredibly long moment, he started again.

"My relationship with Ellen became increasingly estranged. We divorced about ten years ago, but still communicate. We talk almost every night on the phone. In fact, I'm supposed to give her a call in a bit. By the time I realized what devotion to teaching was doing to my marriage and to my relationship with my son, it was past time for me to do much about it. Too late. For a while, I held out hope that when Eddie moved off to college things would be different, that Ellen and I would reconnect and get that vitality back. It was too late. By the time my son was in junior high school, he had sort of closed the door on life with me as his parent. Who can blame him? It's like the title of that book: Dad was too busy raising other people's children. As for Ellen, she didn't get much from me, since there weren't a lot of breaks. I mean there *were* breaks, but I worked right through them, night and day. Then at one point, Ellen developed an interest in fitness. I wasn't there much and she stared going to the gym out of boredom and to get a break from being basically a single parent. She got into triathlons. Suddenly, our scant time together became nothing. When she wasn't working or out of town as part of her job, she was in the weight room or away competing. It was my fault. Not that she got into sports, of course. I was happy she was so excited with a hobby that also helped her health and it gave me more time for my own work, but she essentially left me and married a new life. Who can blame her? I didn't give her much. By the time I realized what I had done and tried to fix things with the two most important people in my life, they had both moved on without me. I remember constantly promising them that the next semester or the next year would be different. That next semester never came. I knew that teaching was supposed to consume you, but I never saw what was right in front of my face. As I learned more and more about the teaching act and what it takes to deliver the goods to kids, my level of commitment to the job destroyed everything else. I divorced my wife and became a stranger to my son for teaching."

Jim changed direction abruptly, shifting easily from soul baring to rationalization: "Also, I'm not overcommitted. There are plenty of teachers more into it than I ever was and more burned by it than I am. They are fat and unhealthy, they eat poorly, they are lonely. This job does that to you." He thought about that for a long ten seconds. "I'm sixty-two now and have been at this job a long time. I am without my wife and my son and I'm not even as excited about teaching as I once was. It is important, teaching, but at what price? The job gets harder all the time because we always hear that we don't know what we are doing. Now it's achievement scores. In the seventies we were told we weren't developing the whole student, we were crushing their souls with rigmarole. Who knows what's next? All I know is that we'll definitely be told we are idiots by a new generation of people who have never taught and won't even take the time to visit our schools. There are no gimmicks, no tricks to being a better teacher, and there are no gimmicks or tricks to being a good father or a good husband. They both take time and there is only so much time. I spent it in the wrong places and here I stand today . . . with nothing."

Jim excused himself to call Ellen. He stood outside in a little recessed alcove near the door of the coffee house that was sheltered from the rain. It was coming down very hard, but at least it was coming straight down. Not much of a breeze tonight. In the Midwest, wind can whip rain at you from all sides; on particularly bad nights, it seems to rise up from the ground. Gutters overflowed in spontaneous rivers and spun bits of trash and leaves in the whirls and eddies. Inside, there were plenty of people around: drinking, studying, eating pastry, playing chess, talking loudly. It was 9:15 now and as I watched Jim's lips through the glass, I wondered what was happening at my home. It was past my daughters' bath time and just before Melanie would be reading them a story. *Hop on Pop? Ferdinand? Berenstain Bears?* Why wasn't I there to read it to them? Daddy's work was too important. Jim mouthed the words "okay" and "sorry" over and over. He closed the phone, looked again at the rain, and turned toward the door. It opened and closed. After a quick step to the counter, he sat down.

"I've been at Wintervalley a long time and have been intimately involved with school reform programs from the get-go. In the beginning I was idealistic and committed, but I've become increasingly cynical and reserved. Reform doesn't work. It's partially the system and partially the individuals in the system. When I was first team-teaching, my partner was a woman who taught history. Her dictum was 'times change, people don't.' I used to answer her from the other end of the spectrum: 'we can all change, intervention and progress is always possible.' But she was right. All thirty years of continuous reform has done for this school is equip us with a language to describe change and no tools to make it actually happen. We know the lingo by now: success for all, team decision making, shared governance, student-centered instruction. We even have a way of speaking about reform that lets us show that we are sensitive to people in trouble: students at risk, SES-challenged students, learning disabled. Personally, my favorite term is 'exceptional,' it's a real doublespeak gem. We can't find ways to actually help these people so every few years we rename their conditions or situations and throw some money or a 'new' plan at them. There's a little activity, like learning to fill out a new form or a new way to deliver instruction or a way to shift of responsibility from parents to teachers or administrators to teachers, but it's all a game. Very little real change comes from this dance. Maybe one teacher gets inspired by something and sticks with it, but that's it. And doing that comes with a price. If teachers do adopt something, they have to change it again within a year, or at least rename what they are doing, or they are labeled as being set in their ways.

"It happened to me. Some of the things I did in the mid-seventies were cutting edge, really progressive stuff. But I wasn't allowed to pursue anything for more than a year or two because we were always on to the next program. My professional judgment meant nothing if I didn't agree that the latest, greatest reform touted by the administration was going to save the school. They'd be there with flags and banners in the early days if something you were doing could be called innovative, but in every case enthusiasm and support waned and eventually I was the only one standing. It happened to other folks, too; sustained implementation comes out of the teacher's hide.

"There's always been a lot going on at Wintervalley. And you know how it is in education; if you are willing to work, show up on time, and mostly know your lines, you will get to participate in almost anything. When I was younger and had a lot of energy and was involved in everything, I went to all the meetings, was involved in steering committees for this or that program and most other things on some level. I made sure that the teacher's lounge had cookies and helped new teachers write $200 grants so that remedial readers got the right books. Other than the principal, no one made more things happen at the school. In fact, in many cases not even the principal was doing as much as me. But over a period of several years I recognized that (a) I was the only one that was doing *all* of it and therefore the only person who had a holistic vision of how the school worked against itself; and (b) people have such damned short institutional memories. From one week to the next and certainly from one year to the next, people forget about our institutional focus or they get impatient or they respond to the impatience of our clientele—which is the rest of the teachers and the students—and we each wander off into some personal or organizational dead end. It's circular too, because then those same people who led us astray complain about the lack of focus and we're right back where we were at the beginning, putting up butcher paper on the walls and writing values and principles in which we 'all' believe. I'm talking about those silly meetings that are made out to be so important where we debate 'what's important' or The Vision or The Mission. These are not meaningful discussions; I sat in the same meetings, *the same meetings*, thirty years ago. These activities are nothing more than desperate attempts to bring things that have never been on target *back* on target, as though we once had a clear direction. But it never happens, partially because through school reform we have learned a language that allows us to name our failures success.

"It takes a long time or a revolution, not a reform, to change a school. I'm talking decades, not hours, not days, not semesters, not years, not one four-year presidential or gubernatorial tenure. But no one has time and there is a system in place that perpetuates the status quo. Principals and superintendents have to make their mark immediately in measurable terms or they are fired. They get in there and have to make it look like they are a catalyst for real change even though they seldom are. Now, with NCLB, the writing on the wall is that teachers face the same fate. If the numbers don't rise, you're gone. I hate to blame the system, but I blame the system. To cope with the pressure, we have all— teachers, administrators, everyone—learned ways to act like we are reforming, to act like we are creating a new future for the children. What has been created mostly is a bureaucracy that is insensitive to individual needs and that is a disservice to student, teacher, and administrator alike. Schools are shrines to alienation; they should be havens of authenticity. Maybe I'm stuck in another time, but I think schools are there to help kids discover themselves and the world, not to score a quartile higher on a test that measures some researcher's or legislator's idea of adequate yearly progress toward achievement proficiency. My students, nearly all students that come to school regularly, make progress of some kind but not all of it turns up on their state test scores.

"I am all for teacher accountability. I welcome anyone into my room to evaluate me and tell me what I do well or poorly. If I'm not up to it, let me go or let me try to improve. No problem. But the people telling me I can or can't teach have never seen me teach. It doesn't make sense." Upon completing this last sentence, Jim shook his head and excused himself from the table for the restroom. I stared past my reflection in the glass, out the window and into the rain.

When Jim sat down again, he had a troubled look on his face. Something wasn't sitting well with him. He had a loose end to tie before we could adjourn. The discussion returned to his family.

"My work at Wintervalley has directly impacted my personal life. The everyday teaching part of it takes enough time, especially for an English teacher, but it's really the reform stuff, the other stuff that breaks my back. As a young idealistic teacher I treated all of it as though it were important. I wanted to help and I wanted to make a difference. I have, but really it's only been in my own classroom with my own kids. I've worked hard and seen quite a few of them respond well to what I was doing. When you are training to be a teacher, they tell you that you work for those few moments when the light bulb goes on over a kid's head and it's really true. I've seen more than my fair share of those moments."

Jim paused. "But every one of those light bulbs has cost me plenty. For every time I helped someone else's kid learn how to write without comma splices or stop using intensifiers with every adjective or vary their sentence structure to keep a reader's attention, I missed picking Eddie up from basketball practice or I arrived home after supper was cooked, served, eaten, and in the fridge. I missed a lot of those moments that make you a husband, that make you a father, that make you a friend. I missed birthdays, I cancelled vacations, and even when I did make it for an event, I wasn't really there; in my head I was teaching. Of course, that's a personal failure on one level, but I can't help but think how my entire life would have been different had I devoted the same fervor to my family that I gave those reforms." Jim's voice trailed off and melted into the hum of rain as he finished: "Not one has lasted. Not one was worth it."

I didn't know what to say. There was a pregnant pause and we both stared outside. A meek and distant thunderclap went boom. Finally, I looked at my watch. Eleven. "Okay, Jim. Let's call it a night." Jim asked if we would meet again before school was out and I told him it was unlikely. I would be putting everything together, but he would get a copy of the study when I was done and I would likely call him to see if I had missed anything. We parted warmly. Jim headed toward the back of the coffee shop and I packed my gear.

The ride home was slick and dreary, and it was hard to see the curves through the opaque wall of waves that pounded the windshield. I passed a grocery, turned left, passed an elementary school, a bakery, and a flower shop—all closed. I turned right. The traffic lights were turned off, blinking either yellow or red. Mine was the only car on the road. I went straight for a mile, past some empty fields, and turned into the driveway. The house was dark.

Melanie and the girls were asleep in our bedroom together; legs, arms, and pillows all akimbo. The baby made little gurgles. Holland snored. When I leaned over to kiss Melanie, she said angrily: "Tonight was very hard. These two were a real handful. I hope your interview was worth it. I'm really tired of these long nights. When will this be over? It needs to stop!" On that last word, Bronwyn started to cry. I brought her into the living room and laid her out on the couch under a small woven quilt her grandmother had made.

I ate whatever was in the icebox and turned on the television to unwind, sitting between my sleeping daughter and my backpack. Liverpool was playing Everton—the Merseyside Derby—but it was a replay from two weeks ago and I had seen it already. I left it on and stared at what I knew would be a boring but spirited nil-nil draw. No beautiful game tonight. I thought I would have the energy to jot down a few notes and I opened my things, but I was exhausted. I opened the bag, but rather than retrieving my notebook, I reached for Bukowski. I flipped to the right page to find out about the "most elevated and lucky moment" of his life:

> for me
> it
> was
> being
> a

very young
man
and
sleeping
penniless
and
friendless
upon a
park
bench
in a
strange
city

which
doesn't say
much
for all
those
many
decades
which
followed.

I closed the book and closed my eyes. I thought back on the interview with Jim as the world faded to gray. Flickering reflections of television light licked pictures of my daughters and wife that perched on top of the armoire. Soon I would sleep. The rain continued to fall.

8

DISTRACTION + DISORIENTATION = DISAFFECTION

I have never let my schooling interfere with my education.

—Mark Twain

Throughout this study, I listened to Wintervalley teachers explain how the lessons of *schooling*, the social processes of working for or attending a particular institution, were different than the lessons of *education*, which centered on authentic and meaningful learning experiences for those same people. When teachers spoke of education, their eyes would light up. Barely able to contain their excitement, they described lessons that had gone well and related their joy when they saw light bulbs figuratively click on over students' heads "when they really got it." There were tales of student improvement, student achievement, and student growth. Teachers spoke in glowing terms about how the students' educations took place both in and out of school. Students had made personal breakthroughs in volleyball practices, in youth service groups, with their garage bands, as authors, fledgling politicos, or in any number of other ways. In addition to the education students received, there were more lessons to learn from the experience of schooling at Wintervalley. Teachers suggested that student schooling lessons were probably equally as useful as their education, but they differed greatly in content and method. Students learned how to function as a member of a large bureaucracy, how to code shift when interacting in different social circles, how to manage their time and resources, and many other "formal" lessons. Students also learned a "hidden" curriculum at Wintervalley High School. They learned about racism, sexism, class biases, and how to work the informal aspects of the organizational system to circumvent operating norms. Teachers spoke freely of student education and schooling, but what of their own experiences? How did teachers experience these as sorts of lessons in their own work?

I began to explore this tension during an afternoon interview with Melissa Francione, a veteran art teacher.

"Right. When you first asked me if there were a hidden curriculum for Wintervalley teachers, I had to stop and think. I'm usually so focused on the kids, especially once the word 'curriculum' comes up, that I sometimes forget that we are all learning. The teachers, parents, administrators . . . everyone. Ever since our first interview, my ears perk up now when I hear the word 'alienation.' I hadn't thought about it the way you explained it to me, the way that sociologist described it as something that happens in many ways. A few of us were talking about your study the other day. Specifically, we were talking about the idea that there are different types of alienation. You can have a feeling that you are kind of floating; but it can also be just moments. Alienation doesn't always mean that it consumes you. I think you said that once, right?"

"That's right," I said. Then I thought better, "Well, I don't know if it's really 'right' but that's the way this philosopher, Richard Schmidt, talked about alienation. He said that you experience it as a situational thing, from moment to moment, and as a global phenomenon, a pervasive, everyday thing."

"Right. We were talking about that because we had all just read another This-is-what-Wintervalley-is-all-about document. We get them about once a month. You know, those 'we believe . . .' memos. We agreed with some of it, but we laughed at some of it, too. There was all this stuff in there about our supposed commitment to multiculturalism. I personally believe in that commitment and work on it in my own classroom, but there is no real commitment to multiculturalism here. We said, 'What is this?' There was just kind of a disconnect between what was there, what was on that paper, and what really happens here."

"What do you mean by disconnect?" I asked.

"There are times that I just literally go, 'Well it's best for me not to even try to voice my opinion because it is not going to make a difference.' I started doing that the first couple of years, trying to explain my perceptions about Wintervalley and discuss my commitment to the things that are dear to me, but I realized that few people were listening and it was always the same people so I just started keeping silent until I was around people who cared about things like multiculturalism and diversity. I remember when Dr. Weleck first came I was full of hope. There was a lot of positive energy, a lot of action. People would come in and say, 'Is this what Wintervalley is all about?' And in the beginning I'd say, 'Yes.'"

Melissa's voice trailed off.

"Now, I say no. I say no, it's not what Wintervalley is about. So it's better for me to disconnect from the people who seem to want to change the way that things are or the way that they see the school. Lots of people seem to be carrying the banner of change but they don't share it. Their grip is firm. Solid. A few people in this school lead change and the rest of us get on board or we don't. It just isn't a big deal. That's part of Wintervalley's hidden curriculum, the distance between what people say and what they do. So much of what is being called reform or progress is actually nothing. Zero. A lot of talk and PR—a lot of nothing. Or, if it isn't nothing, it's a borrowed idea taken from some other 'great school' that the administration wants us to emulate. I've noticed that a lot recently. So many things that we do are appropriated from Horace Mann High, this Chicago-area school. The principal met their principal at a conference a few years ago. They talk and we have even sent busloads of teachers up to Chicago to observe what they were doing, but Mann has totally different issues than we do. All that stuff, Rick DuFour, Peter Senge, all those consultant-researcher types, I mean they have some good ideas, I suppose, but there is no effort to take those ideas and adapt them for use here. A lot of that has nothing to do with what Wintervalley is all about."

"So," I asked, "how do you deal with that? It sounds a little to me as though your domain, so to speak, is not the school. Is it your classroom?

Your circle of friends? It doesn't sound to me like you are finding much but distraction when you go to the school level. But with your friends and in the classroom, you discuss and enact what's most meaningful for you to have your say. Am I getting that right or am I way off?"

"Yes. I think you've captured it well."

"Good," I continued. "Any other thoughts about adopting ideas from elsewhere?"

"To me, it feels like we are doing it, doing most of what we do at the school level, because it was successful at Mann with complete and total disregard to the demographic makeup of Wintervalley High School. We're doing it all out of context. The administration says, 'Well okay, that could work here.' But it's a completely different situation here than it is there. I don't want to teach at Horace Mann South, I want to teach at Wintervalley High School. It seems as though we're trying to fit into the mold whether it's for us or not."

I thought about how many times I had heard teachers evoke the name Horace Mann since I had been at Wintervalley. It was probably more often than I had heard it in my history of U.S. education course. I asked, "Wasn't the whole sophomore retention program based on something they did at Mann?"

"Absolutely, and it has shifted our instructional focus. We are so focused now on the people who might drop out or the ones who might get 1600 on their SAT that I think that there is pretty much about 90 percent of the school that goes through here largely unnoticed. Public education, to me, should be focused on serving that 90 percent. Now if we can keep some of those kids who are dropping out from dropping out, I'm all for that. Also, if we can, we should offer advanced courses and opportunities to outstanding students. If we can make a difference in their lives, then I think that's great—but I think that we are focusing on those groups to the exclusion of the majority of kids that go through this school. I mean, why isn't the foundation of what we do based on that 90 percent?"

"It sounds like you are focusing on the tails at either end of a bell curve and forgetting about the swell in the middle."

"Yes! And we actually have a bell curve here, in terms of student achievement. At Mann, they had a bunch of low-performing students and they brought them up with aggressive programming and academic support. We are starting from a completely different place but we are adopting their orientation and programs. I think we can learn from their commitment, and some of what they do is really innovative stuff, but we have a different set of issues. Still, if it's a big issue up there . . ."

"It becomes a big issue down here," I finished.

"Exactly. So we're doing all these things that Horace Mann High School does. They don't have a high dropout rate there, the community is stable. We have higher attrition partly because of local industry. We have the university and a few colleges. People at universities come and go, and they take their kids with them. We also serve an agricultural community. We have to teach trade skills and some kids leave as soon as they are legally able to help out on the family farm. Even those that stay who live on farms have a different set of issues—they may work forty-plus hours a week and come to school all day. Grueling! At Mann, there's one school campus in the district. One! The elementary, middle, and high school share the same facility. Of course they can have more continuity than us. They can get anything done they need to get done without having to worry about the politics of Owen City or Heskey or Wintervalley or Heskey versus Wintervalley and all that. All their high school kids come from a single feeder school, and the teachers at the feeder and the high school meet for a half-day session once a month! That is great, but it has little to do with us. Anyway, the bottom line is that there's a large majority of this school that doesn't get taken care of because we are enacting a grass-is-greener-in-Chicago attitude. When I feel really alienated is when I start talking about that group of people, that group of students, that majority of kids that to me are underserved."

"Still," I noted, "the test scores here are good, whatever that means, and it seems to me that there are a lot of good things going on. I mean, whether the focus is on certain student populations or not, at least the students seem to come first. People consistently say that the kids are what's most important. It's definitely a nice thing to hear. Maybe people just have different ideas about how best to meet their needs."

"Right. I think they are a priority, they are important. That goes without saying. We all want to have a culture of kindness and a culture of acceptance and I do think we are really working pretty hard to make that happen. Here's my point—if the focus of our effort is borrowed rather than generated by us, it is not only a distraction, like I said, it also be-comes disorienting."

"Disorienting? What do you mean?"

"You mentioned the test. You're out here observing teachers all the time, so what do you see as far as teachers who are starting to have to deal with that?"

"Well," I said, trying to buy some time. I wasn't ready to be the inter-viewee. "That stuff does kind of cut into your time. Teachers are wor-ried about having to teach toward that, and then they are worried about how well the kids do, and I think they are bracing for it to become high stakes in the future even though it isn't right now. That creates a moti-vation problem. The kids know it doesn't mean anything. It doesn't af-fect their grade. It doesn't really count."

"Right. Two of my top students were telling me the other day that they knew it didn't matter, so they just wrote whatever they wanted or marked whatever they wanted or didn't finish. One of them said she an-swered B for everything after the second hour of testing because she wanted to read the book she had to finish for English. Now that [En-glish class] was high stakes to her because there was a grade attached. The test means nothing to her now, so she didn't try."

"Okay," I tried to follow Melissa, "how is that relevant to the teachers' situation?"

"Jeff," she leaned closer, "it has everything to do with us. It is the same for us. We—well, not all of us, I teach art—but most teachers have to spend the year preparing kids for the test, knowing that it is meaningless."

What she was saying was somewhat obvious and somewhat simplistic. I had heard plenty of teachers make that complaint, but it seemed like that, a complaint. Wasn't there more to it than just that? I must have frowned.

"You look like you drank sour milk! Okay, listen." Melissa became an-imated and gestured with her arms in sweeping motions to illustrate her points. "Think about how much time we spend, us teachers, just on ac-tivities related to that one meaningless activity. The Test. We are sup-posed to be creating programs and making decisions about curriculum and instruction based on data that we suspect doesn't reflect what the students are learning and we are certain that the students are not trying.

They have no incentive to work to their potential. We *know* that! It might be different if the test was high stakes, but it isn't. It's insane! Now, the test is a big one, and we talk about it a lot. I suppose it's the number one alienation activity in which we engage, if you want to put it in terms of your study, but look—that's only *one* meaningless activity! One! Look at it like this. We are prodded to teach to the test in spite of widespread and sometimes very open reservations, but while that is happening, we are also being asked to go to meetings that have nothing to do with teaching, we fill out endless forms that have nothing to do with teaching, we go to professional development activities that have nothing to do with teaching, we sit through assemblies that are useless, we get memos that are a waste of time. I ask you—when does it end?" Melissa looked at me expectantly.

"When you retire? When you quit? Change schools? I don't know, I'm not sure." I didn't see it coming, but Melissa had set me up for her favorite little phrase. I had heard her use it before in a few meetings.

"D) All of the above." She continued, "You can quit if you want. There are certainly plenty of people who do that. You can leave teaching or leave the school, but I don't think that's what the majority of teachers do."

"What do they do?" I wondered.

"They disengage. They quit on their feet. They stop caring."

"Disaffection?" I asked excitedly, trying to force a technical sociological term into the conversation.

"Well, I wouldn't use that word, but if I understand what you mean, then that's right. If disaffection means that people stop caring, then yes. If it means that they are jut going through the motions, then yes. If disaffection means that teachers get burnt out and lose the love that inspired them to teach in the first place, then yes."

I scanned through my notes. "Distraction plus disorientation equals disaffection."

"Okay. Let's talk about those committees, the PLTs. You know, sometimes they are good, but most of the time it's 'How can we get these principles of good schools or whatever,' and we spend time rewriting and rewriting objectives for something. We share those objectives with other teachers and they critique ours and we critique theirs and I remember thinking that we were really just fussing over words. And, of course, we can't all meet together, the school is too big. I remember thinking once that we had spent a couple of hours on our PLT work and I didn't know how it had helped any of us. So, guess I kind of wish the PLTs would be a little bit more about encouraging thoughtfulness within teaching and within your own area and less about this idea that we all have to do the same thing and reach consensus. More about what strengths each of us can bring to a problem and less about a normative process."

I asked, "It sounds as if you're saying that one more lesson in Wintervalley's hidden curriculum for teachers is that coming to consensus is more important than actually solving the problem. The process is more important than the result. Since the processes that are used are written up in a way that encourages equal involvement, people don't bring their special skills and insights to the table. Is that right?"

"Bingo. You might not always come to consensus with a bunch of teachers because they are opinionated and come to something from different perspectives. Personally, I think that could be a strength, but I think that using the processes we use here, the only thing you can say is, 'we are willing to agree that we will do this job with long hours and little pay with the belief that we will change a young person's life and that will be enough for us.' I think that's the *only* thing you can get teachers to agree on.

"We talk as though it is, but I'm not sure that it is always good to change. At least when changing means giving in to a process that doesn't work. You know, we are not all lockstep, but sometimes you'd think we were. That's why I wish it would be less consensus building and more about ways to be thoughtful in our teaching and our administration of teachers and how do we work with teachers and students and how do we work with students to benefit everybody? And what is our role individually? Uniquely acknowledging and thinking about our role as part of Wintervalley should be part of the teaching profession, but I think it gets lost in all this.

"I guess I am thinking about teaching and engaging schoolwide issues as a habit of thought, being thoughtful. I wish we could do a little bit more of that. Sometimes, I don't know, I've been on enough state standards committees and stuff like that where you are cross-referencing, say, in English, Objective 6, Number 1, with Number 6, Number 7, and you are filling in those slots. I remember once thinking, this activity is not helping any child read better. The phrase that I use was 'politician paperwork.' I'm not fond of that, but it's a fact of life in schools.

"That's one of the things, the whole focus on the 'what we're all about and all that,' seems to come with a double edge. Because it seems as though there is a sense that we do need to reflect on those things periodically, maybe even continually, as it happens here, but there is also a sense that there are so many iterations of it. There is a covenant and a mission and a vision and all these different things at play here. I know a lot of people who have given up on trying to engage those ideas. If they have to go to a meeting where they are talking about those things it's like, 'I'll go and I'll sit there,' but the exercise has lost a lot of meaning. To me, the best thing about the PLTs is that it gets me into a room with a bunch of other teachers. That's it."

I interrupted. "You just answered the next question I was going to ask you. What policies and practices going on at the school help facilitate a meaningful teaching experience?"

"I don't think there are any. That are *really* meaningful? I'm not sure that there are. I'm not sure if that's just the nature of the relationships between school professionals or not."

"I want to talk a little bit about alienation," I said. "It's kind of a weird concept to get my head around to explain. Let me show you this list of what I'm really talking about. The feeling that your work is not your own; that you don't really have ownership over what you're doing; that important decisions are made by people other than you; choices are restricted; you don't say things because it might be outside popular opinion; anything like that; any of these kinds of ideas. Even the idea that people who were once friends feel strange to you. Things like that? Do you ever have any feelings like that?"

"If I was going to say anything on the list, I would probably say that sometimes potentially important decisions are made for me, especially with regard to the types of things Wintervalley is involved in—like Golden Apple or accelerated schools or the way that PLTs are working or anything like that. Or the committees I'm going to be on or things like that. My choices are restricted along the same lines."

"It's interesting. I know one phrase that Dr. Weleck used to describe what had happened before he came, actually, he said that the school—up to that point—had been characterized by 'acts of random improvement.' It was interesting. In my experience of two years looking around, it's almost as if there is a new set of reforms every year."

"New reforms, new ideas, or new . . ."

"It's to the point where many teachers—some really get into it, buy into it—and go along, but for some, they just end up ignoring everything that happens outside their classroom."

"It does. You pay attention when it really strikes a chord with you, but then, for the most part you just say, 'Okay.'"

"That's what I wonder about the most. When something *does* strike a chord with you, are you able . . ."

"Am I able to say something about it? Yes. But it's just one voice amid the cacophony of everything else that's going along, so you don't really feel like there's much to it. Yes, I can say stuff about it, but where's the forum for it now? We have the PLTs after school and we're supposed to respond to things on e-mail and we are supposed to respond to executive committee minutes on e-mail, the BAT team (which is the Building Administrative Team) minutes by e-mail. I don't have time to read all that stuff and come up with any kind of formulated response to it."

"From what you've told me in the past, even responding to those things wouldn't mean anything."

"I don't feel that it would other than to make me feel better. In the long run, it would probably not end up making me feel better if you just weigh it out."

"People here, especially veterans, are going through the motions. They can look enthusiastic, but the life has been beaten from them. They have learned to say all the right things, but the meaning of the statements is drained from them. All talk, no action. You wonder why teachers burn out? They burn out because of schools, not because of teaching. Burnout has nothing to do with losing a love of teaching, it has to do with working for years and years in institutions that don't value education. They don't value the individual thoughts and growth of teachers. I mean, we talk about professional development, but it's almost entirely a waste of time."

Melissa was in full flow. As a researcher, you are supposed to remain silent in these situations. You are supposed to let the tape run and make sure you catch every word. You are supposed to scribble into your notepad and stay on the edge of your seat. But, being a novice inter-viewer, I was swept away by her energy and interjected, "So, working here, working as a teacher, is more about learning the lessons of school, of *this* school, of Wintervalley, than it is about having the opportunity to actually learn, to actually grow and have an ongoing education as a per-son, as a professional. You are suggesting that the institution is the fo-cus, not the individual. Teachers matter less than the team."

I had, of course, derailed her train of thought. Melissa leaned back.

"Your study seems to be pretty focused on the negative aspects of teaching at Wintervalley. I mean, we've spent a lot of time talking about problems and about the reasons teachers are dissatisfied out here, but it's not all bad. There are a lot of good things about being a teacher here. Now, obviously the students are number one. We have great kids. At least a couple of other things come to mind as well: pretty adequate re-sources, nice building for the most part, among at least certain groups of teachers, there's a pretty high degree of collegiality. I mean, I hope you're capturing that stuff, too."

"I've heard and seen those things. I've written them down. What else about the place is particularly positive?" I asked.

"I think, generally speaking, the quality of the staff is good. You have people who are intelligent and who want to teach and who care about it and who are generally willing to help each other. The building's great, but the building is sort of spread out too. You go for days without seeing people and sometimes you have to make an effort to find somebody. But it's easy to get equipment. If I have a video to show, I don't have to fight for a VCR. There's usually one available. Still . . ."

"Yes?"

"I think your study appeals to me because you are giving me a space to discuss the unspoken aspects of teaching. Ordinarily, we can't talk about any of this because we are supposed to be these happy, thank-ful, subservient noncomplainers. I think teachers aren't allowed to complain about work conditions because if you do it at work you get labeled as a malcontent and fired. If you talk about something like alienation outside of the workplace, people point out that teaching is . . . easy . . . because we 'only' teach for nine months and have the summer off, or because we 'only' have to work until 3 P.M. They think it's a party. Anyway . . ."

"But isn't it like any job? There are some bad and some good aspects of work. There is a paradox in doing something like teaching, which is ultimately focused on the individual student, in an institutional setting. Of course there are positive things about teaching, the intrinsic rewards, etc., but what are some of the most difficult things or some of the worst things about being a teacher at Wintervalley?"

"The time crunch. I think there's not as much clerical help for teachers as there used to be, so it's harder to get things done. There's a little more sort of negotiating about who's supposed to do what because with shared governance there is a blurring of duties and responsibilities. But the biggest thing is that no one knows what is going on. The school has gotten bigger and like always, people come and go. New and bigger office staff, new and bigger administrative team, new and bigger teaching staff. As things get bigger and bigger, people's work becomes more bureaucratized, more differentiated. The bottom line is that as the school has gotten bigger, our jobs have become more specialized. Anything that happens outside your own little sphere of control becomes . . ."

"A distraction?"

"A distraction."

"I mean, you go into the office now because you want to order paper clips. I ask the person who ordered them for me last fall, if they are still there, and they say, 'He's doing the budget. If you want to order something, go ask him.' So I go over to the other guy and ask for paper clips. He says that he does the budget for the administrators, not for teachers. Now, he might have a crate of paper clips under his desk but he wouldn't tell me. Instead, I have to hunt down the right person, fill out the right form, submit it for approval, and then on a good day, having wasted half an hour or more, I get a little box of paper clips. It's nuts. There's just a lot of time spent figuring out who's doing what and the right procedure. Who the forms go to and all that. It may be because I always have to negotiate and fight for materials because I am an art teacher, but I think other people have the same issues. You put that on top of the other things we discussed, like the fact that the building itself is spread out, that we have that test, that we all serve on committees and task forces, and everything else on top of teaching, and it's easy to see why people might be disoriented."

"Okay," I said. "And that disorientation ultimately leads to disaffec—" Whoops. I remembered her earlier reaction to that word a bit too late, ". . . er, burnout? A loss of care?"

"Yes. There might be people that you would want to visit with, but they are on the other side of the building. And I think there is more pressure to be overextended in terms of nonteaching activity. To be on a committee and, you know, be in a planning group, and be in a PLT. To show up and make sure you do it and fill out all the forms. There seems to be a lot more of that to do."

"Do you tell the administrators that? Maybe they would be sympathetic and help out. I'm sure they don't want you feeling that way. Maybe they don't realize that it's happening."

"Well, I used to think that, but interestingly, there's not really a formal way to complain that is respected and honored. Nobody has ever said in terms—at least that I know of—of 'do you have a grievance?' There are the normal channels of your department chair and then the principal and the executive council and board office and whatever, but there has never ever been any, 'if you think this is not good; then you should do this.' It's like trying to contact amazon.com. Have you ever tried to do that? You can't find the customer service phone number on the site. It's buried in some obscure place. I'm sure most people who want to call them give up. Complaining about things here is the same, you just have to figure that out for yourself. You eventually give up. You lose your love."

9

LEADING WITH SMOKE AND MIRRORS: OF MISTY MISSIONS, VAGUE VALUES, AND FLOATING PHILOSOPHIES

The songs, the processions, the banners, the hiking, the drilling with dummy rifles, the yelling of slogans, the worship of Big Brother—it was all a sort of glorious game to them.

—George Orwell

During a planning period, which he called a coffee break, I spoke with Neil Woodcock. Neil was into his nineteenth year as a teacher and his second cup of coffee when I sat down in his classroom.

"There is a great deal of divisiveness and cliquishness in our school. And while some of that is natural and to be expected, some of it is the wolf of power disguised as the sheep of leadership. I think there is a lot of suspicion among teachers about the motivation behind school policies, formal and informal. Who is really in charge? What are they doing? Why are they doing it? Where do I fit in, if I do? I'm not sure if it's always intentional, but among certain factions in the school there seems to be a coordinated attempt to play groups off against one another to try and secure certain shortsighted, short-term goals. I'm on the executive council. Yesterday we had a lengthy discussion about that—about the competing political forces in the school. We talked about who was strong and who was weak. We talked about why that was and we debated strategies for balancing things out through policy."

"Wow," I said. "I wish I could have been there. That must have been quite a discussion!"

"Well, I have to admit that I'm making it sound more civil than it actually was. It wasn't really a discussion; it was really a one-way diatribe by the principal. And, as is often the case, I couldn't tell whether he was really mad because of the uneven distribution of power, which is what he was telling us, or if he was really mad because he was outvoted and didn't get his way on something. I suspect it was the latter. I've noticed that when he doesn't get his way he complains about politics, and when he does get his way he sings the praises of distributed leadership. Maybe all politicians do that, and I think all school leaders are politicians." Neil took a sip of coffee.

"Amazing," I said. "I wasn't aware that conversations like that actually occurred. I thought that was all part of the unspoken culture of a school house."

"Well, like I was saying, this is my take on the meeting. I'm probably reading into it somewhat. Anyway, the way that it works here, formally, is that the Dr. Weleck sits on the EC in an ex officio capacity. In reality, he has a lot of influence over the EC, which is made up of teachers who are elected. At times Dr. Weleck is conscious of his influence, and of what he's doing when he tries to strong-arm the EC. In those instances, I think he generally backs away from it, but at other times when he isn't paying close attention, he can't help himself and he forces things. I can understand that. I am impatient when I want my way, too. Maybe we all are. The difference is that I don't have any power . . . and he does."

"No power? But you're on the EC."

Neil eyed me through the steam rising from his cup. "C'mon, Jeff, no one has any power in a school but the principal. He holds the purse strings. He hires and fires. He controls the language of the schoolhouse. No program ever happens without his say-so. Who are we kidding?" We were both silent for a moment, thinking about that.

I began again. "It's interesting that you bring up the idea that Dr. Weleck controls the language at Wintervalley. I don't know if I ever told you this before, but I'm teaching seventh-grade English part-time at a private school here in town. Earlier in the year we read Orwell's *Animal Farm*. Have you ever read it?"

"Sure," Neil responded. "What's your point?"

"On Manor Farm, the pigs manipulate the other animals by various means, but the most obvious is that they use language to revise history and to change the rules as they go along."

"And?"

"It occurs to me how adept Dr. Weleck is at inserting terms he prefers into conversations. He is very well read in terms of leadership theory and lingo. The first time I met him he gave an impromptu lecture about instructional leadership. Right off the top of his head he knew citations, references; he drew a diagram on the chalkboard, the whole thing. I have to admit, it really impressed me. Based on that meeting, I thought I had met some kind of superprincipal. My point is that he knows what to say, and he can frame a conversation using specialized terminology if he wants to. That certainly doesn't make him like the pigs in *Animal Farm*, but it does make me think that he could use language for manipulation if he wanted to. For example, if you pointed out a fault of the governance structure, I'll bet he could talk to you for a half an hour about how it should work in practice; I'll bet he could cite all kinds of research; this book's good, that book's good; and by the time he was done he might have you convinced that he has some kind of special knowledge you aren't privy to so you'd better just back off and empower him to do what he needs to do. I'm not saying I've seen that, particularly, but just that it's what happened in *Animal Farm* and I think Orwell was making an insightful comment on a leader's potential to abuse authority."

Neil nodded as I spilled my thoughts into the conversation. "So it is. He knows the lingo. As time has gone on at Wintervalley, mainly because of the administration, we have adopted a new language. You hear shared governance, distributed leadership, teacher leadership, and all that kind of stuff. Yet, when you get past the rhetoric, it has become less of a collegial place in terms of what I would consider to be leadership. You know, we have new organizational charts that reposition everyone in a way that looks more even, but I think power is actually more concentrated in the principal's office now than at any time in the school's history. You've heard him, so you can imagine that when we were looking for a new principal he interviewed very well. One of my best friends at

Wintervalley was on the committee that interviewed him. Ben [Weleck] was very good, very impressive. And the other candidate, a woman, was equally impressive. I wanted her as first choice, but we couldn't pay her enough money. She was from the southern part of the state, an assistant principal at a high school down there, and we couldn't pay her enough money to move to Owen. Plus, I think some people were turned off and scared because she would really have shook things up. She was the kind of person who would be out walking the halls all day. In fact, I first met her when she stuck her head in my room when she was here doing a school visit as part of her interview. She was a whirlwind. She master-minded some kind of during-the-day professional development program in her district. She insisted that she do her interview while walking around the building, talking to kids and teachers and things like that. I don't get the feeling that was a show, either. Anyway, she didn't work out and we have Ben."

Neil took another sip from his cup, which I now noticed read, "Every-one wins with Golden Apple!" Below the slogan was a cartoon apple. The smiling head of a little green worm protruded from a tiny hole in the apple.

"Now, Ben's not all bad. Actually, I think we are beginning to turn a corner. The power pendulum may be swinging back toward a more au-thentic kind of sharing, but it's more in spite of Ben than because of him. We've kind of regained a critical mass on the executive council again this year—there are fewer 'yes men' on the EC now. We have a chairperson who is taking all the right steps. He is advising Dr. Weleck, but is also willing to buck some things. So the teachers have a more outspoken leader, but there are also enough of us on the council now that are will-ing to support that kind of dissent. It hasn't been that way for a few years. We are beginning to bring things back into line but Dr. Weleck's resisting. For a while he had a lot of cronies on the EC—including the chair—and I think he's in the habit of getting away with doing a lot of things. Again, I don't think he sees it that way. but that's my take on the situation."

"Tell me more about Dr. Weleck and his leadership style."

"One of my colleagues used to teach in the building where Ben's men-tor was the principal, so she taught for the guy whom Ben holds up as a model. She tells me that the other principal was in tune with the faculty because he was there forever—he stayed put in one place for some twenty-odd years. He took time and built up a working relationship with the teachers. You can't snap your fingers and have that, and maybe that is one of Ben's problems, he's impatient and wants the school to work as though it's run by a long-term administration. It takes time and it takes patience. I think our test scores will buy him as much time as he wants, but I'm not sure if he has the patience. So far, it's been a real battle to work for him, and I've found that you have to be of some use to him if you want to bend his ear on an issue. Once you do that, prove your worth, you can be influential. When you get there, or if you are in some sort of appointed administrative position, then occasionally you are going to have expanded opportunities to be in the loop."

"LMX," I interjected.

"What?" said Neil. "What did you say, BMX? Like motocross?"

"No. LMX. Leader-Member-Exchange theory. It's one way people explain how in-groups and out-groups form in a school. It has to do with the relative strength of dyadic linkages—"

"You just lost me."

"Sorry, it has to do with good or poor individual relationships. In LMX, the leadership depends on the social networks the leader builds up with followers. If leaders do a good job with individual teachers, they develop a strong in-group. If they do poorly then the out-group is strong."

"Okay. There's something to that, but even then, it doesn't work so simply. It shifts. I've seen him turn on some people who I would say are in his in-group when they didn't go his way. He's sometimes going to act impulsively and go outside the system from time to time. Whether you are his friend or not, you're going to get blindsided every once in a while or he's going to do something you sat there and told him not to do. Even worse, sometimes he'll tell you he's going to do one thing but when the policy comes out it has gone another direction entirely. Maybe the real problem is that I'm part of the out-group and I don't realize it! Anyway, I've seen it a lot; he's going to do things at times because he can't help himself."

"Like what?"

"For two years he put everyone on common assessments. That was one bad decision and two catastrophic years. A lot of teachers voiced concern when he announced it, but he was all fired up. He got the mess started and then, when it became apparent that it wasn't working, it was suddenly somebody else's problem to try to fix it. He had seen something about it at a conference or something, got excited, and then there it was. Bam! But he screwed it up because it's a pretty radical idea and we had no professional development or training about it and no time to get together and work through things with other people we should have been talking to. He didn't even understand how he had screwed it up, and it was obvious. He tried to force the pace. He thought you could just say, 'You're going to do this and have it happen and be successful.' Well, you can say you're going to do this and you can do what you can to try to make it successful, but you can't change people's attitudes right away. A lot of us thought it was promising and an interesting idea, but it all happened too fast, so it was doomed to failure right off the bat. People were confused and overwhelmed, so it was an instant failure, a major problem. He didn't give them time to buy in. He didn't give them enough of a security blanket. And he has an incredibly short memory. He never remembers that he was the one who made the decision over other people's objections. He actually said in one meeting that it was 'our' screw up, as a *school*. *We* did it. It really pissed me off that he refused to accept more responsibility on that one."

Neil continued. "I've never had as much power as a principal, so I can't really say what I would do, but I have noticed that Ben uses power in a sort of passive-aggressive way. I've had to keep on my toes on the EC. He will try to use particular circumstances or situations to lure you into supporting his position. Sometimes that's fine, but sometimes it's for the wrong reasons. Maybe he saw his vision for the school clearly when he started, but I think it is clouded now. I think it is as clouded in his mind as it is in everyone else's. Although he probably sees the goals he is trying to achieve when he closes his eyes, when he opens them he can't see the path that will lead him there, lead *us* there. He hasn't lost sight of the goal, I imagine, but he has lost sight of the process. He hasn't forgotten what the ideal school looks like to him, but he has forgotten how to lead."

"So," I asked, "things have changed?" I asked Neil to explain his thoughts about the principal.

"Honestly, Dr. Weleck has the best intentions. He simply does not know how to get there from here. He's a lousy judge of character when it comes to choosing people who can deliver the goods. For a while there, and still now to some extent, he has surrounded himself with people who tell him what he wants to hear rather than what he needs to hear. I suppose that in his position, I might be the same way. It's interesting to me that he has hired and/or appointed an administrative team that has no previous experience in administration, with the exception of one dean. Donna was there before, but she's very reserved and she's close to retirement. She might have one more year. The other people never did administrative stuff before, including one person who's really got his ear—it's become clear to me in the last two weeks just how much that person means to him—and because of her influence we're headed for another debacle."

"Debacle?"

"Sure. We have at least two or three a year because of Dr. Weleck's impulsiveness and impetuousness. He gets excited and chooses the wrong person for something, or does something very dramatic without really touching base and checking out details. He puts his foot into it without really knowing what is going on. His credibility continues to go down and down and down with teachers. I think he senses that, but I'm not sure it changes his behavior. I think he rationalizes it by judging people who question him as malcontents."

I asked Neil for an example.

"Last year, as part of a curriculum project, Dr. Weleck and I sat in on a lot of meetings together. He had called us all together, all of the department chairs. The first time I set foot in the room where we met, I looked up and there was The Covenant, The Mission, and The Vision. There was the Coalition of Essential Schools stuff, and the accelerated schools posters. There were at least six or seven different sets of principles that were supposed to be guiding the school taped up around the conference room. In that meting, Ben suggested that curriculum reform was needed and gave us this, 'if-you-don't-like-it-then-leave' pitch. A few people did leave before we met for a second time and at that next meeting he began by making a flip comment about finally being around people who cared about kids. It was unnecessary. He told them they could leave if they wanted, and they did. He didn't have the right to question their commitment to kids, only their commitment to buying into his vision of how to serve kids. I asked a few people about the comment after the meeting, but only myself and one other person heard him say it. Principles are important, and maybe *Webster's* would tell you something else, but when I will say principles I mean principles in the broadest possible sense. I understand that a mission really is different from a vision, for example. But I care about what they mean in action, not on a poster. When I talk with other teachers about it, when I ask, 'What does the school stand for formally?' People cannot articulate any of the stuff on those posters. Actually, unless you are an EC member you may never have even heard of some of it. But then, that doesn't really bother me because teachers are able to talk informally and touch on a lot of those principles anyway. Like I said, I mean principles in the broadest sense. When I walked out of that second meeting, it struck me that a lot those things intended to bring people together were actually driving a wedge between them."

Having no brilliant follow-up question, I asked, "Really?"

"I think so, "Neil responded. "I think there's a maxin that summarizes a lot of those principles and could guide what we are doing. It could help fix what is happening to the human side of the school: less is more. Simple, huh? I don't think we need the covenant. All we need are the ten common principles from the coalition. Throw the rest away! They say it all. But even so, all that does is describe a focus we had here for many years—many years, I might add, that predate the tenure of this administration."

"Tell me more," I prompted.

"We joined the coalition the year Dr. Weleck arrived. He spearheaded it and we were all impressed and excited. One of the reasons we were so comfortable with the coalition was that it was not prescriptive. It was descriptive, meaning that it described a goal but didn't demand that we get there in any one particular way. That flexibility resonated with the faculty and was in keeping with our values, I think. Some of us, like me, were willing to trust the administration because we acknowledged that those principles were our beliefs and that together we would have a platform from which we could build. It seemed to me that the common core principles would do two things: (1) it would give us something positive to focus on, and (2) it would give us a code of sorts, a contract to point to when those values were violated. It hasn't really worked out that way. I expected there to be more open furor about the informal practices of the school than there was. What I didn't account for was unspoken intimidation, Mafioso management, that kind of thing."

"Wow," I said. "Mafioso? That's pretty dramatic."

Neil said, "Like I said before, this is my take on things. Maybe I watch *The Sopranos* too much, but I call 'em like I see 'em."

"Okay," I urged. "Go on."

"Teachers who have been in a school for a while rationalize poor administrative behavior the same way they do everything else. They say 'this too shall pass.' They say, 'If we can keep our heads above water and suspend disbelief long enough then we'll outlast this program, this administrator, this "new" thing, whatever it is.'"

"What is the new thing at Wintervalley right now?"

"They are always talking about involving teachers in schoolwide decision making. It's the new buzzword—sharing. But it's a selective kind of sharing, and while there are formal procedures in place to facilitate sharing, there are informal forces at work as well. I think that the administration supports people to a significant degree, but it's a surface reinforcement, nothing of substance—a lot of smoke and mirrors."

"How do you mean?"

"Teachers have a psychological need to believe that they are making a difference. From my perspective as a teacher, that's the only reason I want any administrator to come into a school, because they genuinely believe that they can make a difference for the kids. Being a principal isn't supposed to be about the prestige or the money or even the power. You don't get paid nearly enough for what you do at any of those levels, even principals, who make a lot more than teachers. It's all about commitment, and for all his faults, I think Dr. Weleck's heart is in the right place. He's a bit messianic, and he's also fanatic in a sense. Those are marks of a visionary leader, and they aren't bad qualities, necessarily. But he doesn't temper those great visionary qualities with common sense and he isn't reflective. In fact, he's very irreflective about himself. I don't even know if that's a word, but I think it captures the essence of what I'm trying to say."

"I don't know if it's a word either, but it should be."

"Right, irreflective. Also, immaturity is a big factor here. Dr. Weleck is nearly my age and it's just amazing how immature he is. I feel badly for him sometimes, because he has a lot of good qualities, the kind that can make a leader a long-term success, but his tactics have been quick fix and I don't think they match his leadership style. He's just been self-destructive. He's thwarted his own plans, but since he externalizes everything he sees it as other people's shortcoming and not his own."

"That's interesting," I began. "Some leadership theories suggest that leaders are shaped in large part by personal experiences and personal characteristics. You know, that regardless of what they learn in a preparation program or through professional development, they lead based on their own life experiences. What do you think about that?"

Neil paused for a long moment, and then he dropped a bombshell into our conversation. "It took me a while to find this out, but I discovered more or less by accident that one of the things that leads to these often really bad decisions that Dr. Weleck makes has to do with very personal stuff. He lost his sister to suicide, an older sister, when they were in young and in school. I'm convinced that has a lot to do with who he is as a leader. This is awful, but because his definition of kids who are left behind is shaped by an innate desire to save his sister, people who can play that tune—or who are willing to play that tune—can manipulate him. They can get his ear and his sympathy. If they pitch something to him as being a way to save someone, that's his next big crusade. If you get him thinking he can save some students, he just explodes into action. It may be the same day or maybe the next day, but it's nearly always immediate and sometimes out of the blue."

"Does that really happen? Do people really intentionally manipulate him knowing that he is driven by such a personal thing? That's horrible."

Neil drank his coffee. "It is what it is. We're all human. We are all motivated by important things in our life. It's just that most of us don't have the kind of power that a principal has. I think that if I had power, people would try to play me in any way they could as well."

"So what about teachers who aren't willing to play that game, or aren't aware that they can influence things in that way?"

"I think most teachers around here don't trust the administration, or they just don't care. Most of them are so focused on teaching that the rest of the stuff just washes over them; they sort of view leadership as something to avoid. I think that's the thing that matters, the thing that makes real leadership difficult around here right now; there is no longer any trust. I'm not surprised, really, based on what's happened since Dr. Weleck arrived."

"What sorts of things are you talking about?"

"Let's go back to yesterday's EC meeting. It will illustrate some of my points. It started out very collegial, very collaborative. We worked through some low-stakes issues and got some housekeeping chores out of the way. Then, fifteen minutes before the meeting was supposed to end it became something totally different. It became very adversarial because Dr. Weleck was adamant about part of a new initiative that wasn't going the way he wanted. He wanted us to rubber stamp a pretty drastic change, he wanted us to do it right then, and he wanted us to do it without discussion or debate. We wouldn't do it. We wanted to table it until the next meeting because it was too big a decision to make without more discussion. He got frustrated when he couldn't push it through. He even said it himself in the meeting—it isn't really the EC's job to give him what he wants, but he was very unhappy when we refused to vote on his idea. It was not savvy, totally transparent, and really childish, even. He sat there and waited until there was clearly no time for discussion and then introduced a new item and wanted us to vote. I mean, does he think we are stupid? Sometimes I think he does. You know, people know about this stuff throughout the district."

"What do you mean?"

"He's raised a lot of negative things about his reputation in the district in general. I think he is maybe a little bit more aware of that than he used to be. Still . . ."

"Yes?" I asked.

Neil continued. "You have to remember that even with all of this seemingly negative stuff I am telling you, I like him. It's just that he has these faults. Some of us, including me, have tried to alert him to how some of his loose-cannon activities affect his ability to do his job effectively in our building."

"Explain."

"People in other buildings say to people in our building, 'I wouldn't teach where you're teaching. Why don't you get the hell out of there?' I'm sure the word is out among prospective teachers at the universities also." He quickly shot a direct glance at me over the table. "Is it? Do you hear negative stuff about us over at the U?"

"No. But you have to remember that I'm not around the teacher preparation program. I'm studying educational leadership. I don't really interact with those people." I could tell that my answer didn't sit well with Neil. His skeptical glance implied that he had wanted a yes or no. I wonder if he thought I was withholding uncomfortable information? I wasn't. Strange and inefficient as it may seem, the teacher preparation programs and leadership preparation programs at most universities don't interact much. He continued.

"Negative PR has a negative effect on people who work here, whether it's deserved or not. We are proud of our school, but it's hard to feel that way when you feel like you are under personal attack or you feel that everything that has made you proud of your school has been undermined. I don't always feel that way, but sometimes I do. When I speak to teachers from other schools, I always have to defend Wintervalley, even with all of the great things we are doing. I find that a lot of what I am defending is an administrative decision rather than anything the teachers are doing. The problem is mainly that Dr. Weleck is not systematic, he's impulsive, and so even though he has put some useful and positive structures in place, he himself constantly destroys them. I know that there is no grand scheme, no long-term plan, because even though he can dream one up, he can't execute any grand scheme. He's a long-term guy, not a day-to-day guy."

The phone on the wall in Neil's classroom rang. He excused himself, got up, and answered. After "hello," he said "okay" four times. While he listened, I mulled over whether or not to share something with Neil that had recently happened. As I thought, he sat back down and without thinking it through completely, I began speaking.

"Neil, something disturbing happened to me a couple of weeks ago regarding this study. I got a phone call at 11:00 at night from a teacher who couldn't sleep because of something that was happening out here at the school. She told me about a veteran teacher who was basically being forced to quit. The teacher who called was not only disturbed because this person was a close friend, she were also disturbed because she felt it had become a pattern. I don't know how to say it, but she described the relationship between teachers and the administration as a war. I haven't brought this up with anyone else, but I have talked with a lot of teachers who were concerned about my taping them for fear that someone in the administration might get a hold of the tapes. Last week I heard a word that I never expected to hear in any school, much less this one. The teacher I was interviewing said something like, 'You never know who the principal's spies are,' and now I've heard you bring up *The Sopranos*. Is this all a bit extreme or is it really happening? The research I've read in my coursework seldom carries things quite that far. At the very least, you don't see that kind of language. Are you being dramatic? I mean, no one's going to end up at the bottom of the river wearing cement shoes."

Neil thought about that for a minute, looking down into his coffee. "Jeff, look. That teacher who called you, I've got a pretty good idea who that was. I'm also fairly certain I know who the teacher in job peril was as well. The one who called you was right. There is a pattern, but it's not a pattern of abuse as much as it's a pattern of ambiguity. Ambiguity leads to mistrust. The administration and the principal are not terrible people. In fact, even though I am an outspoken critic of this administration I would still argue that every one of them cares deeply about the school, the teachers, and most importantly, the kids. Their hearts are in the right place. The mob hasn't moved into the front office, there is probably no conspiracy, and it is also very likely that there is more to every instance of a teacher getting fired than the rest of us will ever know. There are legal reasons that most of us never see the most important documentation that features in those cases. But really, more important than any of that specific information is the climate of ambiguity created by unclear communication or incomplete information."

"Tell me more."

"Take that teacher who might get fired. He's a good guy. He's been here a long time and while I'm not sure I would say that he's well liked, he is a decent human being. He's not a great teacher, never has been, but he's been here his entire career. He is two years from retirement and based on the few conversations we have had, I think he is more focused on that than on teaching. He's a religious guy and he's very active in church. I think over the years religion has become more important to him than school. Does that make him an awful person? Certainly not. But it does represent a shift in focus, a shift from centering on the kids and the work here at Wintervalley. I think he's probably been retired on the job for a decade or so and is just collecting his check so he can live the rest of his life. Now, I don't think that guy is the victim of a conspiracy; I think he is a victim of himself. I haven't seen the numbers for his students on the state test and I haven't seen him teach in years, but it wouldn't surprise me at all if his evaluations were poor and the numbers were bad. What is the principal supposed to do? Is he supposed to say 'Oh well, let's put up with two more years of poor instruction?' That's crap! Those are two years that 300 kids will lose! No school can afford that. It outrages people looking in from the outside because he's only a few years from retirement, but schools owe nothing to a bad teacher."

"So, let me get this straight. What you're saying is that there is certain information that administrators must take into consideration when making decisions that teachers are not privy to. Since teachers don't have access to that information but they see administrative action, they fill in the blanks with assumptions. They replace ambiguity with fantasy?"

"Well, maybe not fantasy, but with assumptions and guesswork. But isn't that natural? I mean, don't we all try to connect the dots to finish the picture? Some people are more dramatic than others. Some are conspiracy theorists and some are not. The problem is that in the larger picture of what is happening in the school, there is a pervasive lack of trust. We all have to make important decisions: teachers, parents, students, administrators—all of us! We all make important decisions because there is so much riding on what we do. We are shaping students' futures. Test or no test, teaching is a high-stakes profession. Much of what we do impacts the way kids view the world. Principals make bad choices, and this one has made some doozies, but who hasn't? It's difficult to be in that position. Everyone is looking, everyone is waiting for him to screw up."

"Lots of pressure."

"You bet your ass it's a lot of pressure! But here's what has happened, here's why it isn't working right now for Dr. Weleck and his team. They are not open. They play their cards too close to the vest. Since no one is sure what to expect, the level of trust among the faculty has eroded. In the beginning, we were all ready to trust and give him the benefit of the doubt, but as people see more and more decisions made in an ambiguous manner they are less willing to take it in a positive light. Teachers now question his intentions, they question his motivation for doing things, and they question his devotion to the kids. Why? It's because we don't have transparency, because of ambiguity, not because Darth Vader is our principal. When you have ambiguity you have questions and when no one steps forward to answer the questions, they become larger and larger questions until finally the 'big' questions are raised—questions about commitment, about trust, about the direction of the school. So, getting back to Ben, in some cases he may have had good grounds for some kind of action, but who knows? I think what I question about him is not his motives, but the way he way does it and the way he communicates."

"Right. I see what you're saying."

"Here's the problem. The climate of the school is becoming adversarial. It's partially because of leadership ambiguity and partially because the principal is so much more powerful than everyone else. He's just a human being and just like he has this sincere desire to save kids, he also has the capacity to be vindictive, to hate, and to lash out, just like the rest of us—whether he understands it or not, whether he can control it or not, and you don't want to do that."

"I also wonder about whether or not Dr. Weleck took the time to learn about the school. The first time I met Dr. Weleck he started talking in terms of the 'old Wintervalley' and the 'new Wintervalley.' But he talks about it in almost the opposite way from the way veteran teachers do. His favorite thing to say—he has said it to me five or six times now— is that the old Wintervalley was characterized by random acts of improvement. I heard it put so well by one teacher who said, I have to look it up, but it was something like, 'I remember the days of Wintervalley the Republic, but now it's Wintervalley the Empire.'"

"Ha! That must have been an English teacher, or a social studies person or something, that's good. We're certainly struggling with that, this new form of governance, of participation, and we're also struggling with the fact that we're going to continue to get bigger and we're setting some—the school—is setting some unwitting precedents which we may never get over any time soon. Just like it takes time to instill positive change, it takes time to get rid of negativity and some mistakes. We have talked about some of this negative stuff today, and you have articulated other things over the course of our interviews this year. Unfortunately, people are not willing to acknowledge negativity and deal with it or they feel hopeless in the face of it because they are scared or because their first impulse is to place blame and responsibility elsewhere. That issue is not the sole domain of leadership, but since they have all of the power it is at least partially their responsibility."

"Tell me more."

"By the simple defining of a new term or by structure or whatever, you're not accomplishing any real change. You have to build a coalition to change a school, but not the kind of a coalition the people in the office are trying to build. You have to build a community coalition which knows and discusses (a) what you are doing, (b) why you are doing it, and (c) how are you going to evaluate and reevaluate to determine what comes next. Then you become a real collective agent for change because if somebody comes in and tries to undo what you are doing it doesn't depend on one leader, it depends on the process and the will of the group. For example, let's say that someone attacks the way I teach in an overt, direct, and uninformed way. In the system I described, you know how to respond. You have reasons for doing what you do and you invite people to review them through a normal cycle that is long established. They don't have good reasons for why they want you to stop doing it without results that prove what you're doing is wrong. If they do, they look like fools and they go away and they don't come back again. Anyway, I know it doesn't work that way but what is happening now at Wintervalley wears people down. This is why some folks are getting so tired of this year after year. They are led toward burnout. It's a mess, but it has forged a bond among us about our philosophies at the departmental level.

"Principle number one—the preeminent principle of the Coalition of Essential Schools: You don't learn to use your mind well by completing a worksheet and getting attendance forms for showing up in class and then you get butt time credit and you get a diploma and you can't read or write and then we catch hell for that. Then we do badly on standardized tests and people say you don't know what you are doing or you are incompetent or you don't care. It's all of a piece and people don't see that. They don't get it.

"You can talk about involving teachers as leaders all you want. I honestly don't see administrators gaining a new paradigm at all. They are in the same exploitative and manipulative paradigm they always have been in. I think maybe they become corrupted or intoxicated with power; some very good people end up making lousy principals. To some extent, I think I would say the establishment of public education exploits teachers, and maybe educators in general, because they've always gotten away with it. But at Wintervalley I think we are headed for a train wreck because schools cannot continue to demand more and more and more. Besides, we are barely giving kids what they need. We're not going to adjust professional training or adjust the school's mission to give kids what they really need, we're going to try to add more on top of what is already happening. That's the principal's solution—more and faster—ask teachers to do it all. We'll have to wait and see if it happens." Neil chuckled to himself.

"What were you thinking about?" I asked.

"You were talking earlier about *Animal Farm*, but maybe you picked the wrong novel. Isn't *1984* the one with Big Brother?"

"Yes, it's also the one with Newspeak."

"Okay, then that is the right novel."

"Big Brother is watching you," I mumbled.

"Nope," said Neil, "Big Brother is *leading* you."

10

CODA OR REFRAIN? REFORMING AGAIN AND AGAIN AND AGAIN AND AGAIN . . .

Life is just one damned thing after another.

—Elbert Hubbard

It is not true that life is one damn thing after another—it's one damn thing over and over.

—Edna St. Vincent Millay

As the end of my study neared, I shared my findings, in the form of a rough draft of my dissertation, with about a dozen teachers to see if they thought I had captured or missed what was happening at Wintervalley. After about ten days, I began meeting with them individually to get feedback. I have to admit, I was worried. Worried that they would say that I had missed it completely, or worried that they would, at the last moment, demand that I remove the data I had gathered from them because they were scared of keeping their anonymity. The study certainly wasn't all bad. As one of my mentors said to me, "it's not like the school is on fire." Still, I knew the study cast a harsh light on some of the school's imperfections. How would they respond? Admittedly, I gave them the text at a bad time of the year, right near the end. So while I didn't get the 100% response I had hoped for, I heard from half of the

teachers. Four of those had skimmed through the study; the exit interviews I conducted with them left me wondering if they had really taken
the time to read the thing. For the most part, these teachers said, "It was
interesting" or "Looks good and good luck." They had seen research
folks like me come and go, and here I was, another one about to go. Still,
two teachers in particular gave more substantive comments.

"Ha! It's such a *Dilbert* comic strip," said Joan Wilkes. "Anyone who's
worked in a school has to laugh at those *Dilbert* pieces, they are so accurate. I mean, we don't sit in cubicles, but really, what is a classroom?
It's a cubicle. The difference is that I think when people read *Dilbert*
they always identify with Dilbert, the character, when in fact, we are all
probably a composite of characters in the strip. It's easy for someone like
me to view myself as Dilbert, the rational victim of organizational insanity, and view my colleagues as the various inept or corrupt characters
in the strip. You know that manager? The one with the pointy hair? He's
a moron with no leadership skills, and even though Dr. Weleck is actually a lot better than that, and is in many ways a great person, he's a victim of the system just like that guy. He has power, but in a way he
doesn't know what to do with it so he kind of floats from one ill-
informed decision to the next and if the word comes down from above
that he needs to do something, boom! There it is. At the same time, I
have to look at myself here, too. You know that woman in *Dilbert*, the
one who is neurotic? I have some of those qualities. And that little bald
guy who is always trying to abuse the system? I don't do that, but I know
plenty of people around here who do. Anyway, those characters are flat,
and real people are more complex. A lot of what you wrote about in your
study has to do with people who are probably good at heart but are stuck
in an insane system."

"Hm," I mumbled. "Maybe I should have presented that data as a
graphic novel."

"In a way," Joan continued, "that *Dilbert* stuff is a good analogy because a lot of it talks about the life of working in a big, bureaucratic type
organization like a school."

"Okay," I responded, "what I am trying to find out in this study is not
just to point out those absurdities that we all chuckle about, *Dilbert*-type
stuff, but also to find out what it is like to work in Dilbert's world on a

day-to-day basis. What does it do to teachers, mentally, emotionally, professionally? How does it make us feel about how we approach our work? Maybe this is really a Dilbert study, but the characters are not flat. They are real, complex people who don't get to walk away after a four-cell comic. They do it day after day, month after month, year after—"

Joan interrupted and finished my sentence, "Year after year."

"Right. So, what's your impression of Wintervalley? How are you doing in Dilbert's school?"

"I have a lot more work than I did even a few years ago. I think that, personally, I am more confident in what and how I'm teaching. I'm getting a good handle on the material and I think my little team-teaching partnership with Thom is working well. I'm going to take a couple of things this summer on creative teaching, looking at literacy infusion and I think I ought to try to present things in a better way than I've done in the past. Some of those teachers you spoke with are just going through the motions. I don't want that to be me."

When I sat down in Mr. Finnan's room, I immediately sensed that he was unhappy. "Jim, how do you feel about the school's reform efforts? What's next for Wintervalley?"

"Jeff, I read your stuff. You nailed it, that dark side of teaching, but you didn't say it all. Why not?"

I squirmed. "What do you mean?"

"You left out some of the most awful and abusive stuff," he said. Jim looked disappointed.

I knew exactly what he was talking about. In one interview Jim had described, in great detail, how two teachers were intimidated into being fired without due process. In another interview, he had told me why so many teachers in the school were scared to talk about issues of race in the building. A few years before my study, a guest speaker from the university was slated to speak at a Wintervalley assembly during a Black History Month event. Apparently, the speaker had prepared a hopeful speech, something about how great it was that an African American male was invited to speak when only a few decades earlier he wouldn't have been allowed on school grounds. By Jim's account, the speaker abandoned that thesis when he heard some students making racist remarks in the parking lot as he arrived. Instead of using his notes, the speaker used the opportunity to harangue the mostly white faculty and students about their insensitivity and abuse of white privilege. He blasted the "Jim Crow school system" and repeatedly exclaimed that visiting their school was like entering a time warp wherein *Brown vs. Board of Ed.* had never happened. Jim had told me that the speaker started his talk by saying, "So the crackers want to hear from the niggers." Although I couldn't find anything in the local papers when I researched the event, Jim said that the local TV cameras and press were there, and it got ugly. Teachers and students were torn and confused. It took the school a while to recover and many people, especially teachers, were now terrified of discussing race.

"Jim, first of all, I didn't include everything. That's just my dissertation. Second, I asked a bunch of people about it and they wouldn't speak. Even a few people I came to know very well wouldn't comment at all or respond to questions about race. To be honest, I felt a little weird pursuing it too much, being a six-foot-four-inch white guy with a shaved head. I don't know that I really understand how race in general, and white privilege in particular, enter into the interviewer-interviewee relationship. I became fearful that people would stop talking to me. Also, I was worried about compromising anonymity."

"That's all fine, Jeff, but I want to say, for the record, that the race issue is huge—precisely because of people's reactions to your questions, not because of what they wouldn't tell you—no one will engage race and a lot of people feel that since the school is mostly white they don't have to. Not only are they wrong, our students suffer because teachers are unwilling to have open conversations about race in their classes or among themselves because they are scared. I know you are still learning as a researcher. This is your first study, right?"

"Right," I said, suddenly feeling very small, very white, very male, and very qualitatively inadequate. "I promise that if I turn this into a book, this interview will make it in."

"Fine," Jim said, "We'll see. Like I said, I think you got most of it. One more thing occurred to me. History is more important than you wrote in the study. There are a lot of reform efforts going on here, and as a result, there is this continuous dialogue about 'what's important.'"

"Right. Isn't that good? A lot of educational research says that such a conversation is an important first step of meaningful change."

Jim was annoyed. "But it's the *same* goddamned conversation recy-
cled every year. There is no sense of institutional memory and we make
the same mistakes we've been making for decades. It's the same crap
over and over. We are not moving forward, we are moving in a loop, we
are stuck in a rut. Certainly a lot of the dialogue is, 'How can we best
help kids?' and that's good. I think all people go into teaching to help
kids. But beyond that I'm not always sure that our actions match our intent. Sometimes I think some of the PLT work can become a little navel
gazing. To an extent, we should be asking ourselves 'How is this helping?' but we don't always do that. I know what you are talking about in
terms of having an initial dialogue. There's the part where it's a philosophical thing and to a certain point the exploration of philosophical issues is important. But at what point do you say, 'Well, this is the way
we're going to do it here.' And then *do* it? We spend too much time
screwing around. The test scores are good so there's no sense of urgency.
Of course they are good; we teach a bunch of rich white kids! Certainly,
exploring pedagogy makes teachers more thoughtful but I think a lot of
what we do here is not authentic."

"What do you mean?"

"All of that reform stuff is teacher- or administrator-centered
change—where are the student voices in the conversation? I am sure
that if we let students tell us what they wanted and empowered them to
lead change, the school would be a different place. If we actually talked
about race, about social justice, and about equity, this would be a different place. As it is, I think we are maintaining the status quo. We are
keeping the rich, rich and the poor, poor."

"Hegemony," I said.

"What's that?" Jim asked.

"Hegemony is a term used to explain what you are talking about. It
kind of means perpetuating the existing social structures rather than
challenging them—nothing new is allowed to grow in the system."

"Jeff, that's all well and good. But that's one of the problems with research and with researchers. Why can't you just use common language
to describe something so common? I mean, what you just said isn't especially groundbreaking or difficult to grasp. If more research would do
that, speak plainly, it might actually help. I mean, how many studies
have you read about . . ."

"About hegemony? A bunch. There's this guy, McLaren, who writes—"

"That's my point. There's a bunch of stuff out there, but it never makes it to the school. Even in your study, there were a hundred pages of stuff there about alienation before I ever got to the interviews. Maybe you should title your study *The Dark Side of School Reform*, so teachers know what you're talking about, instead of some technical title no one understands."

"Okay, Jim, maybe I will. Thanks."

On a windy day in May, I signed out in the Wintervalley registry for the last time. Walking toward my car, I wondered what the school might be like next year. Would the same teachers be wrestling with the same issues? Would the administration be able to lead the school in the direction they hoped? Would the focus change? Would communication be better? Would alienation be the watchword? Thinking back on my final meeting with Jim, I wondered what the school might be like in twenty years' time. Would the same issues be in the air? Would the same reform tensions exist? Would Wintervalley learn the lessons of history? I opened the trunk of my car and placed my bag among the mess. When I sat in the driver's seat, I noticed that I had left my cell phone on the dashboard. I had been in the school saying goodbye and thanking various people for about three hours. The phone was blinking red, which meant I had a message. I picked it up and listened to Melanie's voice— she was justifiably angry and upset—I had forgotten Holland's lunch box at home that morning when I dropped her off at preschool and her teacher had called to ask what was going on. Melanie's message ended with an emphatic, "C'mon, Jeff, when will this be over!?!!" As I turned the key in the ignition, the radio kicked in and I wondered if I would ever be able to answer that question.

11

TEACHING IN THE SPACE
BETWEEN REALITY AND UTOPIA

I wanted only to try to live in accord with the promptings which came from my true self. Why was that so difficult?

—Hermann Hesse

The previous ten chapters in this book presented findings from the Wintervalley study—an empirical, field-based, qualitative study of teacher alienation during conditions of ongoing school reform in a single public, secondary school. This chapter is different, in terms of both style and substance. When reflecting on the Wintervalley study and considering what lessons educators and researchers might take from this investigation, it is helpful to understand some of the inquiry on alienation and school reform that preceded and informed this work. This chapter begins with a review of literature devoted to alienation and explains how this complicated and often confused phenomenon was conceived in this study. The section on alienation is followed by a similar review of school reform literature. While it may be obvious, I still feel it is important to note that neither of these reviews is exhaustive, and are instead selective (Wolcott, 1994). Research into each of these phenomena has a varied and vast lineage. While I have here organized concepts in a way that I think helps make sense of the data collected during my two years at

Wintervalley, there are certainly a number of other works that could connect to themes developed throughout this book. After these literature reviews, the chapter ends with a discussion of how the Wintervalley study might extend and challenge current thinking about these concepts, plot a course for further inquiry, and inform work in schools.

ALIENATION: EXPLORING THE SPACE BETWEEN REALITY AND UTOPIA

The quote at the beginning of this chapter is posed to readers in the preface of Hermann Hesse's (1965/1999) novel *Demian*. Yet while young Emil Sinclair, the hero of Hesse's story, sought answers to this question amidst the storm and stress of an adolescent search for identity, many public school teachers in the United States are likewise in pursuit of solutions to this enduring dilemma in their professional lives. They ask, "Why is it so difficult to *teach* in accord with the promptings which come from my true self?" Educational scholars have likewise sought to understand why those who work in public schools report acute dissatisfaction with various aspects of teaching. Research on institutional culture in schools (Grimmett & Neufeld, 1994; Hong, 1996), professional community (Bryk, Camburn, & Louis, 1999; Merz & Furman, 1997; Westheimer, 1998, 1999), burnout (LeCompte & Dworkin, 1991; Friedman, 1991), principal mistreatment of teachers (Blase & Blase, 2003), and job satisfaction (Bogler, 2001; Haser & Ilham, 2003) has identified a "dark side" to teaching in contemporary public schools that dramatically affects the way teachers conduct their work and their attitudes toward various educational activities and roles (Blase & Blase, 2002a, 2002b).

A primary purpose of this study was to explore the dark side of teaching vis-à-vis a predominantly sociological conception of alienation developed by Melvin Seeman (1959, 1967, 1975, 1983). According to Seeman, alienation can be conceived as a set of five related empirical subconstructs, or variants. Collectively, these variants comprise an empirical domain of alienation: powerlessness, meaninglessness, normlessness, isolation, and estrangement (Seeman, 1959, 1983). For the purposes of this study, I explored these five subconstructs as distinct forms of teacher alienation. That's all well and good, you may say, but what is alienation in the first place?

General and Technical Alienation

Alienation can be understood to have two types of meanings: general and technical. I have heard the term "alienation" used to explain aspects of professional sporting events (*And by committing that foul, Foudy has alienated herself from the fans*), explain experiences of cross-cultural dissonance (*To celebrate Kwanzaa gave me this sense of alienation. I mean, the other kids were having Christmas*), and to review popular movies (*Jar-Jar Binks alienated legions of* Star Wars *aficionados*). A discerning and perceptive listener will undoubtedly find alienation used in even more contexts, from prescription drug advertisements to songs, poems, novels, or as a means of explaining reactions to political situations. Still, if the term "alienation" is evoked to explain several phenomena, some fundamental questions must be answered if the concept is to be used as a framework for empirical research: What is alienation? How can a researcher recognize alienation as behavior or attitude or when they see it or hear participants describe it? Does alienation even exist? If it does exist, how might we live better or better conduct the work of schooling and educating by understanding alienation?

The italicized examples in the preceding paragraph represent general alienations, ambiguous popular uses of the term intended to relate a sense of separateness, of political, social, affective, or cognitive disconnect. Here, a specific definition of alienation is less important than conveyance of a feeling of ennui, unease, angst, or anxiety—something just doesn't *feel* right because it is more distant than it ought to be. In contrast, technical meanings of alienation are developed through systematic inquiry and seek to apprehend the nature of (dis)connection between alienated and alienating as discrete behavioral or attitudinal phenomena. While general alienations are vague, technical alienations identify specific disconnections and examine the nature and context of that disconnect. Alienation has been treated technically in all the social sciences (Seeman, 1959, 1983; Schacht, 1970), including political science (e.g., Templeton, 1966), anthropology (e.g., Megged, 1999), education (e.g., LeCompte & Dworkin, 1991; Zielinski & Hoy, 1983), psychology (e.g., Fromm, 1941/1965; Horney, 1939, 1945), and sociology (e.g., Bakarat, 1969; Merton, 1957). However, technical meanings of alienation are not the sole property of the social scientist. Alienation has also been studied and developed as a technical phenomenon among philosophers (Beauvoir, 1975, 1982; Buber, 1958; Kaufmann, 1975; Kierkegaard, 1986; Nietzsche, 1967, 1986; Sartre, 1956, 1957; Schacht, 1970; Schmitt, 2003), artists such as Edvard Munch and Vincent van Gogh (Reitz, 2000), and by writers working in many literary genres (Akhmatova, 1989; Camus, 1942/1988, 1955; Céline, 1934; Cisneros, 1991; Gilman, 1991; Salinger, 1991; Woolf, 1990). You may have noticed allusions or references to some of these works sprinkled throughout the study (and even others; note, for example, that the school's pseudonym, *Wintervalley*, is the inverse of *Summerhill*, A. S. Neill's 1960 classic work about educational freedom). While there is broad and sustained interest in alienation and alienation-related themes, there is also variation among technical meanings of alienation. However, certain central tenets transcend field-specific boundaries and are found in nearly all technical definitions of alienation.

Philosopher Walter Kaufmann (1970) named two propositions common to technical alienation studies. The first is that alienation implies a *relationship between a person (or group of people) and something else*. Basically, when studying alienation,

> we are concerned with a relationship between A and B. A is a person or group of persons: an individual, a social class, a whole generation, a people, or perhaps a smaller group. . . . [B is] an individual (for example, one's father, wife, or child); a group (perhaps one's family, fellow employees, fellow students, teachers, employers, colleagues or neighbors); other people in general; the society in which one lives (for example, American or Soviet society); oneself (perhaps especially one's body or some particular aspect of one's character or of one's past); nature (hardly a univocal term, but possibly in the sense in which we speak of nature lovers); or, finally, the universe." (xxiv)

Kaufmann concludes by suggesting that even this is an incomplete base from which to discuss alienation, as "one can also be alienated from what one does (from one's activity, work, or labor) or from things (such as products of one's labor)" (xxiv). Through numerous methodological traditions and discipline-specific applications, alienation scholars have refined their thoughts on the way A's respond to and develop the experience of alienation. They have also added many more B's to this list: affections (Seeman, 1959), skills (LeCompte & Dworkin, 1991), spiritual essence (Kierkegaard, 1986), and so forth. In short, writers and scholars have discovered that any person or group of persons can potentially be alienated from nearly any other person, thing, or action.

The second of Kaufmann's (1970) propositions is that alienation is, in the broadest sense, *the experience of unhappy, unwelcome, and/or indifferent disconnection*. A disconnection between A and B can have any number of related symptoms or be manifest in a number of ways: anger, malaise, disaffection, separateness, but also happiness, or even joy. Importantly, not all detachment results in alienation and detachment in one aspect of life does not necessarily mean one is alienated from everything. For example, the teacher asked to refrain from participation with a particular committee would only be said to experience alienation if he or she were unhappy with no longer being a member. That is, if the dismissal created a sense of separation between the teacher and something he valued, or resulted in indifference toward something he would value under other circumstances, we might call it alienation. A teacher who welcomed this separation would not typically be described as alienated. Writ large, this is alienation: an unwelcome, unhappy, or indifferent relationship between a person or group of persons and another person, group, thing, phenomenon, or entity (Kaufmann, 1970; Rose, 1966; Seeman, 1959).

While technical alienations tacitly agree on this twofold starting point, they do not concur in their emphases or explanations of the nature of the relationship between A and B. That is, while the sociologist may point to alienation as the result(s) of social habitus and process (Powell & DiMaggio, 1991, p. 26; deMarrais & LeCompte, 1999), the psychologist may understand alienation to arise from tension between internal constructs in conflict within the self or between the psychological self and the other (Fromm, 1941/1965; Horney, 1939, 1945); political scientists might identify alienation as an individual's or group of individuals' nonparticipation in a particular political system or policymaking process (Grotius, 1853; Schacht, 1970; Templeton, 1966); and philosophers may interpret alienation as a metaphysical impediment to pursuit of the good life (Schmitt, 2003), or even as the essential tension that defines the human condition (Kierkegaard, 1986; Sartre, 1956, 1957). However, while it is useful to be familiar with the plurality of traditions that inform contemporary conceptions of alienation, it is unwieldy (and probably impossible) to include them all into a single conceptual framework for focused empirical study. As such, while the Wintervalley study was informed and inspired by the preceding conceptual traditions, I would place it in a distinct line of alienation research based on a relatively recent sociological conception that sees the phenomenon as a multifaceted domain of five interrelated empirical constructs.

The Empirical Domain of Alienation

In 1959, sociologist Melvin Seeman's essay "On the Meaning of Alienation" recast the mold of alienation as an empirical subject of study by conceptualizing it as a multidimensional and interrelated "domain" of inquiry. Seeman lamented the disconnected nature of sociological alienation-related studies. Some researchers evoked Marx's notion of alienated labor (Tucker, 1978), others grounded their studies in Durkheim (1893/1997, 1897/1997), Weber (1947, 1986), or Mills (1959), or related an affinity to the social-psychological emphases of Fromm (1941/1965) or Horney (1939, 1945). However, for all the scholarly attention devoted to the study of alienation, few sought to reconcile or make sense of one definition of alienation in relation to another (Seeman, 1983). Seeman's contention was that researchers ignored entire bodies of related literature and inquiry, instead renaming already identified variants of alienation as something else and proclaiming they had discovered a novel construct. Entire subfields of inquiry with "hidden alienation motifs" emerged and developed with little or no regard for classic or contemporary studies of similar phenomena (Seeman, 1983). According to Seeman (1959), sociologists continually reinvented the wheel by renaming it, rather than making the wheel they already had better by refining, extending, or building on extant alienation studies. Among disjointed alienation-related research were strains devoted to locus of control, disaffection, deskilling, helplessness, system blame, anomie, self-efficacy, fate control, and reactance (Seeman, 1983). It is important to note that Seeman focused his attention exclusively on sociological and social-psychological formulations—if his argument were extended to include additional disciplines of the social sciences (or beyond), certainly more would be added to his list. To Seeman, research into these areas could be strengthened by gathering and considering them in relation to one another under an overarching construct: alienation. Through an exhaustive and systematic review of both empirical and theoretical sociological studies of alienation, he identified an "empirical cluster" of five distinct "alternate meanings of alienation" (Seeman, 1983, p. 783). These five variants, or subconstructs, of alienation constitute the empirical domain of alienation: powerlessness, meaninglessness, normlessness, isolation, and estrangement (Seeman, 1959, 1983).

Powerlessness is "the expectancy or probability held by the individual that his own behavior cannot determine the occurrence of the outcomes, or reinforcements, he seeks" (Seeman, 1959, p. 784). This view of alienation is derived directly from Marx's idea of alienated labor; that the worker, as a creative individual, is denied his true nature by a system that deprives him ownership of his products. Yet Seeman, much like Weber, saw Marx as a point of departure rather than a final destination. This strain of alienation studies—powerlessness—includes the school-based work of those who focus on the distribution of power within a social system (see, for example, Bourdieu & Passeron, 1977; McLaren, 1989; Giroux 1983a, 1983b) and its attendant alienating effects on members of said system. Seeman noted that powerlessness, locus of control, and control itself were closely related ideas and suggested that empirical alienation studies should be sensitive to these notions.

Meaninglessness occurs when "the individual is unclear as to what he [*sic*] ought to believe—when the individual's minimal standards for clarity in decision-making are not met" (Seeman, 1959, p. 786). Meaninglessness is distinguished from powerlessness in that "where the first meaning of alienation [powerlessness] refers to the sensed ability to control outcomes, this second meaning refers essentially to the sensed ability to predict behavioral outcomes" (p. 786). Thus, meaningless might alternately be conceived as the individual's "sense of understanding the events in which he is engaged" (p. 786).

Normlessness, the "third variant of the alienation theme, is derived from Durkheim's description of 'anomie' and refers to . . . a situation in which the social norms have broken down or are no longer effective as rules for behavior" (Seeman, 1959, p. 787). In their anthropological study of "student dropouts and teacher burnouts" LeCompte and Dworkin (1991) helped append this definition by suggesting that "under conditions of normlessness rules are either inoperative, such that following the rules will not achieve the goals to which one aspires, or nonexistent, such that the individual can turn to no rule to guide action" (p. 155).

Isolation has to do with an individual's relationship to a community, and for the purposes of this study was conceived as primarily a social and/or physical phenomenon. In its social sense, isolation has to do with the degree to which an individual experiences an affinity to others and/or her community as a whole. Seeman (1959) observed that people and groups experiencing social isolation "are those who . . . assign low reward values to goals or beliefs that are typically highly valued in the given society," (pp. 788–789). Physical isolation is a self-evident notion; that although a member of a given community, conditions are such that the one (or a group) is separated from the many (Seeman, 1975). Two different ethnographic case studies of teachers help clarify the concept of isolation as experienced in school settings, one by Lortie (1975) and the other by Waller (1961). Taken in tandem, these studies examined isolation (albeit as part of a larger conceptual framework) and posited that the phenomenon was a prominent feature of teachers' lives that occurs both in professional and personal interactions as a result of prolonged interaction with students (as opposed to adults), community expectations of teacher behavior, and certain other features of teachers' lives which revolve around the complex nature of professional autonomy.

Finally, in Seeman's (1959) formulation, *estrangement* means "to be something less than one might ideally be if the circumstances in society were otherwise—to be insecure, given to appearances, conformist" (p. 790). Bakarat (1969) poetically explained estrangement as "the distance between reality and utopia" (p. 1). Although studies of teacher estrangement are scant, workplace estrangement has been studied by sociologists such as Dählstrom, who suggested that the estranged worker experienced "involvement in work vs. work seen as instrumental," or alternately, the "absence of involvement in work" (Israel, 1971, p. 213). Put another way, the estranged individual in the workplace is disaffected toward his or her activities; passion is replaced with apathy, care with indifference.

Teacher Alienation and Burnout

If we accept Seeman's categories, many works in the sociology of education (and, of course, other areas of educational inquiry as well) may be conceived as alienation studies. Among important research that connected sociological conceptualizations of alienation to education are deMarrais & LeCompte's (1999) work in which they used alienation (paired with boredom) to denote an "initial phase of resistance" that youths experience as they search for social identity (p. 140). These authors speak of alienation in relation to teacher burnout. Indeed, although sociologists have long asserted that alienation occurs in many forms, as both process and condition, alienation is often conveyed in educational research as being synonymous with burnout—one is either alienated or not, one is burnt out or not. LeCompte's work with Dworkin (1991), which is informed in part by Seeman's theories, connected the construct of alienation to the lives of teachers and students. In an important study, they concluded: "teachers feel that their activities in school have no real purpose and that what they attempt to teach is falling on deaf ears" (p. 157). Powerlessness and normlessness caused estrangement and led teachers to experience alienation as dissatisfaction and disaffection, adopt defensive teaching strategies and ultimately may compel them to either tune out, burn out, or leave the profession altogether. LeCompte and Dworkin write of alienation in relation to classroom autonomy and place alienation-related constructs such as deskilling, "the limiting of teacher autonomy through mandated curricula and policies developed at administrative levels," (deMarrais & LeCompte, 1999, pp. 170–171) at the center of discussions about teachers' lives. Now, I turn attention from alienation to another strain of research devoted to examining the educational space between reality and utopia.

SCHOOL REFORM: A PARADOX OF PROMISE AND FRUSTRATION

The educational history of the United States is replete with legislative, pedagogical, and policy-driven school reform efforts (Spring, 1988;

Tyack & Cuban, 1995; Tyack, Kirst, & Hansot, 1980). Whether we listen to the distant echo of Horace Mann's impassioned calls for the establishment of the common school; recall the proliferation of vocational schools ushered in by the Smith-Hughes Act of 1917; consider Roosevelt's New Deal educational programs, Johnson's Great Society, ESEA, IDEA; or look in today's schoolhouses to witness the unfolding of state responses to 2001's No Child Left Behind Act, it is evident that reform, restructuring, and educational change are longstanding norms (Ravitch, 1983; Strayer, 1933). However, despite this overarching emphasis on change, the preceding list also points out the diversity of perspective among reform strategies. Historically speaking, school reform efforts have focused on changing disparate aspects of education as a means to promote improvement and have varied in scope from top-down whole-system reforms to subtle instructional adjustments borne of individual creativity in single schools (Grant, 1989).

Like their predecessors, contemporary reformers urge educators to pursue school reform from a variety of perspectives. Some focus on facilitating positive change through innovative instructional practices (e.g., Gardner, 2000; McCombs & Quiat, 2002; Swanson & Stevenson, 2002), while others assert that leadership is central to school improvement (e.g., Fullan, 1997; Murphy, Beck, Crawford, Hodges, & McGauphy, 2001; Sergiovanni, 1996). Research also indicates that organizational climate (e.g., Chrispeels, 1997; Fullan, 1993; Smylie & Hart, 2000), high-stakes accountability (e.g., Hess, 2004), or a commitment to multicultural plurality (e.g., Nieto, 2003; Scheurich & Skrla, 2003) are critical for those who seek to promote substantive educational change. Importantly, these various aspects of school reform are not mutually exclusive. While most reformers (I use this term in its broadest sense) call for heightened awareness to one or a combination of these components and still others, they also commonly point out that many factors must be carefully coordinated into a comprehensive model of reform if the work of improving schools is to prove successful (Educational Research Service, 1998).

Ideological debates over how schools should reform have raged for over a century, and solutions and suggestions are vigorously contested from the White House to the schoolhouse (Spring, 1988; Tyack & Cuban, 1995). However, as ideologues wage conceptual battles, thousands of local experiments are already in progress (Ayers, Klonsky, & Lyon, 2000). School-level educational personnel have never waited for consensus or resolution among policymakers before taking action they believe will improve students' educational experiences. In many public schools, teachers, administrators, and instructional support staff embrace change in the name of improvement as an institutional norm. Committed educators in these schools actively seek out and implement reforms that ask them to reconsider or alter central aspects of their professional work. However, while some reforms have inspired positive improvement (e.g., Bensman, 2000), some have failed miserably (e.g., Sarason, 1991, 1996; Fink, 2000), and others have produced mixed results and unintended consequences, both positive and negative (e.g., Brooks, Scribner, & Eferakorho, 2004; Westheimer, 1998). This implementation conundrum—why reforms produce unpredictable results when implemented—has alternately inspired and frustrated educational reformers. While some related questions are answered in research and practice through intense, outstanding, and sustained work, solutions to certain enduring problems remain elusive: How is it that carefully planned reforms implemented by hard-working educators fail to reproduce dramatic results obtained in other settings? What happens when site-based reform implementers attempt to operationalize what appear to be conceptually sound and research-driven improvement programs? In short, what factors facilitate or impede successful school reform and improvement at the building level?

School Reform Implementation: Challenges and Opportunities

Calls for reform of the U.S. education system abound. Some educational stakeholders cite an immediate need to address a slowly improving, but unacceptably large, achievement gap between socioeconomic, racial, and ethnic groups (Johnson, 2002). Business interests have voiced concern that U.S. students are not always at the forefront on analyses of international comparison indicators and that the U.S. educational system is insufficient to obtain desired results in terms of student academic performance (Hess, 2004). Legislative pressure in the form of incentives and mandates tied to increased student achievement, coupled with intensified public scrutiny of student performance at building, district, and state levels has also been a catalyst for an impassioned national dialogue around school improvement (e.g., Gordon, 2003; Glickman, 2004). Importantly, the desire to change and improve schooling for the sake of students comes from within the educational system as well. In many local settings, educators are leading the charge for educational change and reform with exuberance, innovation, and acumen (Barth, 1990; David, 1989). The ongoing "great experiment" of reforming the U.S. education system is well underway in thousands of little red laboratories, as educators "tinker toward utopia" (Tyack & Cuban, 1995).

Nearly all reforms at the school level share the central aim of improving the educational situations of students. However, each reform initiative typically advocates change in different aspects of the school and measures the relative success or failure of the work using dissimilar indicators (U.S. Department of Education, 1998c, p. 7). Depending on the particular needs and resources of the school, many reforms have shown promise. Among strategies reformers promote are systemic reforms (Goertz, Floden, & O'Day, 1995); comprehensive schoolwide reforms (Murphy & Datnow, 2003); restructuring, retiming, and reculturing (Hannay & Ross, 1997); and instructional or curricular alignment (English & Steffy, 2001). Certainly, there are numerous other issues and concerns that demand and receive the concentrated attention of education researchers, policymakers, practitioners, students, and local communities. A 1998 report published by the Educational Research Service summed up much public and professional sentiment:

> Although there is disagreement and heated debate about these issues, there is no disagreement about the central goal: *We should expect more from our students, and schools should be structured in ways that produce high levels of learning for all students* (p. 1).

Yet despite commitment, attention, resources, and widespread agreement that school reform is imperative, some reforms succeed, some fail, and some produce unintended results (Tyack & Cuban, 1995). How then, do seemingly well-designed school reforms go awry upon implementation? Research has identified certain pitfalls that have thwarted successful implementation of many inventive and promising school reform initiatives.

Why Do School Reforms Fail upon Implementation? Educational historians David Tyack and Larry Cuban (1995) suggested that rather than pose the oft-asked question, "How do reforms change schools?" educators should instead try and solve a different quandary: "How do schools change reforms?" Identifying historical patterns in school reform implementation, Tyack and Cuban (1995) observed that "some innovations seem to die on contact with the institutional reality of the school. It is the rare reform that performs and persists precisely according to plan" (p. 60). While the puzzle of site-level implementation failure remains unsolved, one thing seems clear: the importance of the context in which school reform occurs is crucial to realization of reform related goals (Bryk & Driscoll, 1988; Spillane, 2002). Although many innovative and promising reforms have been developed, there is as yet no one-size-fits-every-context prescription for success. A program that helped educators attain goals in one school may fail to produce similar results in another (Little & McLaughlin, 1993). To some degree, building-level school reforms, even if they seem to replicate processes undertaken in other settings, are idiosyncratic and site specific. Put bluntly, context matters. However, researchers have identified several potential barriers to successful implementation of school reform initiatives that occur with some regularity.

Among impediments to successful school reform implementation are:

1. Mismanagement of finances (Odden & Clune, 1995)
2. A lack of value and program commitment among educators (Furman-Brown, 1999)
3. Misalignment of curriculum (Moore, 2001)
4. External politics (Chubb & Moe, 1990; Cibulka & Olsen, 1993)
5. Internal micropolitics (Blase & Anderson, 1995; Hargreaves, 1994)
6. Inequity and inequality related to racial and gender dynamics (Datnow, 1998; Foster, Gomm, & Hammersley, 1996; McLaren, 1989)
7. Incongruence of internal and external accountability systems (Fuhrman & O'Day, 1996; Normore, 2004)
8. Tensions between mandated improvement and the social reality of teachers (Brooks, Scribner, & Eferakorho, 2004; Lieberman, 1999)

9. Poor site-level leadership (Murphy et al., 2001)
10. Limitations imposed by access or facilities (Education Research Service, 1998; Pechman & Fiester, 1994) and
11. Systemic and personal corruption, mistreatment, and abuse among employees in educational settings (Blase & Blase, 2002a, 2003)

Moreover, each school develops its own history of reform, which may make implementation easier or more difficult. In schools with a history of success, educators are more likely to buy into and support new initiatives. Conversely, schools with a poor track record face a greater challenge to implement reforms which will take hold (Comer, Haynes, Joyner, & Ben-Avie, 1996). Some schools seem to get stuck in a cycle. Hess (1999) characterized as "policy churn" (crisis definition → program development → program implementation → program evaluation → crisis redefinition) wherein they fail to obtain improvement and instead return to the point they started when the work of reform began. Churning schools may suffer from years, even decades, of stymied reform efforts despite intense and sustained work. Still other schools establish a history of failure by implementing reforms one on top of each other without ever clearing the slate. Reformers in these schools often encounter layers of bureaucracy and rigmarole left from bygone reforms. Uncoordinated or conflicted programs may persist despite similar initiatives being in place (Bodilly, 1996). Similarly, Newmann, Smith, Allensworth, & Bryk (2001) characterized schools in which "change or improvement strategies that bring attention to a school through numerous program and equipment purchases but fail to build its capacity to improve teaching and learning" (p. 6) as "Christmas tree schools" because programs adorn the school like so many ornaments without having substantive effect.

While lists of key factors gleaned from a review of reform literature are useful when framing a discussion of the challenges facing school reform implementation, they also run the risk of conveying a message that problems are easy to identify and may be dealt with in isolation or in turn. Nothing could be further from the truth. Reformers should expect to encounter a unique conflagration of these challenges, and still others, as they seek to instill positive educational change in a school. As there is no single formula for successful school reform implementation, there is also no prescriptive set of implementation factors that can help reformers avoid failure. However, as researchers have noted potential problems for those who seek to implement meaningful school-level reforms, they have likewise developed promising strategies based on lessons learned from successes.

Successful School Reform Implementation   A great deal of research has focused on the successful implementation of school reforms. While no strategy has emerged as a cure-all, many promising plans and useful concepts have been designed, implemented, and tested (see Pechman & Fiester [1994] for a useful overview).

Importantly, it seems clear that successful reforms are seldom implemented alone or without some kind of agreement (or at least consent) among those who will carry out the plan. McPartland, Balfanz, and Jordan (2002) argue that in order to be successful, "reformers must address school reform at several levels simultaneously" (p. 244). Effective reforms are seldom the work of a few empowered change agents or a single change facilitator. Ideally, all stakeholders should understand the initiative and change their work to support success (Fullan, 1993). School administrators are asked to reconceptualize themselves as facilitator, power sharer, consensus builder, and critical friend (Costa & Kallick, 1993; Crow, Hausman, & Scribner, 2002); staff and the community at large are meant to be fully engaged partners in the educational system (Crowson, 1992); parents are to assume active and supportive roles in the school (Lopez, 2001); and teachers must embrace "a new vision of professionalism," which includes roles such as instructional leaders, curriculum managers, action researchers, technology experts, social justice advocates, and active participants in shared school governance (Spillane, Halverson & Diamond, 2001; Verdugo, Greenberg, Henderson, Uribe Jr., & Schneider, 1997).

Successful school reforms are informed by effective, research-based methods, strategies, and evaluations that examine both intended and unintended outcomes (U.S. Department of Education, 1998a). Although there is widespread disagreement as to what should be measured to adjudge reforms, a common standard is to demand explicitly discernable (i.e., measurable) improvement. Evidence is the watchword of contemporary school reform. While outcome evaluations may focus on student achievement scores on standardized or norm-referenced tests, researchers have cautioned against using such measures as the sole determinant of reform success and instead advocate that reforms seek to capture a more holistic view of school improvement (Murphy et al., 2001). Since not all reforms share the same aim, each should set pertinent and measurable goals and benchmarks according to the scope and purpose of the initiative (U.S. Department of Education, 1998a). School culture, organizational climate, and other indicators may prove useful in evaluating the relative success of a reform (Louis, Kruse, & Marks, 1996). There has been a great deal of reform experimentation over the past several decades, and implementers can draw from many lessons as they design initiatives and adapt them to a specific educational setting (Fullan, 1991). When schools implement research-based reforms, their ability to sustain efforts is enhanced, as implementers are able to learn from the mistakes and triumphs of similar schools (Goertz, Floden, & O'Day, 1995).

Successful school reforms are designed and implemented with aligned components. Whether the reform is comprehensive and school-wide, a single program designed to address a specific problem, or a new initiative that will enhance work already underway, it is important that each reform is incorporated in such a manner that they work together meaningfully (Newmann & Wehlage, 1995). The effective reform is implemented as one in a coordinated collection of integrated components, each of which may directly or indirectly affect instruction, assessment, classroom management, professional development, parental involvement, school management, curriculum, and use of technology. In addition to being a good fit with site-specific educational goals, reformers should also consider how the work contributes to meeting district, state, and national educational benchmarks. By considering reform components in relation to one another, rather than as discrete elements of the educational milieu, school reform can be meaningful, comprehensive, and may have a greater chance of sustainability (U.S. Department of Education, 1998b; Murphy et al., 2001).

A successful school reform receives the support of those who implement the reform, who are in turn supported with adequate resources and by relevant, high-quality professional development (U.S. Department of Education, 1998b). This includes reform-specific training, which may be relatively short and intense, as well as ongoing and sustained professional development over the span of a career. It takes time for educators to learn new content and approaches to the way they conduct their work (Lieberman, 1999). In addition to time, funding is a crucial resource for school reform initiatives. However, it is important to note that availability of funds does not ensure success (Hertling, 1999). Reformers should identify which federal, state, and local resources are available to the school and devise a plan to coordinate these services to support and sustain the school reform effort (U.S. Department of Education, 1998b). Reformers should also pay careful attention to the sequencing of reform elements, and design reasonable and well-timed systems of support that allow implementers to foresee potential areas of need rather than react to crises (Fullan, 1993; Goertz, Floden, & O'Day, 1995).

Successful school reforms seek to build a professional community within the school and also develop stable alliances with external stakeholders such as parents, district personnel, and local and state-level officials (Furman, 2002; Spring, 1988). Transparent, effective, and meaningful communication among all stakeholders is important. Reforms are likely to receive more support if implementers attend to the fluid needs of school professionals while also identifying and supporting the corollary needs of parents and local community stakeholders when planning and implementing school improvement activities. As reforms ask educators to alter their orientation, supporters outside the school system must also learn and change if they are to buoy work done in the school. When relevant and possible, attention should be paid to enhancing the capacity of parents, public, and community organizations and businesses to understand and participate in the reform efforts (U.S. Department of Education, 1998c; Goertz, Floden, & O'Day, 1995).

SCHOOL REFORM AND ALIENATION AT WINTERVALLEY HIGH

Studying teachers engaged in intense school reform through the empirical domain of alienation afforded an interesting lens through which to view their work. Yet, while the sociological theory I used to frame the study initially was helpful, data soon suggested that alienation was (at best) only half of the conceptual framework needed to explain the experience of teaching at Wintervalley. While Seeman's empirical domain of alienation was a helpful way to investigate teacher alienation, it failed to give reasons for too many teacher experiences and could not capture some of the truly rewarding moments teachers related. Wintervalley was a school where teachers were at once occupied with meaningful and meaningless work; were committed to certain values and experienced normlessness with respect to policies and people; were isolated from peers, colleagues, and programs yet were included in some curriculum, schoolwide, and division-level decisions; were engaged with students and colleagues but estranged from some activities they viewed as essential to facilitate an exceptional learning environment; they were also powerless to effect change in some instances while wielding various degrees and types of efficacy in others. Teachers' experiences suggested that in addition to an empirical domain of alienation, there was also an empirical domain of authenticity comprised of efficacy, meaningfulness, value commitment, inclusion, and engagement. I came to suspect that these two empirical domains were in direct tension with one another (see figure 11.1), and while a good deal of data seemed to support my suspicion, I am hesitant to assert more than suspicion until more focused inquiry looks at these relationships. For the most part, teachers' experiences constantly slid back and forth among the ellipses in figure 11.1, moving closer to alienation or authenticity depending on the situation and the individual's reaction to a situation at a particular time.

Alienation	. . . .	Authenticity
Powerlessness	. . . .	Efficacy
Meaninglessnes	. . . .	Meaningfulness
Normlessness	. . . .	Value Commitment
Isolation	. . . .	Inclusion
Estrangement	. . . .	Engagement

Figure I I.I.   The Empirical Domains of Alienation and Authenticity

In the midst of seemingly contradictory yet related states and situations, individual teachers largely maintained a steadfast devotion to classroom teaching. Observation and interview data supported the notion that most teacher alienation occurred in extra-instructional situations. Many teachers reported that various forms of alienation increased in intensity and frequency the more removed an activity was from classroom-based instruction. Teachers were willing to make substantive sacrifices with regard to time and effort as long as there was evidence, or at least a belief, that their endeavor would contribute positively to an enhanced learning environment for students. To this end, many teachers bore arduous burdens—giving up planning time, staying after school, working on holidays and weekends—as long as they felt it was for the sake of students. In a sense, these teachers accepted alienation willingly, engaging in activities they knew would render them powerless, isolated, and so forth for what they believed was the good of the community, a friend, or to facilitate a learning opportunity for students. For certain teachers, such activity strengthened the bonds between them and their peers and students (the bonds between A and B suggested near the beginning of this chapter were fortified).

It is possible that as authentic experiences compounded, teachers came to feel more able to express and explore aspects of their work and professional relationships that seemed previously out of their reach; their practice became more authentic and less alienating. However, while this selfless, collegial, and meaningful behavior was evident in many facets of professional life—most notably among peer teachers in an academic division and toward students—it was not shared across the school. Engagement and inclusion gave way to estrangement and isolation the further teachers strayed from their academic divisions. For example, if asked to serve on a schoolwide interdisciplinary task force, they related a stronger experience of alienation than when working with their content-area peers.

For Wintervalley teachers, alienation existed in relation to both time and space. Most teachers had their own room, or at least a room in which they team-taught. This room was important as a consistent enclave of personal space during trying times. As teachers gained professional experience in the classroom, as a member of their academic division, or as an actor in the schoolwide political arena, they developed values and strategies that would allow them to survive, if not thrive, in other areas of the schoolhouse. Predictably, some teachers possessed or learned more political savvy than others. These more politically involved teachers were able to engage most meaningfully in schoolwork beyond the boundaries of their classroom and division. Teachers with less political acumen, or simply distaste for political dimensions of school practice, often disengaged from the schoolwide community and instead focused their attention on the areas of practice where they felt most duty bound and committed, student and intradivisional personal and professional relationships. For the most part, such teachers still functioned positively and worked hard within their classrooms and divisions, but felt estranged and/or normless in other school settings.

An experience of estrangement, and also of normlessness, seemed more acute among longer serving teachers. Some veterans, though not all, intimated a sense that things had been better in the past—that the school's social structures had eroded as a result of years of dynamic school reform and also because of an increase in the school's student and teacher populations. Seemingly positive changes were often accompanied by unwelcome consequences, and many felt that the school no longer stood for what it had in the past. This caused some veteran teachers to feel disconnected, discontented, and uncertain of their professional futures, or indeed even in relation to their current work. To these teachers, alienation was an institution and constant companion. This particular perception, common among veterans and noticeably absent among younger teachers, may suggest that situational alienating experiences can accrue and become a state of being that permeates professional life (a notion explored philosophically by Schmitt [2004]). Perhaps, as LeCompte and Dworkin (1991) suggested, longitudinal compounding of alienating experiences is a way of explaining the phenomenon of teacher burnout. Another plausible explanation was posited by Huberman (1993), who found that engagement and estrangement were highly correlated in teachers' stories of personal development over the course of their careers. Although the central focus of Huberman's inquiry was neither estrangement nor engagement, he recognized their conceptual connection and suggested that engagement gave way to estrangement, or vice versa, at various points in teachers' careers (pp. 79–81).

As engagement in school reform efforts was a central part of professional life at Wintervalley, school policies related to reform efforts had a great impact on teachers' individual experiences at the school. Structures like professional learning teams, shared planning teams, and team-teaching pairs, all features adopted from various school reform initiatives, were variously alienating or a step toward a more authentic work life. While no policy components were universally alienating or authentic, it was evident that a great number of teachers felt most alienated when forced to work on or with policies that dealt with issues outside of the instructional and curricular areas of their work. This was in part due to an impression that their work in extracurricular committees was not taken seriously and did not impact the policymaking processes of the school. From these teachers' perspectives, the actual shared decision-making processes of the school were a far cry from the scheme portrayed in official documents or embodied in the motivational posters on the walls of meeting rooms. To these teachers, a more accurate metaphor for school decision making might be the garbage can—used by Cohen, March, and Olsen (1972) to describe a process whereby decisions are made without any clear connection between policy production and the decision-making process.

At Wintervalley, power and institutional transparency played significant but ambiguous roles, and this uncertainty had a disparate effect on teachers. For all the talk of schoolwide shared governance, collective decision making, and democratic principles, Wintervalley operated as a top-down, hierarchical organization. Setting the espoused order aside, the principal was nested at the apex, just above (or perhaps equal to) the Star Chamber (see chapter 5). The executive council was below the Star Chamber, with PLTs and SPTs, representing the majority of teachers, at the bottom. Although officially PLTs and SPTs were the voice of teachers in governance, they were connected to the school's informal and systemic elite only by the thinnest of organizational threads. A vast majority of teachers had little observable or reported power to impact school policy.

As the single most powerful individual in the school, the principal played a key role as an agent of alienation among teachers. Importantly, while it would have been easy for teachers to blame many of the school's alienation-related problems on Dr. Weleck, few were willing to do so. While teachers interpreted the principal's behaviors and surmised his motives in different ways, many saw the principal as being as much a victim of alienation as anyone else. In many teachers' eyes, Dr. Weleck was committed to the success of the school, the teachers, and the students, but unable to successfully implement the necessary reforms to move Wintervalley nearer his (or the collective) vision of the good school. He was alienated in that he had an earnest desire to facilitate progress, but lacked the technical or interpersonal ability to realize his vision.

Many teachers commented that the principal's weakness was uncritical gullibility rather then Machiavellian intent. For all his good intentions, Dr. Weleck was easily and consistently persuaded to adopt the agendas of a silver-tongued informal elite (Mills, 1959). To many teachers, this was the key power dynamic that affected the school, an instrumental form of manipulative power exerted by follower over leader. Whether or not it was wholly true, many teachers' perception was that a small cadre of teachers wielded a great degree of control over school reform and policy. In these teachers' estimation, there was an in-group and an out-group that exerted more control than the principal might guess. That being said, most teachers were unwilling to totally excuse Dr. Weleck from responsibility for the ineffectiveness of the increasingly dysfunctional formal governance structure dominated by Star Chamber teachers. Many teachers felt that a principal should be more astute, a better judge of character, and more considered in his decision making than Dr. Weleck. Some teachers even saw Dr. Weleck as an incompetent dupe or simply a person not attuned to the school's real needs (see chapter 7). To these teachers, Dr. Weleck understood only a few people's *wants* as the school's agenda rather than the *needs* of the school community—he mistook the strains of a modest ensemble for the chorus of the choir.

The teachers in this study experienced alienation, but that is only part of the Wintervalley story. Throughout this book are examples of teachers who described meaningful connections to their students while at the same time completely (or partially) disengaging from colleagues in other departments or rejecting certain school policies. Some teachers spoke of the beauty of power wielded toward the end of inclusion and community building and a moment later decried their impotence as "empowered members" of the school's farcical shared-governance structures. To some, the school's community seemed a healthy and vibrant model of collaborative endeavor, while for others the school community made them feel as ostracized as Charlotte Perkins Gilman's heroine in "The

Yellow Wallpaper"—a woman driven mad by stifling conventions insensitive to her unique insight and talent. Moreover, each teacher reacted to his or her experiences of alienation and authenticity differently (e.g., anger, frustration, apathy, self-selected isolation, etc.). As such, while there were some similarities among teachers, in the case of Wintervalley High School, it is incorrect to characterize the entire school community, or even whole subcommunities, as being alienated or free. Wintervalley was a school of *alienations*, not of alienation.

Interestingly, although the principal was formally the most powerful school professional in Wintervalley, it seemed in many instances that he was one in alienation with the teachers. Dr. Weleck was powerful and manipulated, and many teachers characterized him as a victim of his own strength—driven by a desire to move the school toward a positive vision, yet undone by an inability to identify when he was being influenced by members of the school's informal (and, at times, deviant) elite. Like teachers, the principal could not be treated as a flat character but was rather a paradox; his professional existence was in many ways an enigma of confounding qualities, some of which could be explained as operating between alienation and authenticity.

Although education researchers have addressed some of the qualities here associated with alienation, the field has yet to adequately examine the relationships among and between the qualities I suggest constitute these two domains. This study is a step in that direction, but only a modest one. Clearly, this research must be followed by sustained and substantial inquiry if lessons gleaned from this study are to be regarded with any semblance of veracity. Still, while this study suggests avenues for future inquiry, there might also be some points for those working in schools to ponder.

IMPLICATIONS

Findings generated from a site-specific qualitative study such as this should not be generalized to other settings without a great degree of caution (Wolcott, 1994, 1997). However, lessons learned from Wintervalley High may be useful to educators working under or studying conditions of sustained and intense school reform implementation. First, reformers must strive to directly and transparently connect various components and tasks associated with reform to classroom instruction. It is not enough to coordinate various components of a reform with each other; they must also be coordinated with the instructional work of teachers and this alignment should be clearly articulated. Reformers should provide clear answers to the questions that Wintervalley's teachers repeatedly asked: "How does participating in this activity make the school more conducive to student learning?" And, by extension, "How does participating in this reform activity make me a better teacher?" Whenever possible, answers to these questions should be answered with data, gathered and analyzed systematically as a central component of the reform initiative (Johnson, 2002; Murphy et al., 2001). Teachers should be included in all parts of this process when possible, as participating in evaluation of the work can provide ongoing feedback and give ownership of the work to those who implement it.

Second, reformers should be sensitive to how their work, and the work they ask of teachers, impacts the speed at which they conduct daily activities. This acceleration of professional speed is at least a twofold phenomenon. As reform activities may increase the pace of *everyday* work by making time a scarce resource, they may also tend to accelerate the work of the entire institution in a way that also affects teachers *longitudinally* over the course of an academic year and over a span of years. Further research is needed to investigate speed-of-the-day and speed-of-implementation. However, data from this study suggest that teachers may partially adjudge the success of a reform in part based on (1) the way a reform impacts the speed of their workday, and (2) the rate at which new reforms are adopted, abandoned, and implemented. Hurtling from reform activity to reform activity without pause may cause teachers to view changes as a succession of discontinuous failures rather than as an aligned and sustained commitment to improvement.

Third, since there is a finite number of tasks to which a teacher can attend during any given time period—an instructional period, an hour, a day, a week, a semester, a year—reformers would be wise to ensure that initiatives do not prioritize duties in a way that distracts teachers from instructionally related activities. Reformers should strive to remain sensitive to the additional demands that reform efforts place on teachers and consider how reforms intended to facilitate improvement and progress might actually distract teachers from serving students in their instructional capacities. Constant, clear, and honest communication between stakeholders around this issue might help ameliorate teachers' sense of reform saturation (Goertz, Floden, & O'Day, 1995). Perhaps equipping educators with the language of alienation, or at least familiarizing them with the concept of professional saturation (see chapter 2) would help them be more specific in their expression of discontent. Adopting common terminology might be a first step toward overcoming these issues.

Fourth, no school reform or school reform component should be conceived as one-size-fits-all. Reformers might offer varied and/or flexible ways for teachers to contribute to a reform initiative. A teacher may be committed to and engaged in her instructional work and her relationships with peers, students, parents, and administrators, but also feel that a particular element of reform does not contribute positively to her work. Flexibility in implementation, coupled with the realization that disengagement or dissatisfaction in certain domains of professional life does not constitute *total* disengagement or insubordination is important. Rather than creating punitive policies that threaten harsh consequences for teachers who refuse to participate in the "new way," reformers might instead seek to offer several options for teachers to substantively contribute to reform efforts. While some teachers enjoy participating through shared governance structures, others may prefer a different challenge such as peer coaching, curriculum development, or by heading a program they develop themselves that can focus on a particular aspect of reform.

Fifth, it is important for reformers to understand the context in which school reform is implemented. Is there a legacy of success or failure? Wintervalley seemed to be a Christmas tree school (Newmann et al., 2001) trapped in a cycle of policy churn (Hess, 1999), but this possibility was ignored because reform dialogue did not occur in a historical context. Initiatives were not considered in relation to reforms or data gathered in the past and it was common for programs to offer (or demand) overlapping services which led to a multilayered and at times conflicted bureaucratic structure. Some important questions were not asked: Which programs have enjoyed success and what indicators support the notion that they were a success? How will adopting any given initiative add to or detract from the work already in place? Reformers ignore context at the peril of their programs. Taking the time to understand institutional norms before a reform is put in place and then seeking to ascertain how the reform affects those norms during implementation may be a key to success.

Finally, it may be necessary to consider that reforms do not necessarily succeed or fail because of the personnel who implement them, but rather as a result of those people interacting in a particular context at a particular time. This seemingly obvious assertion might actually suggest a radical change in the way reforms are designed and implemented. The Wintervalley study suggests that leadership or reform activities that occur *between* those who implement school reform are at least as critical as the individual characteristics of reformers or the institution of organizational structures meant to encourage effective change. Importantly, in this study alienation was conceived as the "culprit" that undid reform efforts, *not* individual people or organizational units. In many strains of school reform research, individual characteristics and roles are conceived as the unit of analysis (or, alternately, as the dependent variable) rather than the actual activities in which they engage in situ (see Spillane, Diamond, Burch, Hallett, Jita, & Zoltners [2002] and Spillane, Halverson, & Diamond [2001] for more on this concept). This research may urge a rejection of the idea that part of "getting it right" is seeking the proper mix of suitably devoted employees or implementing faithfully each step of an eleven-step reform program. It may be more important to focus on how reformers, whether they "buy in" to what is happening or not, interact in a specific context and destroy or create reforms as a perpetual and nonlinear process. A pedagogical shift toward reconceptualizing school reform as something enacted by individuals and groups—as fluid action carried out in shifting and idiosyncratic contextual environments—rather than as something which flows necessarily out of individual "hero" teachers or administrators, or any particular process or structure, suggests that reforms can fail or succeed anywhere despite the (positive or negative) characteristics of the individuals who implement reform. Considered from this perspective, reform happens in the space between people rather than to them, reform is practiced as engagement rather than enactment, and is organic rather than linear. It has less to do with whether or not people play the proper roles and more to do with the collision of roles and activities in the place we call school.

School reform implementation can be difficult, even when conducted in accord with well-designed, research-driven approaches. As educators seek to identify ways they might improve the educational experiences of students, they should also be sensitive to how implementing reforms changes the daily work and activities of building-level professionals. By designing reforms with flexibility (allowing people to contribute in ways they find personally and professionally meaningful) and paying special attention to the way initiatives impact the manner in which educators conduct their work, the amount of duties they are required to undertake, and the foci of those activities, success might have a better chance to take hold.

METHODOLOGICAL APPENDIX

Merriam (1991) likens a research design to an architectural blueprint. She explains the analogy thusly:

> It is a plan for assembling, organizing, and integrating information (data), and it results in a specific end product (research findings). The selection of a particular design is determined by how the problem is shaped, by the questions it raises, and by the type of end product desired. (p. 6)

The blueprint of this study began, as do all blueprints, with a blank piece of paper and an idea. Jay Scribner, one of my mentors at the University of Missouri, asked me (and fellow graduate student Jite Eferakorho) to participate in a study at Wintervalley High School as a research assistant. Over the course of an academic year, he showed me the ropes and helped guide me through the process of collecting and analyzing data. Jay was an excellent mentor, and although neither of us planned it that way, that year became the first of two years I would spend at Wintervalley; the first under his tutelage and the second on my own for the dissertation. This book drew from data collected during both of those years. For anyone interested in getting a look at Wintervalley from a different perspective, some of our findings from that first year were published in the *Journal of School Leadership* (Brooks,

Scribner, & Eferakorho, 2004). Still, while I was happy with the article and I had learned a lot working with Jay, I was unsatisfied. My discontent stemmed from a certainty that we hadn't captured more than a tiny, albeit useful, slice of what it meant to teach and lead at a rapidly reforming school. My dissertation became an attempt to investigate some of the issues we set aside to focus on teacher leadership.

As that first year at Wintervalley progressed, I began to notice a familiar refrain running through many of the interviews:

"We're trying, but we don't have the support or the resources to . . ."

"The students work hard, but their lives are difficult and complicated . . ."

"The curriculum is fine and our test scores are good, but . . ."

"Our leadership is fine, but . . ."

"I enjoy teaching, but . . ."

"It's a great school, but . . ."

"but . . ."

"but . . ."

"but . . ."

For Wintervalley's reputation as a successful school, and by many measures I suppose it was, something wasn't quite right. Despite the best efforts of hardworking and passionate professionals, there was discontent. But how to study it?

I spent that first year rereading many of the books I had been assigned throughout my doctoral course work, looking for a study or approach that would help provide some direction. Eventually, I came to a short passage about alienation in Kathleen Bennett deMarrais and Margaret LeCompte's (1999) book *The Way Schools Work*. From there, I read a longer study LeCompte had done with Anthony Dworkin (1991) that used Melvin Seeman's work on alienation as a conceptual framework. I was on my way!

I read a great deal more about alienation, school reform, and qualitative research methodology. In this space, I will describe how the last of this trio informed decisions I made throughout the study. You can read what I discovered about alienation and school reform in chapter 11 of this book. I apologize in advance for using too-technical language throughout this section, but in some ways it is necessary to explain exactly how I approached the study.

DATA COLLECTION

I took a qualitative approach to examine alienation among teachers engaged in school reform efforts in a particular public secondary school. I chose these methods because the nature of the research demanded an integrated and comprehensive examination of multiple perspectives and data (Fielding & Lee, 1998; Silverman, 2001). Data collection began shortly before the Fall 2001 school semester and continued through the end of the 2003 academic calendar. During this time, I conducted seventy-two observations in naturalistic settings such as classroom instructional periods, faculty meetings, and curriculum planning sessions (Bogdan & Biklen, 1998, pp. 4–5). In addition to gathering data through observation, I completed forty-two interviews and engaged in countless informal exchanges with school personnel (Bogdan & Biklen, 1998). Interviews were open-ended, and although these went in many different directions as the study developed, I initially prompted participants to explain their perceptions of themes identified through my literature review of alienation and school reform (Silverman, 2001). Interviews ranged in duration from forty-five minutes to three hours, depending on teacher availability, and were transcribed verbatim (Wolcott, 1997).

As the goal was to gather data from as many perspectives as possible, participant sampling procedures were of critical importance in this study. Specifically, I employed a combination of purposive and network selection techniques (Bogdan & Biklen, 1998, p. 65; Whyte, 1993). Initial group observations in various academic departments led to identification of teachers who might be most willing to share and articulate their perceptions about the school's reform efforts. After approaching and gaining access from a few teachers, network selection began, which was characterized by interviewee recommendation. Upon completing an interview, I asked each interviewee to suggest other teachers who might be willing to participate in the study, based on expertise, interest, or accessibility (Merriam, 1991, p. 51). Building on these connections, I interviewed and observed "new" participants and accompanied them to other meetings and informal group events. Approaching teachers in these settings allowed me to meet teachers outside closed or preferential social circles. In addition to building a network through participant recommendation, I also purposively sought participants who were not recommended in order to obtain multiple perspectives. This sampling technique, used in a classic sociological study by William Foote Whyte (1993), allowed for broad data collection from multiple perspectives and also made it possible to create a network of participants that crossed departmental boundaries and social cliques, and was diverse with respect to age, experience, gender, and ethnicity (pp. 279–373).

I also collected technical and nontechnical documents such as memos, strategic planning documents, organizational charts, brochures, meeting agendas, newsletters, participant's notes, and so forth that were germane to the study (Strauss & Corbin, 1998, p. 35).

DATA ANALYSIS

I coded interview, observation, and document-derived data thematically. After gathering data based on questions specific to the empirical domain of alienation, I used open coding procedures to "force open the research by encouraging the analyst to get into the data, to make some initial, if only tentative, interpretations and to gain a sense of where to go and what to do next" (Fielding & Lee, 1998, p. 32). These open codes were established by analyzing data via microanalytic techniques and the constant comparative method (Strauss & Corbin, 1998, p. 57). The resultant open codes were analyzed for thematic similarity, which led to the establishment of axial codes. Once axial codes were developed, relationships between these axial codes were again analyzed for similarity, which suggested broader, more abstract categories of data. Categories are here defined as "concepts that stand for phenomena" (Strauss & Corbin, 1998, p. 101).

As discrete categories emerged, they were explored further through directive field-based data collection. Categories eventually became theoretically saturated, as evidenced by increasingly redundant data (Strauss & Corbin, 1997, 1998). When theoretical saturation became apparent, the empirical and conceptual relationships between categories were explored to develop themes. The themes developed by this process are the chapters of this book.

REFERENCES

Akhmatova, A. (1989). *Poem without a hero and selected poems* (L. Mayhew, Trans.). Oberlin, OH: Oberlin College Press.

Ayers, W. C., Klonsky, M., & Lyon, G. (Eds.). (2000). *A simple justice: The challenge of small schools*. New York: Teachers College Press.

Bakarat, H. (1969). Alienation: A process of encounter between utopia and reality. *British Journal of Sociology, 20*(1), pp. 1–10.

Bakkenes, I., Brabander, C., & Imants, J. (1999). Teacher isolation and communication network analysis in primary schools. *Educational Administration Quarterly, (35)*2, pp. 166–202.

Barth, R. S. (1990). *Improving schools from within: Teachers, parents, and principals can make the difference*. San Francisco: Jossey-Bass.

Beauvoir, S. (1975). *The second sex* (B. Frechtman, Trans.). New York: Philosophical Library.

Beauvoir, S. (1982). *The ethics of ambiguity*. (B. Frechtman, Trans.). Secaucus, NJ: Citadel Press Library.

Bensman, D. (2000). *Central Park East and its graduates*. New York: Teachers College Press.

Blase J., & Anderson, G. L. (1995). *The micropolitics of educational leadership: From control to empowerment*. London: Cassell.

Blase, J., & Blase, J. (2002a). The dark side of leadership: Teacher perspectives of principal mistreatment. *Educational Administration Quarterly, (38)*5, pp. 671–727.

Blase, J., & Blase, J. (2002b). The micropolitics of instructional supervision: A call for research. *Educational Administration Quarterly, (38)*1, pp. 6–44.

Blase, J., & Blase, J. (2003). *Breaking the silence: Overcoming the problem of principal mistreatment of teachers*. Thousand Oaks, CA: Corwin Press.

Bodilly, S. (1996). *Lessons from New American Schools Development Corporation's demonstration phase*. Santa Monica, CA: RAND.

Bogdan, R. C., & Biklen, S. K. (1998). *Qualitative research for education: An introduction to theory and methods*. Boston: Allyn & Bacon.

Bogler, R. (2001). The influence of leadership style on teacher job satisfaction. *Educational Administration Quarterly, (37)*5, pp. 662–683.

Bourdieu, P., & Passeron, J. (1977). *Reproduction in education, society and culture*. London: Sage.

Brooks, J. S., Scribner, J. P., & Eferakorho, J. (2004). Teacher leadership in the context of whole-school reform. *Journal of School Leadership, (14)*3, 242–265.

Bryk, A., Camburn, E., & Louis, K. S. (1999). Professional community in Chicago elementary schools: Facilitating factors and organizational consequences. *Educational Administration Quarterly, 35* (Suppl.), 751–781.

Bryk, A., & Driscoll, M. E. (1988). *The high school as community: Contextual influences and consequences for students and teachers*. Madison, WI: National Center on Effective Secondary Schools.

Buber, M. (1958). *I and thou* (R. G. Smith, Trans.). New York: Scribner's.

Camus, A. (1942/1988). *The stranger* (M. Ward, Trans.). New York: Vintage.

Camus, A. (1955). *The myth of Sisyphus and other essays* (J. O'Brien, Trans.). New York: Vintage.

Céline, L. F. (1934). *Journey to the end of the night* (R. Manheim, Trans.). New York: New Directions.

Chrispeels, J. H. (1997). Educational policy implementation in a shifting political climate: The California experience. *American Educational Research Journal, 34*, 453–481.

Chubb, J., & Moe, T. (1990). *Politics, markets, and America's schools*. Washington, DC: Brookings Institute.

Cibulka, J. G., & Olsen, F. I. (1993). The organization and politics of the Milwaukee public school system, 1920–1986. In J. L. Rury & F. A. Cassell (Eds.), *Seeds of crisis: Public schooling in Milwaukee since 1920* (pp. 73–109). Madison: University of Wisconsin Press.

Cisneros, S. (1991). *The house on Mango Street*. New York: Vintage.

Cohen, M. D., March, J. G., & Olsen, J. P. (1972). A garbage can model of organizational choice. *Administrative Science Quarterly, 17*(1), 1–25.

Comer, J. P., Haynes, N. M., Joyner, E. T., & Ben-Avie, M. (1996). *Rallying the whole village: The Comer process for reforming education.* New York: Teachers College Press.

Costa, A. L., & Kallick, B. (1993). Through the lens of a critical friend. *Educational Leadership, 51*(2), 49–51.

Crow, G. C., Hausman, C. S., & Scribner, J. P. (2002). Reshaping the role of the school principal. In J. Murphy (Ed.), *The educational leadership challenge: Redefining leadership for the 21st century* (pp. 189–210). Chicago: University of Chicago Press.

Crowson, R. L. (1992). *School-community relations, under reform.* Berkeley, CA: McCutchan.

Datnow, A. (1998). *The gender politics of educational change.* London: Falmer Press.

David, J. L. (1989). *Restructuring in progress: Lessons from pioneering districts.* Washington, DC: National Governors' Association.

DeMarrais, K. B., & LeCompte, M. D. (1999). *The ways schools work.* New York: Longman.

Durkheim, E. (1893/1997). *The division of labor in society.* New York: Free Press.

Durkheim, E. (1897/1997). *Suicide.* New York: Free Press.

Education Research Service. (1998). *Comprehensive models for school improvement: Finding the right match and making it work.* Arlington, VA: Author.

English, F. W., & Steffy, B. E. (2001). *Deep curriculum alignment: Creating a level playing field for all children on high-stakes tests of educational accountability.* Lanham, MD: Scarecrow Press.

Fielding, N. G., & Lee, R. M. (1998). *Computer analysis and qualitative research.* London: Sage.

Fink, D. (2000). *Good schools/Real schools.* New York: Teachers College Press.

Foster, P., Gomm, R., & Hammersley, M. (1996). *Constructing educational inequality.* Washington, DC: Falmer Press.

Friedman, I. A. (1991). High- and low-burnout schools: School culture aspects of teacher burnout. *Journal of Educational Research, (84)*6, pp. 325–33.

Fromm, E. (1941/1965). *Escape from freedom.* New York: Avon Books.

Fuhrman, S. H., & O'Day, J. A. (1996). *Rewards and reform.* San Francisco: Jossey-Bass.

Fullan, M. (1991). *The new meaning of educational change.* New York: Teachers College Press.

Fullan, M. (1993). *Change forces: Probing the depths of educational reform.* London: Falmer Press.

Fullan, M. (1997). *The challenge of school change: A collection of articles.* Arlington Heights, IL: IRI/Skylight Training.

Furman, G. C. (Ed.). (2002). *School as community: From promise to practice.* New York: SUNY Press.

Furman-Brown, G. (1999). Editor's foreword: School as community. *Educational Administration Quarterly, 35*(1), 6–12.

Gardner, H. (2000). *The disciplined mind: Beyond facts and standardized tests, the K–12 education that every child deserves.* East Rutherford, NJ: Penguin USA.

Gilman, S. P. (1991). The yellow wallpaper. In J. E. Miller Jr. (Ed.), *Civil war to the present: Heritage of American literature* (pp. 506–516). San Diego: Harcourt Brace Jovanovich.

Giroux, H. (1983a). Theories of reproduction and resistance in the new sociology of education. *Harvard Educational Review, 53,* 257–293.

Giroux, H. (1983b). *Theory and resistance in education: A pedagogy for the opposition.* Hadley, MA: Bergin & Garvey.

Glickman, C. D. (Ed.). (2004). *Letters to the next president: What we can do about the real crisis in public education.* New York: Teachers College Press.

Goertz, M. E., Floden, R. E., & O'Day, J. (1995). *Studies of education reform: Systemic reform, Volume I: Findings and conclusions.* Washington, DC: U.S. Department of Education.

Gordon, D. T. (Ed.). (2003). *A nation reformed? American education 20 years after A Nation at Risk.* Cambridge, MA: Harvard University Press.

Grant, G. (1989). *The world we created at Hamilton High.* Cambridge, MA: Harvard University Press.

Grimmett, P. P., & Neufeld, J. (1994). *Teacher development and the struggle for authenticity.* New York: Teachers College Press.

Grotius, H. (1853). *De jure belli ac pacis* (W. Whewell, Trans.). London: John W. Parker.

Hannay, L. M., & Ross, J. A. (1997). Initiating secondary school reform: The dynamic relationship between restructuring, reculturing, and retiming. *Educational Administration Quarterly, 33* (Suppl.), 576–603.

Hargreaves, A. (1994). *Changing teachers, changing times: Teachers' work and culture in the postmodern age.* New York: Teachers College Press.

Haser, S. G., & Ilham, N. (2003). Teacher job satisfaction in a year-round school. *Educational Leadership, (60)*8, pp. 65–67.

Hertling, E. (1999, July). Implementing whole-school reform: ERIC Digest 128. Retrieved October 31, 2003, from http://eric.uoregon.edu/publications/digests/ digest128.html.

Hess, F. M. (1999). *Spinning wheels: The politics of urban school reform*. Washington, DC: Brookings Institute.

Hess, F. M. (2004). *Common sense school reform*. New York: Palgrave Macmillan.

Hesse, H. (1965/1999). *Demian*. New York: Perennial.

Hong, L. (1996). Surviving school reform: A year in the life of one school. New York: Teachers College Press.

Horney, K. (1939). *New ways in psychoanalysis*. New York: W. W. Norton.

Horney, K. (1945). *Our inner conflicts*. New York: W. W. Norton.

Huberman, M. (1993). *The lives of teachers*. New York: Teachers College Press.

Israel, J. (1971). *Alienation: From Marx to modern sociology*. Boston, MA: Allyn & Bacon.

Johnson, R. S. (2002). *Using data to close the achievement gap: How to measure equity in our schools*. Thousand Oaks, CA: Corwin Press.

Kaufmann, W. (1970). The inevitability of alienation. In R. L. Schacht, *Alienation* (pp. xv–lvii). Garden City, NY: Anchor Books.

Kaufmann, W. (1975). *Existentialism from Dostoyevsky to Sartre*. New York: New American Library.

Kierkegaard, S. (1986). *Fear and trembling* (A. Hannay, Trans.). New York: Viking.

LeCompte, M. D., & Dworkin, A. G. (1991). *Giving up on school: Teacher burnout and student dropout*. Newbury Park, CA: Corwin Press.

Lieberman, A. (1999). *Teachers—Transforming their world and their work*. New York: Teachers College Press.

Little, J. W., & McLaughlin, M. W. (Eds.). (1993). *Teachers work: Individuals, colleagues, and contexts*. New York: Teachers College Press.

Lopez, G. R. (2001). The value of hard work: Lessons on parent involvement from an (im)migrant household. *Harvard Educational Review, 71*, 416–437.

Lortie, D. C. (1975). *Schoolteacher: A sociological study*. Chicago: University of Chicago Press.

Louis, K. S., Kruse, S. D., & Marks, H. M. (1996). Schoolwide professional community. In F. M. Newmann & Associates (Eds.), *Authentic achievement: Restructuring schools for intellectual quality* (pp. 179–203). San Francisco: Jossey-Bass.

McCombs, B. L., & Quiat, M. (2002). What makes a comprehensive school reform model learner centered? *Urban Education, 37*(4), 476–96.

McLaren, P. (1989). *Life in schools: An introduction to critical pedagogy in the foundations of education*. New York: Longman.

McPartland, J. M., Balfanz, R., & Jordan, W. J. (2002). Promising solutions for the least productive American high schools. In S. Stringfield & D. Land

(Eds.), *Educating at-risk students* (pp. 148–170). The 101st Yearbook of the National Society for the Study of Education, part 2. Chicago: University of Chicago Press.

Megged, A. (1999). The religious context of an "unholy marriage": Elite alienation and popular unrest in the indigenous communities of Chiapa, 1570–1680. *Ethnohistory, 46*(1), pp. 149–172.

Merriam, S. B. (1991). *Case study research in education: A qualitative approach.* San Francisco: Jossey-Bass.

Merton, R. (1957). *Social theory and social structure.* Glencoe, IL: The Free Press.

Merz, C. & Furman, G. (1997). *Community and schools: Promise and paradox.* New York: Teachers College Press.

Mills, C. W. (1959). *The power elite.* New York: Oxford University Press.

Moore, A. (2001). Teacher development and curriculum reform. *Journal of Education Policy, (16)*3, 269–77.

Murphy, J., Beck, L. G., Crawford, M., Hodges, A., & McGauphy, C. L. (2001). *The productive high school: Creating personalized academic communities.* Thousand Oaks, CA: Corwin Press.

Murphy, J., & Datnow, A. (2003). *Leadership for school reform: Lessons from comprehensive school reform designs.* Thousand Oaks, CA: Corwin Press.

Neill, A. S. (1960). *Summerhill school: A new view of childhood.* New York: St. Martin's Press.

Newmann, F. M., Smith, B., Allensworth, E., & Bryk, A. S. (2001). *School instructional program coherence: Benefits and challenges, improving Chicago's schools.* Chicago: Consortium on Chicago School Research.

Newmann, F. M., & Wehlage, G. C. (1995). *Successful school restructuring.* Madison, WI: Center on Organization and Restructuring of Schools.

Nieto, S. (2003). *What keeps teachers going?* New York: Teachers College Press.

Nietzsche, F. (1967). *Beyond good and evil* (W. Kaufmann, Trans.). New York: Random House.

Nietzsche, F. (1986). *Human, all too human* (R. J. Hollingdale, Trans.). Boston, MA: Cambridge University Press.

Normore, A. H. (2004). The edge of chaos: School administrators and accountability. *Journal of Educational Administration, 42*(1), 55–77.

Odden, A. R., & Clune, W. (1995). Improving education productivity and school finance. *Educational Researcher, 24*(9), 6–10.

Pechman, E., & Fiester, L. (1994). *Implementing schoolwide projects: An idea book for educators.* Washington, DC: U.S. Department of Education, Planning, and Evaluation Service.

Postman, N. & Weingartner, C. (1971). *The soft revolution*. New York: Dell.

Postman, N. & Weingartner, C. (2000). *Teaching as a subversive activity*. New York: Dell.

Powell, W. W., & DiMaggio, P. J. (Eds.). (1991). *The new institutionalism in organizational analysis*. Chicago: University of Chicago Press.

Ravitch, D. (1983). *The troubled crusade: American education, 1945–1980*. New York: Basic Books.

Reitz, C. (2000). Art, alienation, and the humanities: A critical engagement with Herbert Marcuse. New York: SUNY Press.

Rose, G. (1966). Anomie and deviation—A conceptual framework for empirical studies. *British Journal of Sociology*, 17(1), 29–45.

Salinger, J. D. (1991). *The catcher in the rye*. Little, Brown.

Sarason, S. (1982). *The culture of the school and the problem of change*. Boston: Allyn & Bacon.

Sarason, S. (1991). *The predictable failure of educational reform: Can we change course before it's too late?* San Francisco: Jossey-Bass.

Sarason, S. (1996). *Revisiting the culture of the school and the problem of change*. New York: Teachers College Press.

Sartre, J. P. (1956). *Being and nothingness* (H. Barnes, Trans.). New York: Philosophical Library.

Sartre, J. P. (1957). *Existentialism and human emotions*. New York: Philosophical Library.

Schacht, R. L. (1970). *Alienation*. Garden City, NY: Anchor Books.

Scheurich, J. J., & Skrla, L. (2003). *Leadership for equity and excellence: Creating high-achievement classrooms, schools, and districts*. Thousand Oaks, CA: Corwin Press.

Schmitt, R. (2003). *Alienation and freedom*. Cambridge, MA: Westview Press.

Seeman, M. (1959). On the meaning of alienation. *American Sociological Review*, 24(6), 783–791.

Seeman, M. (1967). On the personal consequences of alienation in work. *American Sociological Review*, 32(2), 273–285.

Seeman, M. (1975). Alienation studies. *Annual Review of Sociology, 1*, 91–123.

Seeman, M. (1983). Alienation motifs in contemporary theorizing: The hidden continuity of the classic themes. *Social Psychology Quarterly*, 46(3), 171–184.

Sergiovanni, T. J. (1996). *Leadership for the schoolhouse: How is it different? Why is it important?* San Francisco: Jossey-Bass.

Silverman, D. (2001). *Interpreting qualitative data: Methods for analyzing talk, text, and interaction*. Thousand Oaks, CA: Sage.

Smylie, M., & Hart, A. W. (2000). School leadership for teacher learning and change: A human and social capital development perspective. In J. Murphy & K. S. Louis (Eds.), *Handbook of research on educational administration* (pp. 421–441). San Francisco: Jossey-Bass.

Spillane, J. P. (2002). Local theories of teacher change: The pedagogy of district policies and programs. *Teachers College Record, 104*(3), 377–420.

Spillane, J. P., Halverson, R., & Diamond, J. B. (2001). Investigating school leadership practice: A distributed perspective. *Educational Researcher, 30*(3), 23–28.

Spillane, J. P., Diamond, J. B., Burch, P., Hallett, T., Jita, L., & Zoltners, J. (2002). Managing in the middle: School leaders and the enactment of accountability policy. *Educational Policy, (16)*5, pp. 731–762.

Spring, J. H. (1988). *Conflict of interests: The politics of American education.* New York: Longman.

Strauss, A., & Corbin, J. (Eds.). (1997). *Grounded theory in practice.* Thousand Oaks, CA: Sage.

Strauss, A., & Corbin, J. (1998) *Basics of qualitative research: Grounded theory procedures and techniques.* Newbury Park: Sage.

Strayer, G. (1933). Educational economy and frontier needs. In *Department of superintendence, official report, 1933* (pp. 138–146). Washington, DC: NEA.

Swanson, C. B., & Stevenson, D. L. (2002). Standards-based reform in practice: Evidence on state policy and classroom instruction from the NAEP state assessments. *Educational Evaluation and Policy Analysis, 24*(1), 1–27.

Templeton, F. (1966). Alienation and political participation: Some research findings. *Public Opinion Quarterly, 30*(2), 249–261.

Tucker, R. C. (Ed.). (1978). *The Marx-Engels reader.* New York: W. W. Norton.

Tyack, D., & Cuban, L. (1995). *Tinkering toward utopia: A century of public school reform.* Cambridge, MA: Harvard University Press.

Tyack, D., Kirst, M., & Hansot, E. (1980). Educational reform: Retrospect and prospect. *Teachers College Record, 81*, 253–269.

United States Department of Education. (1998a). *Schoolwide programs.* Retrieved July 12, 2001, from www.ed.gov/legislation/ESEA/Title_1/swpguide .html.

United States Department of Education. (1998b). *Applications for state grants under the comprehensive school reform demonstration program.* Retrieved September 11, 2004, from www.ed.gov/offices/OESE/compreform/csrdapp .html.

United States Department of Education. (1998c). *Profiles of successful schoolwide programs.* Washington, DC: Author.

Verdugo, R. R., Greenberg, N. M., Henderson, R. D., Uribe Jr., O., & Schneider, J. M. (1997). School governance regimes and teachers' job satisfaction: Bureaucracy, legitimacy, and community. *Educational Administration Quarterly, 33*(1), 38–66.

Waller, W. (1961). *The sociology of teaching.* New York: Russell & Russell.

Weber, M. (1947). *The theory of social and economic organization* (A. M. Henderson & T. Parsons, Trans.). New York: Oxford University Press.

Weber, M. (1986). Domination by economic power and by authority. In S. Lukes (Ed.), *Power* (pp. 28–36). New York: New York University Press.

Westheimer, J. (1998). *Among school teachers: Community, autonomy, and ideology in teachers' work.* New York: Teachers College Press.

Whyte, W. F. (1993). *Street corner society: The social structure of an Italian slum.* Chicago: University of Chicago Press.

Wolcott, H. F. (1994). *Transforming qualitative data: Description, analysis, and interpretation.* Thousand Oaks, CA: Sage.

Wolcott, H. F. (1997). A case study using an ethnographic approach. In R. M. Jaeger (Ed.), *Complimentary research methods for research in education* (pp. 365–369). Washington, D.C.: American Educational Research Association.

Wolcott, H. F. (2003). *Teachers versus technocrats.* Walnut Creek, CA: AltaMira Press.

Woolf, V. (1990). *A room of one's own.* New York: Harvest Books.

Zielinski, A. E., & Hoy, W. K. (1983). Isolation and alienation in elementary schools. *Educational Administration Quarterly, 19*(2), 27–45.

INDEX

ABOUT THE AUTHOR

Jeffrey S. Brooks is an assistant professor in the Department of Educational Leadership and Policy Studies at the Florida State University, where he teaches courses on various aspects of educational leadership. *The Dark Side of School Reform* was based on his dissertation study of teacher alienation and a pilot study that focused on teacher leadership. His work has been published in the *Journal of School Leadership* and the *Journal of Values and Ethics in Educational Administration*. Dr. Brooks received his Ph.D. in education policy studies from the University of Missouri–Columbia and is an active member of several professional organizations, including the American Educational Research Association and the University Council for Educational Administration.